'Brilliant! Alison's book address[...]
effectiveness of the gospel in the li[...]
great stimulator [...]
— JOHN [...]

'Alison Morgan's writing is so winsome that it's easy to be caught up in the beauty
of what she's saying before you realise she's just smacked you between the eyes with
a piece of two-by-four. Like her previous book, The Wild Gospel, which was a
great inspiration to me, this new book presents a deeply radical message in the
most eloquent and seductive manner. You've been warned!'

— **MICHAEL FROST,** AUTHOR, THE SHAPING OF THINGS TO COME

'An excellent analytical summary of our contemporary cultural climate and a
sane yet enthralling account of the reasons we have for confidence in the gospel.
As an apologist for the Christian faith she does for her generation what
C. S. Lewis did for his. I loved it. So will you.'

— **RT REVD JAMES NEWCOME,** BISHOP OF CARLISLE

'This book is hugely important, weaving together powerful stories of people's
experience of faith with deep reflection about culture, the Bible and faith in the
21st century. It is encouraging, uplifting and inspiring.'

— **DR PAULA GOODER,** WRITER AND LECTURER IN BIBLICAL STUDIES

'Timely, helpful and prophetic in starting the work of building confident
disciples who can really engage in God's world.'

— **REVD IAN BUNCE,** HEAD OF MISSION DEPARTMENT,
BAPTIST UNION OF GREAT BRITAIN

'The Church is shrinking and wrinkling because we have taught people to be
Christians and not disciples. Alison Morgan is a disciple who loves Jesus and
loves people. Peppered with stories of changed lives, this book will inspire and
challenge. You gotta read it!'

— **MARK RUSSELL,** CEO CHURCH ARMY AND MEMBER OF THE ARCHBISHOPS'
COUNCIL OF THE CHURCH OF ENGLAND

'The chapter on the Word of God is brilliant.
Only a linguist could have written it!'

— **RODNEY GREEN,** PRIOR OF ST JOHN, CHAIRMAN OF ST JOHN AMBULANCE AND
FORMER CHIEF EXECUTIVE OF LEICESTER CITY COUNCIL

'Important and timely. I believe it will enable us to communicate in more relevant and powerful ways.'

– **LAURENCE SINGLEHURST,** DIRECTOR, CELL UK MINISTRIES, AUTHOR OF *SOWING REAPING KEEPING*

'Her integration of science and theology, of Word and Spirit, of England and Africa, of church and individual, is remarkable and engaging. She writes brilliantly. This is a book to buy, ponder, and share.'

– **REVD DR MICHAEL GREEN**

'This powerful book will help Christians to find new faith and vision in our common call to mission and provides an immense range of resources, rooted in theology and practical experience, to enable us to proclaim the Gospel in new and compelling ways today.'

– **THE MOST REVD DR JOHN SENTAMU,** ARCHBISHOP OF YORK

'Alison Morgan has seen the world and the truth of God with clear eyes. Never abstract and never shallow, The Word on the Wind *brings the fountain-fresh water of the Spirit to an age that's dry, and sick of dusty answers.'*

– **RT REVD PAUL BAYES,** BISHOP OF HERTFORD

'Another inspiring book from Alison Morgan, combining insightful analysis, lucid argument, moving testimony, and a much needed gift of insight from the African church. An encouragement to live confidently for the God revealed in the gospel of Jesus.'

– **RT REVD GRAHAM CRAY,** ARCHBISHOPS' MISSIONER AND LEADER OF THE FRESH EXPRESSIONS TEAM

'An eminently readable, timely, and radical exploration of the power of THE WORD. Alison Morgan draws on a scholarly knowledge of the richness and breadth of meaning of THE WORD in both Hebrew and Greek understanding, as well as a wealth of contemporary experience of people who have known the power of THE LIVING WORD. An exciting and challenging read.'

– **ABBOT STUART BURNS OSB**

THE WORD ON THE WIND

Renewing confidence in the gospel

ALISON MORGAN

MONARCH
B O O K S

Oxford, UK, and Grand Rapids, Michigan, USA

First published in the UK in 2011 by Monarch Books
(a publishing imprint of Lion Hudson plc)
Wilkinson House, Jordan Hill Road, Oxford OX2 8DR, England
Tel: +44 (0)1865 302750 Fax: +44 (0)1865 302757
Email: monarch@lionhudson.com
www.lionhudson.com

ISBN 978 0 85721 015 9 (print)
ISBN 978 0 85721 149 1 (epub)
ISBN 978 0 85721 148 4 (Kindle)
ISBN 978 0 85721 150 7 (PDF)

Published in conjunction with ReSource, 13 Sadler Street, Wells, Somerset, BA5 2RR
Email: office@resource-arm.net

Distributed by:
UK: Marston Book Services, PO Box 269, Abingdon, Oxon, OX14 4YN
USA: Kregel Publications, PO Box 2607, Grand Rapids, Michigan 49501

Acknowledgments

Unless otherwise stated, scripture quotations are from The New Revised Standard Version of the Bible copyright © 1989 by the Division of Christian Education of the National Council of Churches in the USA. Used by permission. All rights reserved. Scripture quotations marked CEV are from the Contemporary English Version New Testament © 1991, 1992, 1995 by American Bible Society. Used with permission. Scripture quotations marked TM taken from The Message. Copyright © by Eugene H. Peterson 1993, 1994, 1995, 1996, 2000, 2001, 2002. Used by permission of NavPress Publishing Group. Scripture quotations marked NIV are taken from the Holy Bible, New International Version, copyright © 1973, 1978, 1984 by the International Bible Society. Used by permission of Zondervan and Hodder & Stoughton Limited. All rights reserved. The 'NIV' and 'New International Version' trademarks are registered in the United States Patent and Trademark Office by International Bible Society. Use of either trademark requires the permission of International Bible Society. UK trademark number 1448790.

The text paper used in this book has been made from wood independently certified as having come from sustainable forests.

British Library Cataloguing Data
A catalogue record for this book is available from the British Library.

Printed and bound in Great Britain by Clays Ltd, St Ives plc.

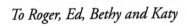

To Roger, Ed, Bethy and Katy

Contents

About the Author

A linguist and medievalist by background, the Revd Dr Alison Morgan has written a number of books, including an internationally recognised work on the poet Dante. She is best known for *The Wild Gospel*, now in its third printing. She is the editor of *Rooted in Jesus*, a discipleship course for Africa currently in use in thirteen countries, co-author (with John Woolmer) of the ReSource healing course *In His Name* and (with Bill Goodman) of the Lent course *Season of Renewal*. A contributor to *Mission-Shaped Questions*, Alison is also a member of the Archbishops' College of Evangelists. After many years spent with her husband in parish ministry, Alison now works for ReSource as a thinker and writer.

ReSource is an independent charity based in Wells, Somerset. Its vision is to help build a church which is diverse, local, renewed in the Spirit, and effective in mission. It works with local churches of all types and traditions, with deaneries, dioceses, and other denominational groupings.

ReSource is based at 13, Sadler Street, Wells, Somerset BA5 2RR. Its website is www.resource-arm.net and its patron is Archbishop John Sentamu. Please do contact ReSource at office@resource-arm.net or on 01749 672860 if you think we may be able to help you.

Acknowledgments

My thanks are due to many people. I have been encouraged, inspired, and challenged by the people I've met and the places I've visited in the course of my work with ReSource and with *Rooted in Jesus*, and I have read many helpful books and web articles. But my particular thanks are due to the other members of the ReSource team based in Wells – Martin and Cesca Cavender, Paula Smit, Richard Thomas, and Roger Morgan – for their constant support and encouragement; and to my son Ed and daughters Bethy and Katy, for their patience. Finally I acknowledge the unstinting interference of my parrot, Alfie.

Most of the stories in this book come directly from those who have experienced them, and every attempt has been made to ensure their accuracy; some of the names have been changed to preserve the privacy of those concerned. Any errors of fact are mine alone.

Text acknowledgments: Poem p.75–76 'Cracks' taken from *Planetwise* by Dave Bookless © Dave Bookless, used with permission of IVP. Poem p.98 'The Abandoned Valley' from *Refusing Heaven: Poems* by Jack Gilbert, copyright © 2005 by Jack Gilbert. Used by permission of Alfred A. Knopf, a division of Random House, Inc. Poem p.119 'The Uninvited Guest' by Thelma Laycock, used by permission of the author. Poem p.138–39 'Guests' taken from *Trouble with Church? Provocative Poems for Thoughtful Christians* by Lucy Berry, published by Kevin Mayhew Ltd. Used by permission of Kevin Mayhew Ltd. Poem p.154 'In Broken Images' by Robert Graves, taken from Robert Graves, *Complete Poems*. Used by permission of Carcenet Press Limited. Poem p.213 by John Leax, used by permission of the author. Poem p.237 'The Other' by R. S. Thomas, © Kunjana Thomas 2001, used with permission.

Cartoon acknowledgments: Cartoon p.28 by Noel Ford, used with permission; cartoon p.80 by Dave Walker, www.cartoonchurch.com, used with permission; cartoon p.123 by Darren Harvey Regan, reproduced from Michael Moynagh, *emergingchurch.intro*, published by Monarch, used with permission; Cartoon p.217 by Katy Morgan, used with permission.

All graphs drawn by the author from published statistics.

Foreword

Nobody much wants to be arrogant or overbearing; and so often we Christians are so concerned not to look or sound arrogant that we can only murmur apologetically about what ought to be infectiously exciting. Finding the right sort of confidence is quite a challenge; but Alison Morgan shows that it is possible in this warm and encouraging book, rooted in extensive experience in both the UK and the younger churches abroad.

She shows us that true confidence comes from inhabiting a story larger than ourselves – so, strange as it may sound, true confidence may be expressed in the happy acknowledgement that we don't know quite how to talk about the reality that has overwhelmed us. Part of the strength of this book is that Alison is determined that we shan't confuse loyalty and obedience to Scripture with a myopic focus on unimportant details or a style of reading that ignores what sort of text is in front of us – any more than we should confuse common sense and imagination in reading the Bible with a particular style of scholarly fashion.

And of course if we find ourselves in the middle of a story that our minds can't quite get themselves around, we should not be too surprised to find ourselves being – well, surprised: surprised by joy, by grace, and yes, by miracle. Such surprise needs to be chronicled as much as the challenges that we face in a confused and rebellious age. Alison pulls no punches about the scale of these challenges and about our reluctance as churches to respond with the sort of creativity and fullness of heart that we need, but she also pulls no punches about the scale of the transformative power of the Gospel.

This is a welcome and invigorating contribution to the mission of the Church in the UK and elsewhere. I hope that it will be blessed in finding the readers who most need to encounter its message, and that it will be used by God to motivate anew all those who are trying to share the indescribable riches of God in Christ with their neighbours.

+Rowan Cantuar:
Lambeth Palace
Lent 2011

Introduction

Johann Sebastian Bach used to set musical exercises and scales for his very musical sons and wrote "To the Glory of God" at the top of every page he put in front of them on the piano. Whether they thought they were doing their scales to the glory of God or not I do not know, but the theology was right – even if the parenting skills might have needed a bit more help.[1]

"To the Glory of God" is at the heart of this book by Alison Morgan, as it was for her previous offering *The Wild Gospel*. That's what drives and informs it, what gives it life and eloquence, grace and truth; and what rams home its inescapable challenge. Here is the "reckless, adventurous life commitment… filled with the laughter of forgiveness and the conversation of grace."[2] Here is the journey from what is known to what is not, which is in Alison's own words, "a bit like being in a room full of immensely complex and interesting things, and then opening the window to find yourself gazing in astonishment at a whole new realm outside it". This is the beckoning to life in all its fullness.

Alison is the thinker and writer of our team at ReSource. As a team we have learned a lot from our time on the road together for the last several years. That learning has included not only work at many levels and across traditions and denominations in this country but also living and serving alongside clergy and lay-people in places like Rwanda after the genocide, Mozambique after the civil war, urban South Africa, Argentina, rural Zambia and Angola, Kenya and Cambodia. Cross-cultural engagements with people like Martin Mlaka (Chapter 12) bring a proper humility to our dealings and dismantle some of the card-houses of Western understanding we have taken such pains to build. All this has grown in us a new desire to wait on the Lord of creation to open the mystery to us as we journey with him. There is always more with God.

That may all sound a bit high-flown but it is part of the discovery that, as Alison says, "…the kind of learning we do as disciples is a travelling kind of learning". The Christian Gospel is one of movement, change, watersheds, new vistas and landscapes. It's about making a journey, about going somewhere – and doing so intentionally. The travelling is not some worthy and earnest, work-ethicky, proof-text, points-ticking trip towards perfection. It is, as Alison also says, an apprenticeship in community, a hand-holding, laughing, food-for-the-journey sort of ramble with companions, eyes open to the wonders of "the whole new realm outside us". It's the call to holiness, and it's fun. It carries that joy and laughter which is the one constant mark of a healthy church. It is also a reminder that Jesus is not only the truth; he is also the way and the life.

Watching people making a real, gutsy journey together like this is immensely attractive to those "outside" the Church, because "when the Church becomes a house of prayer people will come running."[3] There is, in this twilight of atheism, a genuine desire for spiritual answers to the questions of life.

I have noticed this when running a parenting course in

a village in Oxfordshire: the unchurched parents who came not only wanted answers for themselves but were also looking for a big story, a star by which they could guide and nurture their new children. Roger Morgan of ReSource has found it in speaking with children and staff-members in local schools and seeing them come to faith. I have seen it when mentoring and coaching in large companies for a Christian management consultancy, particularly in discussing questions of purpose, meaning and principle in relation to recruitment; and a Christian understanding of forgiveness in order to counter the insidious, profit-damaging dangers of risk aversion. It is a constant for us all on the road. It's in the air.

The Gospel story is the alternative story, to be spoken afresh into the culture, which, if it ever knew it, has forgotten it. The spoor of the searcher, the tracks of the spiritual explorer, are all around us – in the fierce debates over religion and the vehemently held views on television and in the other media, alongside the prime-time offerings on the Monastery, or the Miracles of Christ, the Passion or the Nativity. They are there in the world of films, too, with a constant refrain of searching and redemption, violence, sacrifice and the beauty of moral duty in movies like Clint Eastwood's *Gran Torino*, or *The Shawshank Redemption*, *Avatar*, *The Lives of Others*, *The Matrix*, *The King's Speech* or *Toy Story 3*. To visit the cinema/multiplex/local movie house or fleapit these days is to partake in a worship experience. It is a truism that people are seeking spirituality but not religion, spiritual experience but not Church. It is also a mighty truth that the Church constantly misses that which is right in front of its face, or perhaps in the street outside. That's also what Alison is talking about.

This book concerns the Word on the Wind, the crucial

interaction of God's Word and God's Spirit which alone can bring transformation and life. Word and Spirit are the very stuff of the Church of God but sometimes one could be forgiven for missing it. I went with an unchurched, enquiring friend to Christmas Eve Midnight Communion in a church in Oxfordshire last year, and he came out saying, "Well, that sucked all the life out of me". I felt the same. There hadn't been much display of Robert Lewis's "living proof of a loving God to a watching world."[4] Indeed, the watching world had had all its prejudices neatly if rather painfully confirmed.

Mission is not something the Church does but something it is. People can recognise the community which has a purpose, the *communitas*, and they do come running. Witness the Tubestation surfing church in Cornwall where they've had to build decking outside to accommodate the overflow, or the effect "Living Proof" had in the schools in a deprived area of Cardiff, or Alpha in prisons, or Messy Church, and all the other fresh expressions. Witness, too, the little inherited, traditional forms of local church across the country where they have discovered afresh the forgotten ways and opened themselves to the power of God's Word and the breath of his Spirit. This is the cure of souls, which is both healing and saving. The Word is on the Wind in these local churches and all their parts, and the searcher can tell the difference from a mile away.

Alison points us to those forgotten ways and challenges us to rediscover what is already in our genes as a Christian Church. She invites us to unearth again all those elements which have been so efficiently leached out of us by fist-waving atheistic scientists or media-chattering rationalists. She reminds us that we have "To the glory of God" stamped on our spiritual passports. Alison is telling us that we need to go back, look again, reclaim, re-source ourselves in the roots-in-the-living-water life that has always been there. Perhaps we need to stop looking back with yearning to the Acts of the Apostles and realise that, to borrow the words of Archbishop Rowan Williams, we may still be the early Church. We need to inhabit the space prepared for us individually and as a body by Jesus Christ.

The Christian Bible is littered with people called to "go back" – Moses past his old bedroom to get to Pharoah; Elijah from despair at the mouth of the cave to anoint his successor; Gideon to his own home before he takes on the Midianites; and then Jesus himself to the Jordan; the lost son to his father; Lazarus from the tomb; Mary to tell the news of the resurrection; the two on the Emmaus road running back to speak their eye-witness in Jerusalem. We re-member the living Jesus Christ. The going back is never for nostalgia, but always for a purpose.

When ReSource came to life in 1994 we had a particular going-back verse of scripture in mind – "Isaac reopened the wells that had been dug in the time of his father Abraham, which the Philistines had stopped up after Abraham died, and he gave them the same names that his father had given them" (Genesis 26:18, TNIV). When I had first read those verses I was given a vision of all the churches of this country, of all traditions and denominations, reopened for the provision of living water for those who sought God. The words re-echoed for us when we felt called by God to move the ReSource office to a place named Wells.

Going back, to deep confidence in the Gospel of Jesus, to find again what it means to be the bride of Christ in this beautiful world in which h

e has made us. J. S. Bach had it so right, and so did the hymn-writers Crosby and Doane.

To God be the glory, great things he has done – so loved He the world that He gave us his Son, who yielded his life an atonement for sin and opened the life gate that all may go in.

Martin Cavender, Wells, Somerset
March 2011

Part I

A Confident Gospel

Chapter 1

Understanding the issues

It's possible to live in a place and not notice the changes which take place all around you. Sometimes we don't notice because there are so many of them that only the biggest and boldest stand out. Everyone noticed Canary Wharf as it thrust its way into the skies of London, its summit winking red in the sunlight to warn low-flying aircraft of its sudden intrusion into their domain; but few observed the quiet passing of a row of old brick terraced houses in nearby Greenwich, or the careful fencing of an ancient oak in the park. And sometimes we don't notice because change comes to a place slowly, imperceptibly: a new sign here, a freshly weeded garden there – minor things compared with the passing of the seasons with their shifting shapes and colours, and mere human wrinkles on the surface of a world which is itself in constant motion.

The city of Leicester is the first kind of place. I lived there for eighteen years, and watched the redevelopment of the river with its new university buildings and waterside plazas, the shiny silver rising of the National Space Centre beside the old Abbey Pumping Station, the sleek arrogance of the windowless casino built in curious anticipation of changing legislation. And yet other things I did not notice. One of these was the Holiness Chapel. Despite its location on the London Road, the old Victorian artery leading from the southern suburbs down into the city centre, and despite its fluorescent green poster proclaiming that those who wait upon the Lord shall renew their strength, the Holiness Chapel remained curiously unobtrusive. Until one day in 2006 a large notice went up: For Auction.

I looked it up. Properly known as Thanksgiving Hall, the chapel opened in 1925 as the first building of the Independent Holiness Movement, a charismatic renewal movement of which Leicester became the founding centre and which was to spread all over the United Kingdom. I was not the only person to have failed to notice it; although meetings were still being held there, those occupying the buildings on either side were unaware of them. One report noted that 'No recruitment or ecumenical initiatives have ever been known.' The chapel was sold for £500,000 and is now home to the halal Al Mashriq restaurant, whose owners are happy to comply with the clauses written into the documents of sale which forbid drinking, gambling, and lap dancing.

And yet this quiet, nondescript building had been, in its heyday, the thriving headquarters of a national renewal movement. 'God First', proclaims a carving over the door. It became, for me, something of a symbol: the symbol of a church which failed to adapt, and perhaps more widely of a society in which the Christian faith is in decline. What happened to these people who believed that those who wait upon the Lord shall renew their strength, and yet who seemingly disappeared without trace in little more than a generation or two? And will that same thing happen to us, so that what even today seems alive and vibrant will tomorrow look like the established habit of a bygone era?

It is often said that we must change in order to remain the same. What may appear static rarely is; even the ground on which we stand is spinning, despite all apparent evidence to the contrary, at an alarming rate beneath our feet.[1] Leicester's motto is 'Semper eadem' – 'always the same'. And yet of course Leicester has not been always the same. Turn back the pages of its history and you find a Celtic tribal settlement, Roman baths, a Norman castle, an Augustinian abbey, and grand new Victorian parks. Its streets have been at different times full of sheep, of fighting Parliamentarians and Royalists, of ragged factory workers, of the carriages of comfortable Victorian middle-class families, and of Gujurati-speaking immigrants. Today Leicester is home to seventy language groups and many religious faiths. Stay the same and you will find that everything changes around you, that the rushing waters will sweep on and leave you high and dry; that you leave no greater trace than that left by the faithful members of the Independent Holiness Movement.

I work now for ReSource, a small but ambitious charity whose aim is to support ordinary churches as they seek to minister confidently and effectively in a changing context. Sometimes it is hard to know what should change and what should remain the same; hard to know how to keep a constantly sharpened cutting edge whilst remaining faithful to a shared history which goes back 2,000 years. Some of us in the church seem to want change for change's sake – is it possible to be authentically Christian in today's society without an amplification system, a youth band, a programme of social engagement? Others of us resist change doggedly, as if our faith somehow resides in the medieval flagstones, seventeenth-century liturgies, or Victorian pews of buildings, which in fact mostly date from well over a thousand years after the death of Jesus. To change or not to change easily becomes an argument about style, the style not of our discipleship but of our gatherings. It's all very confusing.

Over the last seven years ReSource has worked in dioceses,

deaneries, and local churches, with Anglicans, Baptists, Methodists, Catholics, and New Church denominations all over the country. For me it's been a fascinating process, after years given primarily to writing and ministry in a single parish. What is the issue the church finds most difficult today? Tim Sledge put his finger on it as we ate sandwiches together in Northampton. It's confidence. We live in a culture which dents and knocks our confidence as Christians. And so 'does this stuff really work?' is probably the question to which most ordinary Christians in this country would like to hear a convincing answer. It's expressed in different ways, but whether people are asking us to help them to know how to find ways of reaching out to others, or to deepen their relationship with God, or to pray for healing, what they really mean is perhaps just this: can we actually have confidence in this ancient faith of ours? Do we really have something which people out there need and want – or not?

I think we can answer that question in two very different ways. Firstly, we can answer it through experience – it has changed me; let it change you. We all have our own story to tell, and it is important that we tell it; the good news is not just something we believe but something we live – it changes us, and therein lies its power, its attractiveness, its uniqueness. We are not those odd people with a peculiarly antiquated sense of how to have a good time on a Sunday morning, we are – or should be – living witnesses to the power of God to bring healing and transformation to ordinary lives.

Often I meet people who have encountered Jesus in this way. I think of Kevin, who told me he'd just become a Christian. How did that happen? I asked. Kevin is an ordinary bloke, an odd job man, not very articulate. He didn't want to tell me, he said; it'd cause a riot. No, go on, I said. Kevin explained that his life had been in a mess. His wife had run off with another man and he'd been forced to find himself lodgings. He was having nightmares – dark figures running towards him, with faces like the face in *The Scream*, he said, twisting his face into a contorted, open-mouthed expression of anguish. One night Kevin was having this nightmare, and suddenly he was aware of another figure, and a great sense of being overwhelmed by love. He woke up. "I thought it was a woman," he said. "I thought it meant I was going to find another woman. I've only ever known that kind of love with a woman – but this was different. I can't describe it, but it was bigger, much stronger." The couple he was lodging with were Christians. Kevin realised the figure offering him this love was Jesus. He's a rough and ready kind of guy, not the kind of guy you'd expect to find in church. But there he was, three weeks later, talking about how love is the only thing that matters.

But important and encouraging though Kevin's story is, it's not enough. If we have no story to tell, perhaps we have not yet grasped the full potential of what is available to us in Christ. But even if we have, we need to be able to look critically at the bigger picture. So secondly, we need to be sure that we are talking not just about our own experience, something that worked for me but might not work for you, but about something universal; something much bigger, something into which our individual stories fit like pieces of a jigsaw. To do this, we need to be able to understand and respond with confidence to some of the intellectual challenges our culture throws up to the gospel, to know why and how it is that we genuinely do have something powerful and true to offer. We need to be able not just to encourage those around us with our real life stories, but also to help them through the tangle of voices which press in on all of us, voices which offer illusory and ultimately unsatisfactory answers to the big questions of human existence. In many places that's just what's happening. In others it is, as yet, not.

What stops us? Many things, of course, but I think that two in particular erode our confidence. The first is to do with the church itself, and in particular with our experience of steady numerical decline. Falling numbers are not good for morale, and in particular they are not good for the morale of church leaders. The second is to do with the fast-changing cultural environment in which we live, and the wide acceptance of values which are in direct conflict with those of the gospel. These all too easily slip under the radar of ordinary Christians who do not have the skills or theological experience to evaluate them, and who therefore find themselves giving in to the invisible pressure to conform to the norms which surround us, or subsiding into an unwilling but confused silence. To put it another way, we are so unnerved by Richard Dawkins – who is not interested in the possibilities of the gospel – that we fail to offer it to Kevin, who is.

Life on board the *Titanic*

Perhaps the biggest challenge to our confidence comes from the visible weekly reminder that church is losing its appeal; such is the scale of the problem that statistician Bob Jackson warns that the figures should not be read by those of a nervous disposition. The basic facts are these. Peak attendance in the UK in the twentieth century was in the year 1904, when 33% of adults were to be found in church on any given Sunday; this already represented a steep decline since the mid-nineteenth century. By 2006 weekly attendance had fallen to just over 6% (see Figure 1). Membership of the Church of England declined by 14% in the 1990s alone (28% for children).

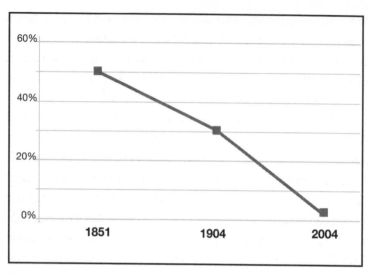

Figure 1: Proportion of UK population in church on a typical Sunday.

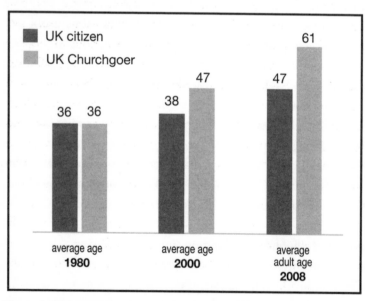

Figure 2: Rising average age of UK Churchgoers compared to the national average (2008 figure relates to the C of E).

Some denominations are doing a little better than that, others a little worse. The average age of churchgoers in all denominations is rising: in 1980 it was 36 (the same as the national average), but by 2000 it was 47 (compared to 38 nationally). The most recent figures available for the Church of England relate to the year 2008, and show that the average adult Sunday Anglican is now 61 years old (compared to 47 in the general population), and that two thirds are female (see Figure 2). Half of all Anglican churches have no work amongst children and young people, and only one in three hundred 18–24 year olds now attends a weekly Church of England service.[2] Whilst thousands of young people gather each year at the inter-denominational Soul Survivor and Momentum events in Somerset, they come from a tiny minority of mostly urban churches, and represent a fraction of their generation. It's a small community – my son Edward was one of 3,500 students attending Momentum last year; expecting anonymity, he reported the curious experience of constantly bumping into people he knew from all over the country. And it's not just the overall numbers but, more worryingly, the proportion of young people in church which is shrinking. Often it's not so much hostility to the gospel as ignorance of it. I was talking recently with Eleanor, a vicar in Carlisle. Eleanor had just been approached by a woman who wished to have her baby baptised. What do you know about God, Eleanor had asked gently. "Well, nothing really." What about Jesus, then, do you know anything about him? "Well, no, not really." Looking for common ground, Eleanor suggested she did know something about Jesus, because she knew about Christmas. "Oh yes, I suppose I do," said the woman, furrowing her brow in puzzled thought.[3]

Meanwhile those who do know these things continue to leave – the fastest growing sector of the Christian community is said to be those Christians who no longer attend church. A recent survey concludes: 'Britain is currently experiencing an unprecedented cultural and social change. The nation, Christian, at least in theory, for the last 1,300 years is demonstrably no longer so. The last fifty years have seen churches empty, the Christian worldview cannibalised and abandoned, Christian institutions lose their historic influence, and the birth of generations almost completely ignorant of the Christian story.' It has been suggested that if the current rate of decline continues, there will be no institutional Christian presence in this country by 2050.[4]

With the best will in the world it's hard to feel positive about these statistics. Lesslie Newbigin remarked long ago that the Christian faith is now regarded as 'a good cause in danger of collapsing for lack of support.' The Bishop of Durham has written that it's seen as 'an upmarket version of day-dreaming for those who like that sort of thing.' And that's the charitable view. A member of a lively church in Maidstone suggested more robustly that 'the church has done for Jesus what *Jaws* did for swimming lessons.'[5] Whatever the cause, public interest in church is probably at its lowest ever point. Church leaders who try to reverse the trend by dint of sheer hard work sometimes succeed; others do not. One vicar, leader of seven rural parishes with slowly growing congregations, confessed to us recently that were he not required to attend, he wasn't sure he'd want to. For others it's tougher even than that: a few months ago we worked with a group of hard-pressed clergy in a Midlands industrial town – committed to their calling, their general demeanour was one of men resigned to their fate.

And yet this is not, as we shall see, the whole picture, for God remains active not just in the dreams of people like Kevin but in and through even our most traditional expressions of faith. Sometimes the very church buildings which so often seem a burden to small congregations responsible for their upkeep seem to have a strange, almost tangible power to move those, ignorant of what they represent, who nonetheless find themselves crossing their thresholds – as if at the moment of entry into their prayer-soaked space, the Spirit of God in some way meets with the human longings of those who do not yet know him. I remember walking years ago into Christ Church cathedral in Oxford, watching the sunlight stream multicoloured through the deep, rich hues of the stained glass windows, and beginning to wonder if beyond the barrier of my atheism there did not lie some greater reality, some kind of love, which I did not understand but which I could almost feel pressing against me, unknown and unlabelled. Perhaps it was a similar sensation which drew friends of mine, not churchgoers, to take each of their newborn children into a side chapel of Wells cathedral and pray the only prayer they knew, the Lord's Prayer. Even church gates and porches can be hosts to the unexpected. Lisa, a single parent with a history of abuse, violence and drugs, began the journey which led her to Christ when she stopped to talk to a woman arranging flowers in the porch of a Leicestershire village church. "I managed," she said later in a heart-stopping account of her story, "to get an invitation to church" – a phrase I shall never forget; how many people are there out there longing for an invitation to church? Church led to Alpha, Alpha led to Christ, and Lisa is a different woman; "I was looking in all the wrong places and with the wrong people for a thing called love. God set my heart on fire and his love, patience, kindness, grace and mercy poured into my life repairing all the damage that fear, guilt and being chained to my past behaviour had caused," she wrote.[6]

Another member of our church was Tony. Tony, a recovering alcoholic, reluctantly agreed to accompany a friend to a Sunday service in rural Norfolk. 'We walked through the quiet village in the direction of the church bells of Holy Innocents, a magnificent medieval structure that dominates the local landscape. As we entered the gate, without any warning, it happened – a gentle, warm feeling of "coming home". Peaceful, saved, call it what you will, but it's never left me. Some time later, I was baptised and said goodbye to my old existence. Emerging from the water, I felt cleansed of my past and reborn into a world where faith and Christian values would underpin every new day on God's earth.'[7]

But whilst stories like these remind us that God is still

clearly at work amongst his people and encourage us to believe that, whatever the national statistics, people are still open to his touch, they don't describe the reality experienced by most churches and church leaders. On the whole statisticians like Peter Brierley, Lynda Barley, and Bob Jackson find themselves issuing more of a trumpet call for action than a pat on the back for achievement. Most people are not looking to the church to provide answers for life's questions; on the whole it is neither fashionable nor desirable to go to church.

Cultural climate change

We once had a small cottage in a Northamptonshire village. It had a greenhouse. One Christmas Eve, pressed for time, my husband Roger found himself in the local branch of Boots looking for Christmas presents. He came up with a book on greenhouse gardening. So with the first hint of spring, I set to. I replaced the broken glass, pruned the vine which took up most of the space, bought seeds and trays and compost, and planted everything from Busy Lizzies to aubergines. The Busy Lizzies did fine, and so did the tomatoes. The aubergines and peppers grew into fine strong plants, produced flowers, developed promising little fruits. Looking forward to a summer of Italian cooking, I watched as the little fruits grew into slightly larger fruits. As a cold June was followed by a wet July, they reached the size of, say, gooseberries. Then they stopped growing. I suppose it was obvious, but perhaps a small Midlands greenhouse cannot, even with the holes stopped up, replicate the climate of the Mediterranean. Environment matters.

Sometimes it feels as if we are attempting to live out and to share a Mediterranean gospel in a Northamptonshire greenhouse. Plants grow better in some environments than in others, and the cultural environment in which we are currently living is a tough one. The air we breathe is full of pressure, debate, hostility, misunderstanding, indifference. There's the scientific fundamentalism of the new atheists. There's the pressure of Islam and the threat of faith-based terrorism. There's the secular liberal call for us to unite around a shared belief in nothing, a position held up as the epitome of maturity and tolerance by a media machine which delights to report the decline statistics we've just looked at, but shows little interest in reporting the good news stories of those who do come to faith.[8] And then there's the pick and mix world of enticing alternative spiritualities, most of which demand no time-consuming commitment and threaten nothing more dangerous than idiosyncrasy. "How can you believe in God," asks a fifteen-year-old student at our local school, "when there is so little evidence for him?" – a student who with no apparent sense of contradiction dabbles in tarot, writes elvish, and sleeps with a sword under her pillow; and who experiences, on entering a church, the opposite sensation to that described above: a sensation of nausea, trembling, faintness. Two generations ago she would have thought it natural to be a member of her village church; today, she is pressed upon by other forces – forces in which she doesn't really even believe.

One of the difficulties we have is that the world we live in is changing so fast. One of the biggest changes was triggered on 11 September 2001, when two planes hijacked by members of the Islamist terrorist network al-Qaeda crashed into the Twin Towers of the World Trade Center in New York. Almost overnight, the ideological lines which had dominated our lives for the best part of a century were redrawn: instead of a world stage dominated by the competing secular ideologies of capitalism and communism, we suddenly found ourselves living in one dominated by competing religious faiths. Religion is now on the agenda; if ever we thought that faith was a private matter, now we are forced to realise otherwise. One month after what we now know simply as 9/11, the US invaded Afghanistan; two years after that, Iraq. In multicultural Leicester, Muslims and Christians redoubled their efforts to respect and affirm one another; in other places, on buses, in trains, a culture of fear was sown. 'Welcome to the age of insecurity,' the headlines said as they looked back on the first decade of the new millennium.[9] By 2006 *The Times* was remarking that 'faith is returning to the centre of public debate.' Archbishop Rowan Williams returned from a visit to China and offered the reflection that anyone landing in Britain would assume that we were in the middle of 'a general panic about the role of religion in society.'[10] A British Airways check-in clerk was sent home for wearing a necklace with a cross on it; a social worker in Wandsworth was sacked for 'gross misconduct' after asking a suffering client if she had considered placing her faith in God; a nurse from Weston-super-Mare was suspended after she offered to pray for a patient, and a teacher was dismissed by North Somerset Council for suggesting she might pray for a pupil.[11]

The 'general panic' affects not just individuals expressing their faith in these seemingly innocuous ways, but also the role of religion in the public arena. In recent years student Christian Unions have seen their right to exist challenged in four universities. In 2005 Torbay Council removed the cross from its crematorium and renamed the chapel 'the ceremony hall', and in 2006 the Post Office decided to leave the birth of Christ out of its range of Christmas stamps. Dundee, Perth, and other city councils rebranded Christmas as a Winter Light festival, and in 2007 70% of Bolton employers decided to ban Christmas decorations for fear of offending members of other faiths. By way of rejoinder the Christian Muslim Forum sent a circular letter to every town hall in the country condemning the 'secularising agenda' which seeks to suppress religious symbols and festivals despite the 77% majority of people who claim religious affiliation; and in Oxford a united protest from all religious faiths resulted in the renaming of the 2008 'Winter Lights' celebration – in 2009 the city celebrated 'Christmas in Oxford'.

So suddenly, everywhere, people seem to be asking the question – is religious faith a legitimate part of a twenty-first-century democracy, something which needs and demands a public face; or should it rather be seen as legal but slightly reprehensible, to be practised in private, or at most in those specially designated religious smoking areas known as churches? As I write this, the BBC is screening a programme entitled *Are Christians Being Persecuted?*, which suggests that it is not just religious pluralism that has led to the changing values of our multicultural society but, more alarmingly, the increasingly prescriptive Equality legislation which, in seeking to ensure freedom from discrimination for minorities, actually undermines the religious freedom of the majority. Vincent Nichols, the Roman Catholic Archbishop of Westminster, points out that equality legislation is not value free; it is itself part of a secular ideology.[12]

The result of all this is that we increasingly find ourselves living in a cultural climate which has been, not unreasonably, described as 'totalitolerance'.[13] For those who still wish, like the builders of the Holiness Chapel, to put God first, it's dispiriting.

What is the gospel?

Taken together, these two problems – declining numbers and an increasingly complex and antagonistic social environment – have the effect of seriously undermining our confidence as Christians, and therefore our ability to share the gospel with others. Aware of all this, in 2004 the Archbishops of Canterbury and York set up a working party whose brief was to find ways of enabling the local church to become more effective in mission. The working party came to the following conclusion: 'We lack the skill and resources to speak confidently and coherently with our contemporary society. At the heart of the issue is our (lack of) confidence in the nature and content of the gospel.' Their recommendation was that 'the Church needs to develop a greater understanding of the gospel so that it can present to all people of England the good news of Jesus Christ.'[14]

Kevin, Lisa, and Tony represent millions in this country who harbour no suspicion that God might be willing to meet with them personally, and yet who may in fact wish to respond wholeheartedly to him. Kevin lodged with Christians who listened to him. Lisa talked to the woman arranging flowers in the porch because her next-door neighbours, kept awake at night by her drugs parties, had been putting Christian literature through her letterbox. Tony reluctantly agreed to accompany a friend to church. Each then found themselves caught up into a powerful encounter with God – but in each case it was the Christians they knew who made this possible. Many Christians now lack the confidence to reach out to others in this way; and yet if we share the gospel, people will respond to it. They always have, and they always will.

So let's start by taking a step backwards and thinking for

a moment about this gospel which we wish to present to the people of England. What is it, exactly?

The word 'gospel' just means good news. At its simplest, the good news is that Jesus Christ, the Son of God, was born, died, and raised again, and that this changes everything. This event is offered by those who first spoke and wrote about it as a simple, historical fact – the kind of fact which could be put on the front page of a newspaper. The complexity for us is that we live in a world which dislikes the arrogance of facts, and prefers the opportunity to choose between values. A fact does not permit choice. A fact, derived from the Latin word *factum* (from the verb *facio, facere, feci, factum*, to do or make), is something which has been done. The gospel is not fundamentally about values, beliefs, concepts, or choices: it's about events. The gospel is about something which was done, something which *happened*. And that is the first key to our confidence. Something happened, and it's something which makes a difference to your life and to mine – something which is not just a global event but also good news to an individual. Something which changes both the history of humankind and the story of each person who hears and responds to it; something which brings liberation, hope, love and resources for a new way of living – as it did for Lisa, Tony, and Kevin.

In summary

We live in a world which is changing incredibly fast. And history shows that it's at times of big cultural shifts like this that the church faces its greatest challenges. Increasingly theologians are suggesting that the challenge facing the church now is greater than that posed by the Reformation.[15]

If we are to speak with increasing confidence and clarity into our contemporary society, we need to try and make sure that every Christian has both a clear and confident understanding of their own faith and an effective and growing daily relationship with God. If we have truly received something life-changing, it should not be difficult to share it in sensitive and appropriate ways with others – if there's a great film on at the cinema, as Jesus might have said, it's not hard to let our friends know about it.[16] If on the other hand our faith is no more than a Sunday habit, or a belief that we rather hope might be true against the apparent evidence that it probably isn't, then we will not succeed in making Christ known to men and women as the hope of the world.

Secondly, we need to understand what it is that is holding people back. We will not speak meaningfully into our current situation if we do not have a clear and critical understanding of it. What are the voices shaping it, the assumptions underlying it? Remembering that Jesus said "I come to seek and to save the lost," what are the ways in which people in our communities are lost – spiritually, mentally, emotionally, physically?[17] What are the pressures upon them which make it hard for them to put their faith in Christ?

The Bible often compares a person to a tree. A forester knows that if you want a tree to grow to its full potential, you need to assess the environment in which it is planted and make sure it can access the nutrients it needs. If we want people to flourish like trees, we need to do the same. We must think about the invisible pollutants which make it hard for each tree to access the nutrients it needs, and we must find new ways of delivering clean air to the leaves and pure water to the roots. The biblical message is that the tree will then be able to flourish and bear fruit even in hostile conditions.[18]

The aim of this book is to look at both the tree and the soil, at both the personal and the environmental aspects of faith today; and to do this not sequentially but by weaving them together, in much the same way as they are woven inextricably into our daily experience.

Good news for Nicky

At the age of thirteen Nicky Cox was found to have a highly unusual cancerous lump, a synovial sarcoma, on her knee. This is an extract from an email Nicky wrote eighteen months later to an atheist friend.

> *How do I know God exists? Well, I was not brought up particularly Christian, so when I got old enough to decide my own faith, I chose to be an atheist. My brother, who I am extremely close to, got cancer when I was about eleven. It was a brain tumour – pineal germinoma if you want the medical name. Anyway that crushed any remaining faith in me. Thankfully he was cleared after chemo and radiotherapy, but is still suffering consequences. Anyway in year 7 Katy came to my school and we became actually very close towards the end of the year – she seemed to think this religious stuff was a big deal and even now I can remember her on a boat on the way back from Normandy asking if I had changed my mind about Christianity, and I can remember thinking – so what? It's just religion! Anyway I'd also been having ongoing medical problems concerning my left leg, which in April 2007 was*

diagnosed with cancer – synovial sarcoma. I was quite shocked, not surprisingly, and there was no history at all in our family so this was incredibly strange. Anyway, someone told me to pray – so I did. I prayed that if God were to take away my cancer I would seriously look into Christianity. And I was cleared, it's an altogether confusing story that even some of my closest friends who were there the whole time don't understand, but in short I was cleared without need for radio or chemo, and I am just monitored regularly. So I stuck to my word and looked into it a bit but sort of pushed it away.

At school there had been a huge argument between Katy and my other friend Tessa. And this (totally my fault) effectively ended my friendship with Katy for a good few months. When I began to talk to her again it was completely about Christianity. I challenged her as much as I could and she was annoyingly good at answers. I don't know what happened inside me, which must be incredibly frustrating to hear but something just said to me "Yes, this is right! This girl has got something fantastic here!" Seriously, just ask questions!

So that was my first encounter of healing and an answer to prayer. The second was when a lump formed on my wrist (my immediate reaction being cancer – had the same symptoms). To cut a long story short – I was invited to the Morgan household where their family and I prayed together on Friday night. By Monday morning the lump had completely disappeared along with the pain. Now many will say and you may well say, it could have been anything, that proves nothing, and to that I have no answer, but all I will say is "it takes much more faith to believe there isn't a God, than to realise there is." It's a terrifying concept, which is why people dislike it, but it comforts me to know there's someone out there that cares about me and is looking out for me, and you. There are so many things I won't understand in this life but that's OK, you just need faith.[19]

For reflection and discussion

PAX

All that matters is to be one with the living God
to be a creature in the house of the God of Life.

Like a cat asleep on a chair
at peace, in peace
and at one with the master of the house, with the mistress,
at home, at home in the house of the living,
sleeping on the hearth, and yawning before the fire.

Sleeping on the hearth of the living world
yawning at home before the fire of life
feeling the presence of the living God
like a great reassurance
a deep calm in the heart
a presence
as of the master sitting at the board
in his own and greater being,
in the house of life.

D. H. LAWRENCE

Is faith based on thinking or feeling, or on both? Where does your own faith find its roots? Does the way we think as a society affect people's ability to understand the gospel?

How positive do you feel about the future of the Christian faith in this country?

What is the good news that we wish to present to our friends, workmates and neighbours? Do you think they are interested in it?

'How are they to believe in one of whom they have never heard? And how are they to hear without someone to proclaim him?' (Romans 10.14). How confident do you feel about sharing your faith? Find one other person and explain to them, without using religious words, what difference it has made to you to know Jesus.

Chapter 2

Two world views

Making sense of life

Making sense of life is more complex than it seems. Take, for example, the physical environment in which we live. Apparently only the simplest, single-celled animals experience things as they really are. For higher animals such as ourselves there is no such thing as an uninterpreted world; every sense impression we receive is edited, arranged, and integrated with pre-existing information by the brain. Research done with newly sighted people offers a fascinating insight into this process – one patient described lemonade as 'square' because it pricked on his tongue as a square shape pricked on his hands; another regarded depth as a form of roundness; another interpreted shadows as random black patches strewn oddly about a flat and otherwise coloured world. For the newly sighted, vision is sensation unencumbered by meaning.[1]

If we engage interpretatively even with the simple, objectively existing matter of the world we can see and touch, we must do so even more as we enter the mental world of thought and belief – a world which is itself built largely upon the foundation of our physical experience.[2] The way in which interpreted sense experience underlies the way we think not just about the world we live in but about our own role and status within it, our own meaning and purpose, is illustrated by the simple but historically cataclysmic question 'Does the sun go round the earth, or the earth round the sun?' Direct observation suggests that the former is the case; and the discovery that in fact the opposite is so caused a whole world view to be thrown up in the air and painstakingly rearranged – not without conflict – when it came down again. Man, for centuries the centre of his own cosmos, suddenly found himself on the edge of an infinite universe.[3] Nothing had changed: the earth continued to spin gently beneath his feet, sparrows continued to chirp in the hedgerows, farmers ploughed their fields as usual; but philosophers and theologians began a long, reflective re-examination of everything they (in western Europe) had believed about human existence and its relation to the divine (for of course in the East and in Africa they had believed quite different things, and continued unperturbed to do so).

In order to make some kind of sense of life, every human society has to come up with the answers to two basic questions: how do we know things (a question about knowledge), and how do we make sense of them (a question about purpose). The answers to these questions provide a kind of map or compass which allows us to navigate through our daily lives with some vague sense of being in control, of coherency. Together they form a world view, one which most people never examine, but which they live by nonetheless.[4] A world view serves as a framework, and in some sense even a religion – a philosophy of the nature and meaning of life.[5] Developing it is a process which we engage in not just individually but collectively, in dependence upon one another. As a society we are in the process of changing our world view. It's very confusing; like living through an earthquake, standing on the shifting tectonic plates of different ways of doing things.

Scylla and Charybdis

Between the coast of Sicily and mainland Italy lie the twin dangers of Scylla and Charybdis – a sharp rock (or, following Homer, a six-headed monster) and a dangerous whirlpool. Easy to deal with independently, they become a double threat when confronted together – as any navigator who chooses to sail through the Straits of Messina must. Passing from nature to legend and finally to metaphor, Scylla and Charybdis will do us service as features of a physical and mental landscape by which we may for a moment chart our passage – for we too are navigating in new and complex waters.

Historically our culture is founded on two quite different world views. Using shorthand to summarise them, the first was the Hebrew, or Judaeo-Christian, world view. It offers faith-based answers to the fundamental questions of life. In particular, it holds that we know things through revelation: 'In the beginning was the Word, and the Word was God, and the Word was with God.' What we know, we know because God reveals it to us; and he does this through story. The scriptures are the word of God, and they tell the story of the relationship between man and God in the context of a bigger story which runs from the creation of the world in time right through to its recreation in eternity. Jesus is made known through story, and we find meaning for our lives through finding our own part in the story.[6] From Genesis to Revelation we watch groups and individuals learn, sometimes joyfully, sometimes painfully, to see themselves and their lives in this way. The process begins with the Pentateuch, the first five books of the Bible, in which God painstakingly teaches the Hebrew people to trust, follow and obey him, to understand their identity with reference to him, to expect their lives to unfold in line with his purposes. Reading them is a bit like watching a boy patiently placing and replacing his Scalextric car on the tracks he has built for it, learning to make it take the corners neither too fast nor too slow, finding out how to navigate the overhead loops, discovering the laws of motion and of gravity and how to work within them. So the people learn, as they wander in the desert, that the God who has liberated them from Egypt can be trusted; that he provides; that he must be obeyed if they are to have any kind of meaningful future. They learn to live their life on his tracks. Reading the gospels is the same: we watch person after person encounter Jesus, and re-evaluate their own understanding of relationships, priorities, choices in the light of that encounter. None is left unchanged, neither those who follow nor those who do not.[7] It is the same for us too; as I learn to live my life within this God-centred and God-narrated world view, I find that it takes a shape radically different from the one I had expected. I discover that the values by which I find myself living diverge increasingly from those of the majority who do not live in this way. Once fiercely determined to make my own choices, to seize life by the throat and shake it into conformity with my own ambitions, I now realise that my life is lived in the knowledge that what is required of me is not to create my own meaning but rather to discover it. Learning to live as part of God's story is an interesting and strangely satisfying process.

Many people in all periods of history have lived fulfilling and satisfying lives within the parameters of a faith-based world view, finding their own part – often somewhat to their surprise – within God's story. One of my heroes is Mary Slessor, born in

1848 as the daughter of an alcoholic shoemaker, sent to work in a Dundee mill from the age of eleven, who realised that God was calling her to travel to Nigeria as a missionary. She spent her entire adult life there, working amongst the Efik people whose lifestyle (when she arrived, but not when she left) included slave trading, cannibalism, witchcraft, trial by ordeal and, particularly irksome to Mary, the killing of all twin babies. Another hero is William Wilberforce, a young MP who said openly 'my own distinction was my darling object' and who yet found himself, as a new Christian, realising that God had another plan in mind. 'Who knows that but for such a time as this God has brought you into public life and has a purpose for you,' hymn writer John Newton told him. Setting aside his own ambition, Wilberforce spent the next twenty years campaigning against the slave trade, and the rest of his life against slavery itself. He died in 1833, aged seventy-four, two days after it became clear that slavery would be abolished by law in all British territories.[8]

We are of course not all called to be Mary Slessors or William Wilberforces; but it is open to all of us to find our own place, however modest or unexpected, in the grand scheme of things. Our small core ReSource team consists of a lawyer, a university lecturer, a children's nurse, a management consultant, and a surprised South African administrator; none of us planned to be doing what we are now doing. I remember, as a sixteen-year-old atheist, thinking how odd it must be to be a Christian minister, and to have a job which was all about nothing – only to find myself, years later, doing that same job (and finding that it is in fact about rather more than I had bargained for). I know a businessman who realises that his purpose is to finance God's work all over the world; a pensions adviser who discovered herself called to be a pastoral rock for teenage boys in a school boarding house; a dentist who finds himself running free clinics in Tanzania as an addition to his work in the UK; a check-out clerk whose ministry is to look customers in the eye and smile at them. It is open to every Christian to become, as Thomas Merton puts it, God's 'word', spoken freely in our own personal situations.[9]

Looking back, then, at our two basic questions (how do we know things, and how do we make sense of them?), it's clear that the Hebrew world view offers excellent answers to the second question, the one about purpose. According to this world view, any individual who chooses to recognise it finds his or her own place in the history of the cosmos, known and defined before birth, to continue after death; and therefore a meaningful role in the present order of things. My purpose is my part in the story, a story overseen by God and into which I am drawn through my relationship with Jesus. Thomas Merton explains how it works: 'The secret of my identity is hidden in the love and mercy of God. Therefore there is only one problem on which all my existence, my peace and my happiness depend: to discover myself in discovering God. If I find Him I will find myself and if I find my true self, I will find Him.'[10]

But if we turn to the first question, the one to do with knowledge, the faith-based world view is much weaker. Attempts to understand the world we live in within a revelation-based epistemological framework have led to controversy and ultimately to its rejection. Revelation does not help us to understand the inner workings of the atom or the laws of gravity. It may offer a coherent story within which to live a meaningful life, but it's no use at all when you are looking for a cure for AIDS or a solution to the problem of global warming. Revelation does not help us to understand and manipulate the world we live in. It doesn't even try.

And yet the question remains. And so from about the thirteenth century we turned to a different world view: that which was born in Ancient Greece. The Greek approach to reality is very different. It's based not on revelation but on human reason. Natural philosophers such as Aristotle, Archimedes, Euclid, and Pythagoras had tried to understand reality not by trusting in it but by thinking about it. Much of their work, lost to the Latin West, now became available through translators working from Arabic versions at the courts of Sicily and Spain, contact points between the civilisations of West and East.[11] Medieval scholars pored in excitement over Aristotle, and gradually a new, empirical approach to the fundamental questions of life was born. It is possible to stand today in the Museum of the History of Science in Florence and admire the astonishing display of new mathematical and scientific instruments from the following centuries: the first thermometers, compasses, and astrolabes.[12] Galileo – whose middle finger sits rather unnervingly in the museum alongside his instruments – looked through his new, precision telescope and came up with confirmation that Copernicus was right, and the earth does indeed go round the sun. Isaac Newton, sent home from Cambridge during an outbreak of plague, sat in a Lincolnshire orchard watching apples fall from the trees, and came up with the laws of gravity from which the science of mechanics was born. Charles Darwin sailed to the Galapagos Islands, and began to think about the evolutionary adaptation of the flightless cormorants and the various species of finch he found there. These men and many others followed in the footsteps of the Greek natural philosophers despite the anxious protests of the Church, and a new, scientific world view was born. Modern science is built to this day on a foundation of Greek speculative enquiry: reality is that which we can investigate through human reason and experimentation.[13] An indication of how recent it is as a world view is revealed by the word 'science' itself: it was first used by William Whewell in the year 1834.[14]

The advantage of the scientific approach to knowledge is that it offers a clear methodology for accessing and exploring our physical environment. Following in the footsteps of the Greeks has enabled us to make astonishing advances in our ability to understand and manipulate the world we live in. Modern science, technology and medicine all bear witness to that. But the weakness of the scientific approach is that it has nothing at all to say to us about meaning. It simply is not the case that if we understand the movements of the moons of Jupiter or the adaptive specialisation of finches we will be any the wiser about the big questions to do with meaning, purpose, and our place in the midst of this complex universe. Darwin himself recognised this, declaring that 'Dr Pusey was mistaken in imagining that I wrote the Origin with any relation whatever to Theology. I should have thought that this would have been evident to anyone who has taken the trouble to read the book.'[15] Darwin would have been astonished to see some of the philosophical edifices which have been built on the foundation of what, for him, was a straightforward scientific theory to do with the mechanisms by which species diversified.

Sensing the rising tide of unanswered questions, some scientists have tried to extend the boundaries of science beyond the 'how' questions into the 'why' questions. Best known among these is Darwin's disciple Richard Dawkins, geneticist turned scientific philosopher, who claims with increasing stridency that everything that needs to be known can be known through science – indeed, he claims that God himself is a scientific hypothesis.[16] The difficulty is that while Dawkins' grasp of genetics is presumably impeccable, his philosophy or theology is surprisingly amateur; it's been likened by one commentator to the kind of science which might be produced by a theologian in triumphant possession of a single copy of the AA *Book of British Birds*.[17] Most scientists have a more modest view of their remit: Nobel Prize winner Peter Medawar points out that 'the existence of a limit to science is made clear by its inability to answer childlike elementary questions having to do with first and last things – questions such as "How did everything begin?"; "What are we all here for?"; "What is the point of living?"'[18]

It seems clear that if faith-based thinking does not adequately answer questions about the nature of the physical universe, scientific thinking does not properly aim to answer questions about the purpose and meaning of life. And so we find that our tendency to view science as the gateway to understanding has produced a society which is strong on reality but weak on meaning. Despite its many astounding achievements, and despite the platform of sophisticated technological security it has created for us on which to build our lives, modern science offers no coherent answer to the fundamental questions of what it means to be alive here, now, in this place. It leaves the emotional and spiritual landscapes of life unexplored. And yet, as Solomon remarked long ago, 'God has set eternity in the minds of men' – we just aren't wired up to live in a world with no greater dimension than today.[19] Indeed, it has been said that we are the only people ever to have tried to do so – the only human society in history to have supposed that a mechanistic and individualistic understanding of life offers the way to become fulfilled and whole persons.[20] Faith offers inadequate answers to questions about the physical universe – so we dismiss it in favour of scientific materialism. But scientific materialism offers inadequate answers to questions to do with the needs of our souls. We have thrown the baby out with the bathwater.

Increasingly we are realising what we have lost; but we can't wind the clock back. The Hebrew world view now seems ancient and outmoded; and yet our sophisticated modern science cannot even begin to answer the question to which a faith-based approach did offer a comprehensive and convincing response – the question framed in the simplest of words by Heidegger, one of the greatest philosophers of the twentieth century: 'Why is there being rather than nothing?'

So there's a fundamental polarity in the genetics of our thinking. Do we go for 'Greek' knowledge, or do we go for 'Hebrew' purpose? Because we don't seem to have found a system which allows us to do both at once. We are in something of a crisis. How do we know things? And how do we make sense of them? We thought we knew. Then we changed our minds. Now again we aren't so sure. We are, it's been said, the 'people of the parenthesis', at the end of one era but not quite at the beginning of the next.[21] If Scylla leaves us high and dry in our quest for knowledge and understanding of the world we live in, and Charybdis threatens to suck us into a whirlpool of meaninglessness, what is the way forward? Can we find some kind of balance as we navigate between them?

Caught between worlds – the vacuum within

The result of the shift from a faith-based to a science-based world view is that we now live in what Chinese philosopher Carver T. Yu has called a society of technological optimism and literary despair.[22] In the West at least, we inhabit an environment shaped by immensely sophisticated technological resources, we enjoy a level of material prosperity not even dreamt of by our forebears, and we are accustomed to making daily choices not just about practical matters such as where and how we live, but more fundamental ones about the role and identity we wish to adopt. And yet…

The state of a society's soul is mirrored in its art, and it's no accident that throughout the twentieth century art became increasingly disjointed and depressed. Gone are the shining golden haloes of the medieval period, the simple Renaissance clarity of madonnas holding goldfinches and silhouetted against blue skies, the tranquil landscapes of the eighteenth and nineteenth centuries; now we have fractured images and controversial installations exploring what one commentator calls 'everyday alienation'. Many of them go on display in London each year as entries for the prestigious Turner Prize – pickled cows, soiled beds, empty rooms with the lights going on and off.[23] And it's not just the Turner, with its deliberate attempt to push its way through conventional boundaries. I went a few years ago to the Tate Modern in London to see an exhibition of the work of the modern artist Mark Rothko. Rothko claimed to see art as a religious experience, but drew his inspiration not from Jesus but from the German atheistic philosopher Friedrich Nietzsche. As I gazed at wall-sized murals of dark red squares enclosed in thick black borders, I could feel myself being sucked into a world without light or hope. Apparently Rothko had wanted people to stand in this room and feel like hitting their heads against the walls. Singularly successful in this endeavour, he committed suicide in 1970.

Other artists, less depressive, use their art to offer a visual protest against the way things are. Long queues formed in Bristol to see the first ever public exhibition by graffiti artist Banksy, whose work offers an overt commentary on the corporately sanctioned images of a materialistic society – images which in one way we would like to believe, but which we know in our hearts are little more than glossy idealisations with hidden agendas lurking beneath their attractive surfaces.

So all is not as well as it may seem. We may have BlackBerries®, Wiis, four-wheel drives and surround sound, but what are our lives all about? However much we have and know, there's no point having or knowing it if we have no idea what it's all for. Our enthusiastic, fascinating, and enriching pursuit of science, economics, and materialistic philosophies has had the unexpected side-effect of creating an existential vacuum. The situation we are left in if we adopt an entirely scientific world view was unwittingly summed up by a soldier who said, "I want to believe something, but I'm not sure what it is." All the indications are that he speaks for an awful lot of people; and yet as Christians we so often find ourselves lacking the confidence to help them. This is without doubt in part due to the factors discussed in the last chapter, and to the realisation that our efforts will not always be well received. But then, Jesus never said they would be.[24] Perhaps we need to remind ourselves that we are people, living amongst people, and that many will be interested in our faith story, as long as we share it in simple, personal, and unthreatening ways. Susan Hope summarises the situation well: "There is at present a great deal of concern and anxiety about how to reach a postmodern culture for Christ. While this concern is legitimate, the anxiety is regrettable. The anxiety, in part, seems to be rooted in a crisis of confidence in our ability to communicate with a postmodern culture. But postmodern people [are like] us. They are made of flesh and blood. They laugh. They cry. They sweat. They get puffed when they run for the bus. Their hearts beat faster when they are afraid. They like to be liked. When they feel peckish, they'll open the door of the fridge and have a little snack. They are glad when Friday comes."[25]

In the gospel we have the answer to their needs.

Good news for Paul

Paul Taylor was a bank manager with NatWest. Martin, a Christian, had just moved house; he made an appointment to see him. They got talking. Paul seemed interested in Martin's faith, so Martin gave him a copy of my book *The Wild Gospel*. A few weeks later Martin's phone rang. It was the bank manager's PA. Could she make another appointment for Martin to see the bank manager, please? Unsure what the problem might be, and apprehensive at being called a second time to see his bank manager, Martin found himself again in Paul's office. The conversation went something like this: "*Oh, hello, it's you – didn't we see one another quite recently?*" "Yes, so I wasn't quite sure why you wanted to see me again?" "*No, that's strange, neither am I; but while you're here, can I say I've been reading that book you gave me last time, and I'm about halfway through.*" He paused, then said, slowly, "*It's true, isn't it!*" "Yes." "*It makes me think I'd like to do something other than what I'm doing, because this is all rather hollow, really.*" "What sort of thing?" "*Something with meaning, a purpose to it.*" "Is that just an idea, or do you want to do something about that?" "*I do.*" "Would you be happy for me to help you with that searching?" "*Yes I would.*" "Would you be OK if we prayed about that now, or would that seem strange to you?" "*No, that would be good – but I should tell you that I haven't been to church for years and years.*" "That's OK – it's not about church, it's about you and God and finding fullness of life." "*Yes, that's what I want.*" Martin prayed for Paul, and Paul said "*Amen*". He went on to share how excited he was, a man of fifty-three, divorced with three children, now living alone – and feeling himself to be standing on the edge of something really significant. He gave Martin his personal contact details, and asked him to travel with him. A couple of weeks later, over dinner at Martin's house, Paul gave his life to Christ.[26]

For reflection and discussion

THE GOLDFISH BOWL

Thought wanders
unconfined
peaceful
over the white page
but once
it was not so.
When I was little
I saw the world
from behind glass
and thought lived
detached
in the goldfish bowl
of my mind.
When I grew bigger
I discovered Plato
and learnt about
Shadows and Forms
and things not being real

and so I settled
for the idea
that the goldfish bowl
was the way things were.
Then one day
I stood in a church
and watched rays of sunlight
melting through
the soft rich colours
of stained glass
and falling
in pools of glowing red and orange
on tombs
in the stoneflagged floor.
And I knew there was something
behind the glass
trying to get through
and that it was love.
The love was pouring
through the window
onto the tombs
but the glass was
in between.
Later I found
what Plato never knew
that the love is God
that love is life
and that the life
is mine
and I swam out
of the goldfish bowl.

ALISON MORGAN

Can you identify the 'Hebrew' (faith-based) and 'Greek'
(science-based) world views in the people you know? Try
looking through today's newspaper – which world view
dominates? Thinking of your local church, is the balance the
same or different?

Do you agree that science is limited in its ability to answer some of the most fundamental questions about life? What elements of human experience cannot be adequately discussed from a scientific point of view?

'The world in all its fancy wisdom never had a clue when it came to knowing God.... We of course have plenty of wisdom to pass on to you once you get your feet on firm spiritual ground, but it's not popular wisdom, the fashionable wisdom of high-priced experts that will be out-of-date in a year or so. God's wisdom is something mysterious that goes deep into the interior of his purposes' (1 Corinthians 1.20, 2.6–7, TM). Where do you look for wisdom today?

Chapter 3

A gilded cage

King's Parade is the artery of historic Cambridge. Flanked by the butter-gold stone of King's College and the delicately carved pinnacles of the Chapel, punctuated by daisy-flecked lawns and backed by the serene gardens which blossom beyond the gentle lapping of the river, it represents centuries of peaceful scholarship and the pursuit of academic excellence. Future archbishops, prime ministers, poets and novelists have lived and studied in King's, and generations of choristers have sung beneath the beautiful fan-vaulted ceiling of the magnificent chapel. But whilst the setting has changed little over the last few hundred years, the college itself has changed profoundly. Founded by Henry VI for the scholars of Eton, King's now hosts a wide variety of students from all walks of life and from many different cultural backgrounds. Many are politically active and involved with campaigning organisations of one kind or another. And so it was that one day I walked down the broad pavement of King's Parade to find my way obstructed by a large wooden cage, and in it a man. Organised by the university branch of Amnesty International, the cage represented a protest in support of the many people imprisoned around the world for their political or religious beliefs. The cage protest has taken place termly ever since, and has become a well-known part of Cambridge life.

As I reflect upon it now, it seems to me that the cage does

not only represent a protest; it also asks a question. Who are the caged in our own society? It is, to be sure, harsh and unjust to be imprisoned not for your illegal actions but for your peacefully held beliefs, and we are right to stand up and say so as loudly as we can. And yet I cannot help remembering the well-known words of the seventeenth-century poet Richard Lovelace, himself imprisoned for political activism: 'Stone walls do not a prison make, nor iron bars a cage.' Prison, said Lovelace, is not external but internal; it is determined not merely by where your body is but by what is going on inside your head. You do not have to be in a cage to feel trapped.[1]

We live in a society which has taken the art of cage making to the highest possible level. To be sure, our shopping malls, advertising hoardings and even insurance companies all claim to offer choice and freedom – but is it real freedom, or merely the illusion of freedom? I may be free to wander beneath the elegant glass-roofed arcade of Bristol's magnificent Cabot Circus shopping centre, but am I free to feel I have no need for the products on sale there? I may be free to enjoy one of the highest standards of health care the world has to offer, but am I free to face death with an untroubled mind? I may be free to change my spouse or my job or the town in which I live, but am I free to experience the joy of committed relationships, to contribute appropriately to society, to belong to a genuine community? Freedom is not necessarily the same as choice, and it isn't necessarily related to economic activity or physical well-being.

The iron cage of rationalism

One hundred years ago sociologist Max Weber warned that developments in modern culture, as it moved increasingly firmly from a world view based on faith to one based on human reason, would eventually result in people finding themselves locked into an 'iron cage' of rationality which would threaten all meaningful human existence. Life in this new world of scientific materialism, he wrote, was already beginning to reveal itself as 'dreary, flat and utilitarian, leaving a great void in the souls of men which they seek to fill by furious activity and through various devices and substitutes.'[2]

Looking back on those words with the benefit of hindsight, experience suggests he was right. We are discovering, as we try to meet our needs with money, education, higher living standards, better medicine and a greater variety of lifestyle choices, that there is more to life than a rationalistic and scientific world view can offer. Put simply, it leaves stuff out.

What are the signs that this is so? The symptoms of dissatisfaction with the 'Greek' world view of scientific rationalism are all around us. The aspirations of our young people are changing. In a recent survey, primary school children were asked what they wanted to be when they grew up. They didn't want to be engine drivers and nurses, or even scientists and bankers; they wanted to be famous, they said. They wanted to be celebrities. Or, in some cases, WAGS – wives and girlfriends of celebrities. And as they pointed out, you don't need qualifications for that, you just need to get yourself on TV.[3] At secondary school, the number of A-level students opting for science subjects is in steady decline, whilst those taking sociology, media studies, art and design and psychology increase year by year – to the point where, in 2009, 14% of schools did not enter any students at all for A-level physics.[4] University applications tell the same story: numbers wanting to study science and engineering remain approximately constant, whilst applications to study media studies, journalism, and art and design subjects are rocketing – despite the fact that subsequent employment rates for those graduating in such disciplines are painfully low.[5] For young people, scientific investigation seems less exciting than self-expression.

At the same time, science itself is moving on. It takes time for cutting edge discoveries to filter down into popular consciousness, but scientists themselves, and in particular physicists and mathematicians, are increasingly aware that the physical world is not such a clear and certain place as had been supposed. Based on centuries of empirical investigation, the popular concept of science is that it works by an objective process of gradual discovery, peeling back facts like successive layers of an onion; and this leads us to assume that as we penetrate further and further into the depths of the onion in question we will gradually achieve greater and greater clarity about the world we live in.[6] And so we watch physicists and biologists trying to understand the world by breaking it down into its smallest constituent parts – from chromosomes to strings of DNA to individual molecules, and from atoms to protons and neutrons, and from those to leptons and quarks, mesons and bosons and gluons. And yet not only is the process less objective than is popularly believed, it seems too that the closer in they get, the less certain it all seems to become: it appears that mystery, not in the sense of something not yet understood but in the far more challenging sense of something that is by its very nature inconsistent and unpredictable, is built into the universe at its most fundamental level. One biologist concludes that 'the universe is not only queerer than we suppose; it is queerer than we *can* suppose.'[7]

To what extent can science explain reality? Well, it is hard to explain the distinctiveness of human life in purely physical terms when it turns out that we have the same number of active genes as the fruit fly.[8] And it is hard to feel that we have got our minds round the mechanics of matter when the empirical evidence we have from subatomic research is not so much incomplete or even unlikely as intrinsically self-contradictory. We know, for example, that light is simultaneously wave and particle, and that matter is not a series of building blocks but 'an affair of changing relationships between non-material entities.'[9] We now suspect that the fundamental unit of the physical world is not a particle but a dance performed by strings vibrating within subatomic particles. And when we raise our heads from the microscope or stand back from the particle accelerator and seek answers not in component parts but in whole organisms, we find ourselves facing the complication that whereas a man-made machine, say a jet engine, is the perfectly predictable sum total of its various parts working together, this is not so for any organic system. Natural wholes, from living organisms to ecosystems to galaxies, operate differently; each of them is more than the sum total of its parts. And if this is so, the whole enterprise of reductionist science, however valuable for other reasons, will never offer any more than a very partial explanation of the reality that underlies our living universe – a universe which one scientist has suggested is beginning to look more like a great thought than a great machine.[10]

So if science is not to proceed by reductionist investigation, how does it proceed? Einstein, whose work burst through the predictable bounds of mechanical science and launched physicists into a new world of quantum uncertainty, said that science proceeds not by logic but by intuition. Philosophers say that almost all intellectual advance, scientific or otherwise, in fact takes place by means not of investigation but of metaphor; it is only through the imaginative possibilities opened up by the use of metaphor that we can escape the straitjacket of previous thinking.[11] And indeed it seems that the most startling scientific discoveries of our time can only be talked about in metaphorical terms – the Big Bang and the expanding universe; string theory; the curving material of space-time. Gone, in common consensus at least, is the feeling that we will get to the bottom of things by opening them up; to get to the bottom of them at all may indeed, suggests President of the Royal Society, Martin Rees, be beyond the capacity of the human mind.[12]

All this has brought something of a revolution in the way we understand reality. Many scientists have responded by concentrating in ever more specialised ways on their own particular fields of research, reminding themselves that physics is descriptive and that it is not, and never has been, its job to ask why. Others, increasingly recognising the limitations of a reductionist approach but not wanting to reject the modernist dogma that science is the source of all knowledge, have tried to stand back and look at the big picture. Scientists are reinventing themselves as philosophers – or even as what one commentator calls 'a new priesthood celebrating the sacred and baffling mysteries of creation.'[13] Physicist Paul Davies suggested over twenty years ago that 'science offers a surer path than religion in the search for God.'[14] Stephen Hawking, until recently reluctant to venture over the boundary which separates science from religion, has now joined the fray: 'Where did all this come from? Did the universe need a creator? Traditionally these are questions for philosophy, but philosophy is dead. Philosophy has not kept up with modern developments in science. Scientists have become the bearers of the torch of discovery in our quest for knowledge.'[15] Stephen's Catholic wife professes her anxiety as her atheist husband writes about God; journalist Bryan Appleyard just comments drily of Hawking and Davies 'both men are physicists, and neither knows what he is talking about.'[16]

The most familiar voice claiming that science alone contains the answers to all dimensions of human life is Richard Dawkins, who has suggested that there is no place for God in a world which contains scientists; and yet whose crusading determination to disprove God has led not only other scientists but even other atheists to denounce him as 'a great embarrassment'.[17] Meanwhile the Advertising Standards Agency disallowed the British Humanist Association's bus advert 'there is no God' and forced the amendment 'there probably is no God', on the grounds that the first could not be verified (a nice later twist to the story came when the free and happy children featured in a subsequent advert turned out to be the offspring of a well-known Christian musician). Mary Midgely, reviewing Dawkins' book *The God Delusion* in the *New Scientist*, described his philosophy as a 'scientific fundamentalism' based on the sweeping assumption that science is the only possible source of knowledge and that nothing can exist outside it – whereas in fact, as she points out, 'science is only a small, specialised, dependent part of what anybody knows.'[18] Others have observed that Dawkins and other God decriers demonstrate not so much secularism as a curiously vehement theophobia.[19] A more personal reaction was given at a men's breakfast in the Cotswolds at which Martin Cavender was speaking on 'The Evidence for Jesus'. After the event a man came up to him. He was the chairman of an IT company, and for thirty minutes he disagreed with everything Martin had said – God, Jesus, the lot. Eventually he said, "Thank you. I'm afraid

I've got to go now – but that was very helpful." Martin, reeling a little, asked "*helpful*, how had it been *helpful*?" "The trouble is," said the man, jabbing his finger in the air, "I want to believe Richard Dawkins. But he's not happy, and you are!" "Well, that's scarcely evidence," said Martin, who used to be a lawyer. "It'll do for now!", came the reply.

So, it seems that reality is a lot more complex than we had ever dreamed possible; the further we push against the boundaries, the more it seems that the 'Greek' view of reality is ultimately as incomplete as the 'Hebrew' one. Francis Collins, Director of the Human Genome Project and a committed Christian, acknowledges that 'one of the strongest motivations of humankind is to seek answers to profound questions,' and suggests that the way forward is not to pit science against faith but rather to draw on the insights of both: 'we need to bring all the power of both the scientific and spiritual perspectives to bear on understanding what is both seen and unseen.'[20] A church notice board put it more succinctly: 'There are some questions that can't be answered by Google.'

The submerged forces of evil

One of the more unexpected consequences of our obsession with material reality has been an increased awareness of evil. For several hundred years now we have persisted in the belief that economic growth and technological advances would bring increased peace and prosperity, enable us to reach our potential as human beings, and make the world a better and safer place for us all to live in. Not only has this clearly not happened, the reverse seems to be the case. In the twentieth century alone, 167 million people were killed by ideologically or politically motivated tyranny, more than in all the previous centuries put together.[21] The wave of international terrorism which was unleashed in the wake of the September 2001 attack on the Twin Towers has led to a level of insecurity greater than that at any time since the Second World War, and perhaps further in its reach due to its hidden nature – for every person killed in a suicide attack, fear is sown in the hearts of millions more. Our secular philosophy seems to leave us with little real idea what to do about it all, except perhaps, as Tom Wright remarks, drop bombs on it.[22] Meanwhile occult thrillers are standard fare in our cinemas and even in the teenage reading section of our public libraries. The world of childhood is getting darker and darker; when the new 3D release of *Alice in Wonderland* feels it necessary to include a scene in which Alice kills the Jabberwocky, we know that somehow things are going wrong.

At the same time, violence and uncertainty seem to be an increasing part not just of human society, but of the natural world itself. As earthquakes, tsunamis, and volcanic eruptions bring destruction and disruption by land, sea, and air, the wonders of our sophisticated technology seem to offer an ever thinner skin between us and a world of chaos. The 2009 Turner Prize shortlist included an installation by Richard Hiorns, who covered half a gallery floor with the black and grey metal dust of an atomised passenger aircraft engine, in a work 'designed to question our faith in technology and remind us of our own mortality.' The cracks are beginning to show through the wallpaper.

Taken together, these things worry us. Opinion polls suggest that people's personal awareness of evil is increasing with every passing year. A poll commissioned by the BBC in the year 2000 found that 25% of people said that they have had direct personal awareness of an evil presence – a 100% increase since the same question was asked only thirteen years previously.[23] My own experience as a Christian minister is that there is a steady increase in people requesting prayer for release from disturbing spiritual forces. Some report the sensation that there is something dark lurking beneath their bed, or interfering with them physically as they sleep. Others report nightmares, hallucinations, visions of shapes, and obsessive experiences of words and numbers. Some find that there are cold patches in their houses, that computer and electrical equipment behaves oddly and erratically, or, like the teenager in Wells, that they tremble and feel sick when they try to attend church or to pray, as if there is something within them which is in some way spiritually allergic to this kind of activity. Some experience distressing and compulsive temptations or addictions from which they seem unable to free themselves. Sometimes there are psychological causes for these things; but in many cases the symptoms disappear when a simple prayer for release in the name of Jesus is prayed, with a command to the unwelcome spirits to go – perhaps in the context of a service of communion or a meditation on the cross.

Many people stumble into this kind of experience by mistake. A couple of years ago Fran came to see me. Fran came from a difficult family background. Her father, a senior Freemason, was sometimes violent; her mother had suffered from depression throughout Fran's childhood and remained emotionally dependent on her. Encouraged by an early and accurate experience of having her palms read, Fran herself had been involved in many different occult activities; in particular she had discovered that by using a pendulum she was able to tell whether a forthcoming baby would be a boy or a girl, by means of some force which she realised was not a benevolent one; "it wasn't me, and I knew it wasn't God." When she became a Christian Fran found that her inner turmoil only increased. She too became depressed, and was unable to work. She began to suffer from psychotic experiences in which she heard and saw things which were not there, and she experienced severe and distressing nausea every time anyone prayed for her. Clinging to the reality of her new faith, Fran had believed that God was 'stripping her down'. As we prayed, she felt the familiar sickness, and then a sensation which she described as being like a fire burning her on the inside; and a great darkness. As we continued in prayer, she began to experience first warmth, and then light coming in from the direction of those praying. We prayed on, banishing any evil spiritual forces and asking that she be completely filled with the Holy Spirit. For the first time in her life Fran felt an overwhelming sensation of peace. The sickness went and she was able to forgive her parents. Her face transformed by broad smiles, she looked up: was there anything she could do for us? Fran has now established a small Christian community from which she also runs her own business.

A society based on scientific materialism which focuses its attention on the visible does not thereby ensure that the invisible does not exist; good or bad, it merely forces it underground. The results are becoming increasingly violent and alarming, and it is time we recognised that as Christians we do have some good news to speak into the turmoil. 'Progress might have been all right once,' quipped Ogden Nash, 'but it's gone on far too long.'

Life behind bars – a lost sense of purpose

We saw in Chapter 2 that a 'Hebrew' or faith-based world view provides clear and coherent answers to questions about meaning ('how do we make sense of things?'). It enables us to make sense of our own lives by learning to find our own particular part in God's purposes. We saw too that because this world view fails to provide answers to questions about knowledge ('how do we know things?'), we increasingly abandoned it as we set about the task of investigating the world we live in through a new scientific approach based on human reason and experimentation. The result is that, some seven centuries after we rediscovered this 'Greek', science-based world view, we are finding as a society that we have lost what for centuries we seemed to have in the bag – the sense of purpose and identity which comes through relationship with God. This has left us in what Gerard Kelly neatly describes as a 'cultural millenopause' – a deepening existential discomfort. Looked at from the outside, our society appears prosperous and contented; beneath the surface, we find that things are not so good. What are the signs that all is not well?

A couple of years ago I led a retreat for a group of curates. One was called David, and he told us that before he was ordained he'd spent ten years as a stockbroker, working amongst men and women whose lives were outwardly highly successful. When the time came for him to leave his job for theological college, David's colleagues came to say goodbye. It was a crowded office, he said, just as you might imagine, with desks rammed up against one another and absolutely no space between them. So as his colleagues came one by one to see him, they knelt by his desk to talk; and one after another, David noticed that they were upset, even in some cases in tears. Touched, he asked them why. It turned out that they were crying not because he was leaving but because they were staying. Their lives of financial success and high social status weren't doing anything for them; inwardly they felt trapped. They longed for the purpose and meaning they saw in David's life. "We wish we could have your faith," they said. Modern life, observed Jeremy Clarkson as he constructed a parable out of Sir Ranulph Fiennes's recent journey on foot to the North Pole, boils down to little more than this: 'We get up in a morning, we trudge through the day, with no sense of purpose or ambition, and then we die.'[24]

One of the most insightful writers on contemporary Western reality is philosopher Alain de Botton. Commenting on what he describes as 'the dwarfing complexity of the modern world of work', Alain remarks on the extraordinary claim of the workplace to be able to provide us with the principal source of life's meaning. Released from the need to spend all our waking hours providing ourselves with food and shelter, he suggests that all too often we find not freedom but incarceration: 'The brightest minds spend their working lives simplifying or accelerating functions of unreasonable banality. Engineers write theses on the velocities of scanning machines and consultants devote their careers to implementing minor economies in the movements of shelf-stackers and forklift operators. The alcohol-inspired fights that break out in market towns on Saturday evenings are predictable symptoms of fury at our incarceration. They are a reminder of the price we pay for our daily submission at the altars of prudence and order – and of the rage that silently accumulates beneath a uniquely law-abiding and compliant surface.'[25] The cage may be gilded; but it is still a cage.

The problem is purpose. Science does not look for purpose, merely for explanation.[26] But purpose remains an inescapable element in life, even if we no longer have a language in which to talk about it. People need purpose, and so, as Lesslie Newbigin has remarked, 'a strange fissure runs right through the consciousness of modern Western man. We all engage in purposeful activity, but accept as the final product of this purposeful activity a picture of the world from which purpose has been eliminated.' An odd state of affairs, to say the least.[27]

Devices and substitutes

We saw earlier that Max Weber warned of the great void which a purely rational world view would generate in our souls, a void which we would seek to fill 'by furious activity and through various devices and substitutes'. If he is right, the signs of those devices and substitutes should be apparent all around us – and they are.

Last year we were doing some work in Newcastle. Somerset is a long way from Newcastle, so we went by plane. On the way home I looked at the departures board. All seemed as expected: the usual ordered, illuminated columns showed the airline, the flight number, the destination, the time. Reading on to find the gate number, however, I found myself gazing at a column I had never seen before. It said 'shopping time'.

If work fails to fulfil us, shopping is on offer as the main alternative. Like work, shopping seems to promise freedom, this time not in the form of personal fulfilment but in that of choice and possession. Through buying things we are invited to build an identity, to gain respect, to find happiness. It's another gilded cage; countless surveys show that beyond a certain minimal level, increased wealth makes no impact on our wellbeing.[28] Indeed, it turns out that the second happiest people in the world are the Masai, whose spending power is amongst the lowest of any people group. But the myth is strong, and it is reinforced to us daily by advertising, the fastest growing form of communication in the world. It is estimated that the average Briton faces 3,000 marketing messages a day, all promising that through making this or that purchase we will find confidence, relaxation, love, freedom from stress, peace, fun, status, happy families, secure friendships, health, personal attractiveness and a host of other intangible benefits.[29] Alan Storkey comments, 'the appeals of consumerism are pathetic in that they are not true. Consumer goods and services cannot give the qualities they claim, and can often not even contribute to them. So we have an invasion which landscapes the mind, emotions and inner character of millions of people, even though it is fabricated of lies.'[30]

A few years ago I was speaking at an Alpha course in Leicester. On the Alpha course was a woman named Dawn, and Dawn told me how it was that she had come to join the course. Each year on Good Friday, Leicester city centre hosts a re-enactment of the Passion of Christ. It's always packed; many people have the day off work, and the city centre is thronged with crowds. Dawn, who had gone into town to do her Easter shopping, found herself caught up in the procession. As she followed Jesus and the soldiers from the trial before Pilate in the Town Hall Square to the scaffolding of the cross outside H&M, Dawn had found herself gazing unexpectedly and momentarily into the eyes of Jesus. Suddenly, she said, it seemed that Jesus was really there, that he was speaking directly to her, and that he seemed to be asking a question, demanding a response. Overwhelmed by this experience, Dawn found someone to pray with and committed her life to Jesus. What then? Well, she said, she bent down to pick up her shopping. And as she stood there, her heavy carrier bags in her hands, she had a thought she'd never had before: why on earth had she felt she wanted to do all this shopping, to buy all these things she didn't need? A lie had met the truth.

What's going on, as we work and shop and fail to find

fulfilment? Perhaps it's that beneath the quest for purpose and meaning there lies a deeper malaise: a quest for identity. In a fast-changing world with no coherent philosophy of meaning, we are left wondering who we are, trying to cover the holes which peep through the gaps in the daylight. Not everyone minds – this is Bob Dylan, who so often seemed to speak intuitively for a whole generation: "I don't think I'm tangible to myself. I mean, I think one thing today and I think another thing tomorrow. I change during the course of a day. I wake and I'm one person, and when I go to sleep I know for certain I'm somebody else. I don't know who I am most of the time. It doesn't even matter to me." But if Dylan could sing his way out of angst, not everybody can. For many, a bottle of wine after work is the only way of stilling the universe before climbing back onto the treadmill. Increasing numbers are turning to alcohol as the leisure activity of choice. "We couldn't think of anything to do," I heard a young man in a pub say recently, "so we came in here and got drunk." According to the *British Medical Journal*, the number of deaths in Britain directly attributed to alcohol almost doubled between 1991 and 2005.[31] It's an easy solution to a difficult problem.

Meanwhile life gets faster and faster, as we substitute hurry for purpose. I stood the other day on an escalator in the London Underground, realising as the adverts flashed past me that the escalators now move at about twice the speed they used to when I was a teenager. It all reminds me of the Red Queen in Alice in Wonderland, running faster and faster in order to stay in the same place. In other cultures people do not live like this. I remember the sight of a Tanzanian bishop staying with us, coming out of the house with a broad smile and a readiness to leave for the drive to a three-day conference in Canterbury. He was bringing all he needed in two plastic carrier bags. In the car he told me something of what it feels like to arrive in a country where everything is so complicated and fast moving: confusing, alarming, and demanding. A few years later I stood on top of the mountain overlooking the Tanzanian town of Masasi, having set off at dawn up a path winding between hard volcanic rocks and carpeted with tinder dry leaves scorched by the rising sun. As we walked up, others came down: men, tired, smiling, laden with bundles of firewood they would sell for a pound each in the town, one or two warning us to avoid the tree by the muddy spring where a mamba had coiled overnight. Birds sang in the green trees which still coated the upper reaches of the mountain; an eagle floated overhead. Reaching the summit, we sat amongst the birdsong and found ourselves looking down on a valley dotted with mango, cashew and coconut trees. This is where our UK palm crosses are made; and yet it's a world as remote from ours as can be imagined, far from competition and consumerism, a world where the only sounds rising from the valley below were the voices of people and cockerels, misty in the distance. Beyond them, silence stretched in waves to the blue brown horizon of an ancient continent. Reflecting that it was days since I had seen an advertisement, I realised how insidiously our culture draws us away from God, and, as Father Francis led us spontaneously in prayer by the cross on the summit, how thin the boundary between us and God actually is, once we strip away the impenetrable barrier of clutter with which we feel it necessary to surround ourselves. Sometimes it seems as if we have gained possession of the world and lost our own souls. Perhaps our hands are full of so many things, our hearts of so many cares, that we have forgotten how to stand naked before God, to look at what he has made, and to listen to the silence in which his voice whispers the story of our lives.[32]

Good news for Tim

Rob was a member of our church, and he lived in a block of flats in the city centre. He got to know Tim, who lived in the same block. Tim had been depressed for years. One day Rob dropped in on Tim, and noticed that his curtains were still closed. He said brightly, "Let's let in a bit of light, shall we?", and swept them open. What Rob didn't know was that the curtains had been closed for the past five years. As he spoke, the words seemed to come alive for Tim. Light, he thought – yes, that's what I need. He began to talk to Rob, sharing something of his history and telling him about his depression. Rob didn't really know what to say, but he invited Tim to join an Alpha course. On Alpha Tim became a Christian. A few weeks after that we spoke to Liz, another member of the Alpha group. Liz had missed a couple of weeks. She said that when she came again, she was astonished by Tim – now freed from his depression, he seemed to have become a completely different person.

For reflection and discussion

There are cracks in my world
I noticed them one day and now they are everywhere:
Sinister hairline cracks that start and finish out of sight
cracks that grow and gape and laugh at my certainties.
My world has been declared unsafe.

I have tried to paper them over,
paint them out,
move the furniture to hide them,
but they always return,
cracks that hang like question marks in my mind.

And now I begin to think:
Why do the cracks appear?
From where do they come?
They have made my room unsafe
BUT

They have thrown it open to new horizons,
drawn back curtains
raised long-closed shutters.
One day I looked and a crack had become a window.
Step through, it said, what have you to fear?
Do you wish to stay in your crumbling room?

And then I remembered a childhood dream.
watching the egg of some exotic bird
oval and perfect, spotted blue and cream
I wished to hold that egg and keep it on a shelf
BUT

As I watched it, cracks appeared.
Tiny fissures spread like zigzag ripples.
It broke in two and life struggled to its feet,
wet and weak and blinking at the world.

Without those cracks that egg could hold
no more than rotting stagnant death

Without its cracks my world would be
a room without a view
Cracks may be uncomfortable, disturbing gaps
BUT

Could it be I need them?
Do you believe in cracks?
Because I keep searching for God in the room
and find he is hiding in the cracks

DAVE BOOKLESS

**Do you identify with the poem? Do you share Dave's view that
it is the very fact of imperfection and uncertainty which makes
it possible to find God?**

Reflect on the reaction of David's colleagues to his ordination. Do you think your own colleagues feel similarly trapped, and that they might be open to the idea that there is a greater meaning to life than can be found in the simple earning of money?

Many Christians see blessing in material wealth – what do you think?

'What kind of deal is it to get everything you want but lose yourself? What could you ever trade your soul for?' (Matthew 16.26, TM). Meditate on this verse.

Chapter 4

The search for more

The search for an appropriate spirituality is one of the signs of our times.

Albert Nolan[1]

Over the last twelve years I have worked, for short stretches of time, in various parts of Tanzania, Zambia, Mozambique, Malawi, and Kenya, supporting the ministry of the Church through the African *Rooted in Jesus* discipleship course of which I am the editor. It has been an enormous privilege to be welcomed by people whose lives are so different from mine, to receive their hospitality, to learn from their way of life, to work in partnership and to watch what God is doing among them.

One year we visited a small community near Kibaya, in a remote and sparsely populated part of the Masai steppe, where Bishop John Hayden was to conduct a baptism service. To get there we drove through pathless gaps between dry, spiky acacia trees and scattered thorn bushes, following the directions of the local evangelist who had been working with the villagers, all members of a single extended family group. Navigating carefully over a sandy riverbed, we finally arrived to the sound of drumming and singing, as men, women, and children surged forward to greet us. Delighted to welcome the first white people and the first vehicle many of them had ever seen, they led us triumphantly into the thorn enclosure which marked the boundary of the village, and then to the woven wicker church they had begun to build and in which the baptisms were to take place. Afterwards the evangelist told us how he had been visiting the village week by week, walking miles on foot through the scrub, in order to share the gospel. The elders had considered the good news he brought and had decided to embrace it. Eventually, speaking for the entire village, they had announced their conclusion: "We have decided to become a Christian." Hence the baptisms; and the establishment of a *Rooted in Jesus* group which would help them discover what it meant, in their own context, to accept Jesus, receive the Holy Spirit and grow together into the love of God.

That day was remarkable in many ways. They were as fascinated with us as we were with them: a young man stroked Kim's blond hair, and an elder offered his daughter in marriage to Nick, who was making a film about the life of the diocese; Nick's camera, he suggested with rare cultural flexibility, would be entirely acceptable as bride price in lieu of the customary cows. Children could scarcely be prised from our wing mirrors, and John was formally welcomed in a ceremony of eldership in which he was presented with a stick, a traditional red blanket, a zebra hair fly swat and a pipe with a beaded case and thong. But what had struck me most was not any of this. What had struck me most was the single sentence which had led to the whole event: "We have decided to become a Christian." It was a simple sentence, but not one which could be even conceived in any Western society. It was the voice of a community.

I AM TRYING TO
ADD MORE FRIENDS
Dave Walker

If in the West we suffer from a loss of purpose, it is clear that we suffer also from a loss of community. The cultural ideal of the Western industrialised world is the self-sufficient, autonomous individual. We believe that an authentic identity is found not by being part of a community but by exercising our own choices. In the last half century we have created for ourselves more personal freedom than ever before; but as our freedom increases it seems also that our communities weaken. The result is a curious kind of crowded isolation. One church we worked with did some door-to-door visiting, and found that 90% of people in a single street asked them to pray about their loneliness. Statistics tell the story: the amount of time we spend in one another's homes has fallen by 45% in thirty years; a third of people in the UK have never spoken to their next-door neighbours; and a third of us now live alone. More and more of us spend our leisure time watching television or surfing the internet; it's been said that we are becoming a nation of solitary people dependent on multimedia communication. A recent survey by the Mental Health Foundation found that two out of every five people in the UK has felt depressed because of loneliness (and yet one in four said they would be embarrassed to admit feeling lonely – we are all supposed to have lots of friends). Younger people are more likely to experience loneliness – perhaps because they spend more time on virtual relationships than on face-to-face ones. 'Loneliness,' said Mother Teresa, 'is the leprosy of modern society.'[2]

Seen through African eyes this is simply incomprehensible. Africans believe that we become a person in and through other people, and many who come to Western countries are shocked by the lack of connectedness which they find. A Nigerian journalist working in London shares his astonishment: 'People walk so fast. And they do not talk to each other. Even first thing in the morning they do not greet each other. I came to the office in London and the people working there did not even greet me or each other.' And the most puzzling thing? 'I was lost and I walked up to a man and asked the way. He did not reply. He did not even look at me. He just walked away. Like that.' Richard Dowden, author of one of the most compelling recent portraits of African society, comments, 'When he goes home to Nigeria and tells that story they will not believe him. They know that some Europeans are not kind to Africans, but to be so trivially inhuman to each other is shocking.'[3]

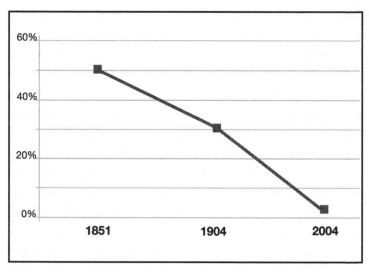

Figure 1: Proportion of UK population in church on a typical Sunday.

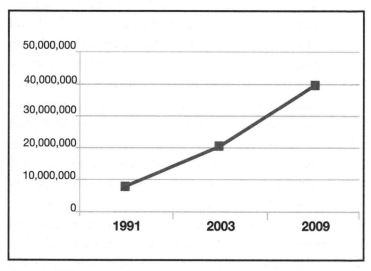

Figure 2: NHS prescriptions issued in the UK for depression.

It is the same everywhere. In northern Natal, South Africa, the normal greeting is "I see you", and the expected reply is "I am here". In Tanzania it is "What news?", and the reply is "Good news", often with a following conversation about the well-being of the family. In Zambia our little team was greeted each day by the collective exclamation "Chikondi, chimwewe, mtendere, umodzi," (love, happiness, peace, unity), followed by an expansive outward wave of both hands and the smiling exhalation "Aah!" It's heart-warming, it's personal, and it's astonishingly welcoming. In Africa you are a person because you are in relationship with others, and it is impolite to engage with others in any way without first exchanging proper greetings, or to part without proper expressions of appreciation. The word for this sense of relatedness is *ubuntu*, and it is expressed in the continent's overflowing churches as clearly as it is in people going about their daily business; the Kenyan communion liturgy includes the words "I am, because we are."[4] If ever that was the case in Western countries, it certainly no longer is. A five-year study into the effects of individualism in the United States identified alienation, loneliness, unhappiness, and an inability to maintain relationships as the price we pay for individual autonomy; it would seem that those who most seek self-fulfilment are the most miserable.[5] Across Africa, by contrast, hundreds of millions of people are in touch with who they are and where they have come from. It's like walking into yesterday – and it's infectious.

As followers of Jesus, we are supposed to know better than to pursue hedonistic individualism. We do not have to live like this; there is an alternative, and it is to be found through becoming part of the body of Christ. It is open to us to discover that to be a Christian is not to visit a building once a week in order to engage in the merciless kind of hymn singing and passive listening to which we have so often reduced our understanding of the Christian faith, but rather to enter together into a relationship with a God who is himself a community, Father, Son, and Spirit – and so to discover what it truly means to be a human being, fully alive. It is further open to us to carry that understanding into the world in which we live. I always return from Africa with better manners and more love; and it is nice to watch the surprised smiles on the faces of people in shops, offices, and garages as I begin to treat them not as objects but as people with histories and feelings. This, in Africa, is routine. In Africa, people are interested in one another.

The search for more – renewed questions about human happiness

A few years ago my printer packed up, and I went to a computer store to buy a new one. "Is it Miss, Mrs, or Ms?", enquired the sales assistant as he reached for the certificate of purchase. I confess I never manage to enjoy this question; so I said, as I normally do, "Dr, actually." I get various responses to this. Sometimes it's slight embarrassment; "Oh, I'm sorry." Sometimes it's very matter of fact. Sometimes it's sheer incredulity. But on this particular occasion I got a brand new response: "Oo-er, lots of money!" Not quite sure how to react, I just said, "Well, no, actually, I'm not a medical doctor, so I'm afraid not." The sales assistant seemed disappointed; what sort of doctor was I, then? "It's a PhD." "What in?" Oh well, he's asked for it, I thought. "Medieval Italian Christian literature," I said, knowing from experience that this is usually a complete conversation stopper. But no; the young man persisted. "But can't you go into interpreting and that sort of thing with that, doesn't that pay a lot of money?" he asked, brightening slightly.

The conversation may have been unusual, but the sentiment which lay behind it was not: not only is earning power the hallmark of social status, but the possession of money has become indelibly associated with happiness. And yet once again the statistics show the falsity of the assumptions. For years we have believed that increasing prosperity will lead to increased well-being. But survey after survey shows that money beyond a certain minimal level has no bearing at all on happiness; indeed, it seems that the reverse is true, and that as our wealth increases, so our happiness decreases. One seventy-year survey was summarised in the following headline: 'The good old 30s. It was the era of Depression, unemployment and poverty. But we were happier then, say researchers.'[6]

Over the last few years, prompted perhaps by the rising incidence of depression, there has been a growing re-evaluation of happiness and how it is to be found. Over the last decade or so a whole discipline of 'positive psychology' has come into being, initiated by Martin Seligman whose research on happiness was the subject of a 2006 BBC series called *The Happiness Formula* – which found that a sense of purpose and a network of relationships, and not money, are key factors to our level of happiness. 'Happiness,' summarised Sarah-Kate Templeton, 'is the new economics.'[7] Far from being seen as the solution, it seems that money is now for the first time in centuries beginning to be regarded as part of the problem. In 2007 Oliver James published a book called *Affluenza*, in which the desire for money is portrayed as a kind of virus: 'the Affluenza Virus is a set of values which increase our vulnerability to emotional distress. It entails placing a high value on acquiring money and possessions, looking good in the eyes of others and wanting to be famous.' It often leads in practice to stress, depression, and even illness. "You cannot worship both God and money," said Jesus; and so perhaps we should not be surprised at James's finding that religion acts as a powerful vaccine against affluenza.[8] Once again, as Christians we are supposed to know these things, and we need to look not only to the economically marginalised in our society as we offer the love and life we have found in Jesus, but also to the millions trapped, as David's colleagues felt trapped, in a world which prioritises money over relationships. 'If the aim of life were to enjoy oneself, Africa should send us missionaries instead of the other way round!', Victorian explorer Mary Kingsley remarked long ago.[9]

The search for more – a renewed interest in spirituality

We have built ourselves a world of astonishing choice and complexity; and yet all the signs suggest that something is missing. Abandoning a faith-based world view for a science-based one leaves a hole in the middle of our humanity; we live now in an age of dissatisfaction. It's leading to the asking of new questions – and not just questions about happiness, but questions once again about that old, once familiar spiritual dimension of life which we threw out so magnificently with the bathwater as we moved from the Hebrew to the Greek world view. Is there something missing, people are beginning to wonder?

All the signs are that whilst traditional churchgoing is declining, we are witnessing a massive rise in spiritual awareness and experimentation. Opinion polls and research projects over the last twenty years tell the story. Figure 3 shows the results of a survey commissioned by the BBC in the year 2000 and compared with the same questions asked by a Gallup Poll thirteen years earlier. On every question, the proportion of people reporting a spiritual dimension to their lives had risen significantly. Nearly 40% said they have a personal awareness of the presence of God, 37% said they have experience of answered prayer, and 25% reported sensing the presence of evil. Taking all the questions together, 76% identified a spiritual dimension to their lives, up from 48% in 1987.[10]

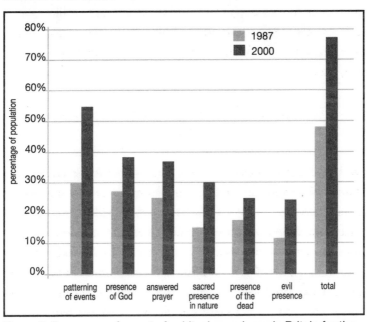

Figure 3: Frequency of report of spiritual experience in Britain for the years 1987 and 2000.

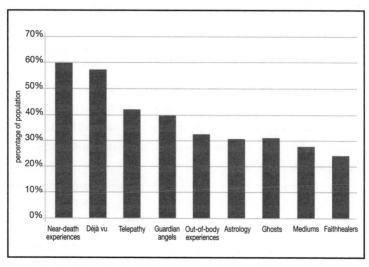

Figure 4: Belief in spiritual phenomena, MORI 2003.

Other research supports these findings. A poll commissioned by Lloyds TSB in 2005 found that half of homebuyers now believe in ghosts.[11] A MORI poll conducted in 2003 (Figure 4) found that huge numbers also believe in near-death and out-of-body experiences, déjà vu, telepathy, guardian angels, astrology, psychic powers, and faith healing.[12] Some 70% now believe in a soul, and 58% define themselves as either 'a religious person' or 'a spiritual person'. Belief in God remains constant at over 75%.[13] We live in a society which may be spiritually stunted, but which is perhaps not as secular as we assume. It is estimated that nearly one in five people attend church at Christmas (in December 2010 one in three said they planned to do so). Nearly a quarter say they sometimes feel drawn to go into a church as they pass by, and over 85% attend a church event each year. By contrast, membership of the British National Secular Society stands at 3,000.[14] We are witnessing, Professor Alister McGrath has suggested, the twilight of atheism and the beginning of a new world.[15]

Evidence that he may be right is not hard to find. Films such as the groundbreaking *Avatar* offer an unexpected insight into this new, spiritually minded world. Billed as 'science fiction', *Avatar* is in fact about the defeat of science at the hands of the spiritually literate and eerily beautiful blue Na'vi tribe, who with the aid of a human defector overcome the mechanical might of the technologically sophisticated mission of human soldiers and scientists wanting to plunder their mineral resources in order to save the exploited and dying planet Earth. Technological might, suggests the film, is not right; it is not even desirable. Released in December 2009, within a few months *Avatar* had become the highest grossing film of all time.

Even the advertising industry is catching on to the new landscape. Buy this, advert after advert now suggests, because it will add meaning and fulfilment to your life; it will meet your spiritual needs. 'Warm your Soul Soup and Toastie,' proclaims a poster in a motorway service station café. 'Harbourside flats – shaping a soul in the heart of Bristol,' says a property developer's billboard. 'There are countries that nurture the soul – visit Morocco,' urges an ad on the London Underground. Soup, flats, and holidays are unlikely to do the job; the only real nurture is to be found in Jesus. And yet it remains clear from the church attendance statistics we looked at in Chapter 1 that it is not to Jesus that people are looking; or at least, that this increasing awareness of the spiritual dimension of life is not being reflected in increased Sunday attendance. What then are people doing to further their spiritual search?

A couple of years ago we moved from Leicester to Somerset.

In Leicester I had been increasingly used to praying with people whose spiritual experimentation had led them into deep water, but apart from the odd shop selling crystals and the occasional advert for cure-all acupuncture or a weekend psychic fair there was little visible sign in the city's streets of any vibrant alternative spiritual scene. This, however, is not the case in Glastonbury. Somewhat to the embarrassment of many of the town's residents, Glastonbury High Street offers a comprehensive and visible picture of the hidden spiritual searching of an entire nation. Here you can buy crystals, tarot cards, dreamcatchers, charms, and talismen; you can visit a miracles room or sign up for courses in anything from practical witchcraft to craniosacral therapy. A single edition of the local free magazine, the *Glastonbury Oracle*, advertises Medicine Wheel teachings with a Native American leader from the Bear Clan, Theta healing and Angel healing, Tibetan pulsing for emotional transformation, sound healing, and Shamanic workshops including tantric healing massage, soul readings, emotional block release, psychic rune readings, cord removal, and soul retrieval. If you think this sounds like a rather wacky minority interest confined to the smaller towns of the West Country, do visit the NHS website and browse its list of complementary and alternative medicine. Thirty-two healing therapies are described, including reiki, crystal therapy, flower therapy, iridology, kinesiology, and shiatsu.[16]

Another survey, conducted in Kendal, Cumbria between 2000 and 2002, suggests that 6% of people have experimented with crystals, 16% with astrology, 16% with reflexology, 17% with tarot or fortune-telling, and 39% with alternative medical therapies of one kind or another. Significantly, 22% had also tried meditation, and the biggest group of all, 41%, had tried prayer (Figure 5). When asked whether these things had become important to them, only prayer produced a majority 'yes' response, with a staggering 25% of people saying they had found it effective.[17]

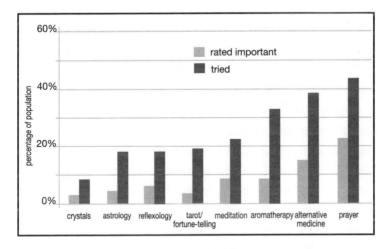

Figure 5: Spiritual experimentation, ORB 2000.

In one sense all this is very encouraging – people are increasingly open to investigating the spiritual dimension of life. In other ways it's alarming – most of these things leave people feeling dissatisfied, and for some they are followed by varying degrees of mental, emotional or spiritual breakdown. Any Christian minister is aware of this – but I was surprised to find it acknowledged in the *Glastonbury Oracle* itself: 'Many people are "called" to Glastonbury from all over the world. Some feel that they know why they have come here – whilst others have little idea. It is as if they have been drawn by that special "Energy" that is to be found in Sacred Places all over the world. Some of these visitors stay for a few days. Others settle in Glastonbury. Many of those who settle here find themselves subjected to various bouts of painful emotional, physical and spiritual stress, a phenomenon which is sometimes called their "Glastonbury Experience".'[18] The article was advertising a workshop to help people cope with the distressing side effects of their misguided spiritual experimentation.

It is clear that the search for an appropriate spirituality is one of the signs of our times. Who would have thought that a modern, secular society could be the scene of such burgeoning experimentation? Tom Wright observes that 'the phenomenon of religious belief in the western world, so far from withering on the vine as so many assumed it would through the second half of the twentieth century, has been making a significant come-back.' Not only are we the host to practitioners of many other religions, 'we have a culture in which "spirituality" is suddenly something everyone wants, even if there is considerable confusion as to what it is and how its different varieties might stack up. It looks as though secularism functioned like a long winter in which nobody dared to explore the landscape of the spirit for fear of being frozen to death, and now spring has arrived and everyone is going off in all directions to see what was there all along under the snow and ice.'[19]

The signs are all around us, even in the hallowed halls of the workplace and the shopping centre. *The Sunday Times* carried the following profile of a typical young spiritual searcher:

> *Louise Jones is a successful marketing executive who can handle stressful board meetings with nonchalant panache. She has a secret, however. Before walking into meetings in her offices in Holborn, central London, the immaculately dressed executive will quietly lock herself in the ladies' lavatory, kneel in the narrow cubicle and start praying. It steadies her nerves. 'I'm not sure what*

I believe in,' said Jones. 'But praying helps. It sounds silly, but it only works if I get down on my knees. I pray before a situation to ask for help to do the right thing. It is to try to stop myself from taking over a situation. The praying is like a pause in the mad rush of life.'

Jones, who does not go to church, has experimented with a medley of other spiritual fixes. She has consulted psychics, herbalists and reiki therapists, practitioners of an eastern form of 'energy healing'. Jones belongs to a new kind of pilgrim, the spirit seekers.[20]

Louise Jones, who is what we might now begin to call a post-shopper, uses her money not to pamper herself with material acquisitions but to book therapy sessions which will help her explore her spiritual self. She is not alone: British women apparently now spend £670 million a year on spiritual therapies. A similar pattern is emerging in the workplace: as people become ever more aware of the gaping lack of purpose offered by their daily employment, companies are increasingly turning to specialist providers to help meet their needs. Apple schedules a daily thirty-minute meditation break for its employees, management consultancy McKinsey sends its executives on spiritual intelligence courses, and even the World Bank has set up its own 'Spiritual Unfoldment Society'.[21]

All this offers an enormous opportunity to us as Christians. People don't *expect* to find the answers to their questions through the Church, but there is no reason why we should not share with them the good news that we have received and introduce them, through relationship with Jesus, to a genuinely life-enhancing encounter with the Holy Spirit. Most are not hostile; indeed, prayer is far and away the most widely valued spiritual experience in Britain. Different surveys come up with different figures, but polls in 1998 and in 2005 found that two thirds of adults pray, and an unlikely recent finding by the RAC was that 73% of motorists sometimes pray while driving.[22] Meanwhile public displays of religious interest are becoming more common. More than 11,000 people turned out to venerate the relics of St Thérèse of Lisieux in Birmingham in September 2009, and the local church is increasingly acting as a focal point for the community following public disasters and tragedies. Furthermore, the local attendance statistics do not tell the whole story: whilst adult attendance dips gently downwards in the average parish church, the opposite is true in cathedrals, where attendance at regular weekly services has increased by over 30% in the last ten years. Nobody knows why – the anonymity, perhaps? The professional standards of the music, the soaring beauty of the architecture, the sense of mystery which you just don't get in the high street? Perhaps we should ask some of the twelve million people who visit a cathedral each year – half of whom say they light a candle or say a prayer.[23]

Our current situation is neatly summarised by journalist Clifford Longley: 'Having constructed a society of unprecedented sophistication, convenience and prosperity, nobody can remember what it was supposed to be for. Just enjoying it does not seem to be enough. Indeed enjoyment as an end in itself quickly turns to ashes in the mouth. Not only is it boringly bland. It is even more boringly purposeless. There is more to human life than comfort, entertainment and the avoidance of suffering.'[24]

Helping people with their questions

About fifteen years ago now Holy Trinity Leicester began to hold a regular event which we called 'Questions'. We laid the church out like a restaurant, with white tablecloths and complimentary glasses of wine, and we invited our non churchgoing friends and colleagues for a meal and a multimedia presentation on a topic of common concern – not 'religious' topics, but life issues such as stress, conflict, the management of change, extremism, how to reach your potential, how to make the most of relationships; we even did one on 'money, sex and power'.[25] Each presentation was followed by a short talk and a discussion. We began with an attendance of sixty to seventy people, mostly church members. Soon we found ourselves running each event twice and welcoming a full house of over 250 to each one, half of whom were not Christians. Our aim was to help people get their minds round some of life's big issues, and to show that as followers of Jesus we have not just a sensitive and thoughtful approach to people but also something to offer; 'take home value' was how we thought about it. We wanted to demonstrate that in a fragmented society which has forgotten how to talk about the real issues of life, our faith-based framework still enables us to live coherently and meaningfully. Many of those who came returned regularly to subsequent events, and many accepted the invitation to join an Alpha course where they could talk in more depth. At one stage we were running twenty such courses a year through the church's cell group system, with many people coming to faith.

One of the most popular evenings we ran was called 'Science and Spirituality – is Dawkins right?' This is an extract from an email I had the next day from a man named Adrian:

Thank you so much for giving your talk yesterday which
I listened to earnestly. Simon [the church member who
had invited him] and I, along with another friend,
discussed this at length on a number of occasions and
they opened my sceptical eyes again, and your talk also
really helped. It has helped me make a large leap from
atheism to becoming an agnostic and now to the eye
opening and fulfilling warmth of God's embrace …
almost. I have a loving Christian wife, a wonderful
four-year-old daughter and I have been so fortunate
that my wife is now expecting our second child. I am a
solicitor and I have loving parents and close relatives.
As you referred to in your lecture, I have everything
material and importantly I have more earthly love than
I probably deserve; but I then sit there and feel a hole
and something missing – but I didn't know what. I do
sometimes taste ashes in my mouth. I feel I am nearly
there. I have always read the Bible out of interest, but I
am now beginning to read it with my eyes wide open. I
desperately hope I can hold on to the faith to make that
next connection.

Adrian came to church the next Sunday, and then joined an
Alpha course in order to continue his journey.

I have found the same combination of fascination and
confusion working with teenagers in Somerset. When we moved
to Wells, our daughters Bethy and Katy joined the Blue School,
a Church of England comprehensive with a long history and
an excellent reputation. Coming from a school where nearly
half the pupils were from Muslim or Hindu backgrounds,
Katy and Bethy were looking forward to being part of a church

school again. It came as a bit of a shock to find that of the 1,500 students at the Blue, only a handful identify themselves as having any kind of faith, and that whereas in multi-faith Leicester it's normal to talk about God, in a cathedral city it's definitely not cool to be Christian: church, in Wells, is for the retired. Aware of the need to develop the spiritual side of the school's life, the head had just appointed a school chaplain, and we joined with her to put on an evening event called 'The Big Debate – has science made God unnecessary?' We found ourselves welcoming some seventy students to pizza, fruit salad, and a chocolate fountain. I spoke for thirty minutes, after which we opened it up for discussion. What followed was I think the most animated, engaging, and searching debate I can remember, as seventy teenagers, most of whom had no church background, bombarded us with questions. In the end we had to ask them to stop. Teenagers may not be keen to go to church, and they struggled to find words in which to discuss the spiritual side of life – but they had more thoughtful and original questions about it than any group of people I have ever met.

Good news for a boy in trouble

Ann works as a Street Pastor in Leicester city centre. She and her partner were walking through the city at 2 a.m., the time when the pubs and clubs close and young people pour out unsteadily onto the streets. As Ann and her colleague passed the taxi queue, a group of youths called out to them. One looked at Ann, with the Street Pastor logo on her jacket, and said "Hey, you're a Christian, aren't you?" "Yes, I am," said Ann. "Well, do you see this scar?" (pointing to a scar on his left temple). His mates nodded; the one he'd got in the fight he had told them about.

The young man continued. "Yeah, that's what I told you, but that's not actually what happened. I had cancer when I was nine. I was terrified. I had to have an operation, and they were going to cut out the lump from my head. They thought I might lose my sight. I prayed, God if you are there will you get me through this? I didn't lose my sight and I was cured of the cancer. I was so grateful to Jesus that I went out and bought this" (he dug under his clothing and pulled out a cross on a chain). By this time, Ann said, his mates were staring in amazement and disbelief, spluttering "We didn't know you'd got that!", trying to get their heads round what they were hearing. "Yes, and I've got this too" – and he opened his black jacket to reveal a white T-shirt with a big black cross on it. "I don't know much about it, but I reckon there's someone up there looking out for me." At that point a taxi drew up and they all got in and sped off. Ann was left with two thoughts – one, that she'd have loved to hear the conversation in the taxi as they drove home; and two, that her only contribution to this astonishing conversation had been to say "Yes, I am."[26]

It is time to introduce people to Jesus.

For reflection and discussion

THE ABANDONED VALLEY

Can you understand being alone so long
you would go out in the middle of the night
and put a bucket into the well
so you could feel something down there
tug at the other end of the rope?

JACK GILBERT

Mother Teresa said that 'loneliness is the leprosy of modern society'. Do you agree?

It has been suggested that the mantra of our age is 'I still haven't found what I'm looking for.'[26] How can we help?

Do you agree that as a society we have become spiritually illiterate? How easy do you find it to talk about your inner life?

'I came so that they can have real and eternal life, more and better life than they ever dreamed of' (John 10.10, TM). What does that mean for you?

Chapter 5

Telling a different story

For I decided to know nothing among you except Jesus Christ, and him crucified. I came to you in weakness and in fear and in much trembling. My speech and my proclamation were not with plausible words of wisdom, but with a demonstration of the Spirit and of power, so that your faith might rest not on human wisdom but on the power of God.

1 Corinthians 2.2–6

We began this book by looking at some of the pressures which cause us to lose confidence in the gospel – an increasingly complex and antagonistic social environment and a gradual decline in church attendance. We suggested that these new circumstances have their roots in the fact that history has provided us with two very different ways of answering the fundamental questions of life: a Hebrew or faith-based world view which offered a coherent and satisfying way of thinking about meaning and purpose, and a Greek or science-based world view which offered a coherent and satisfying way of thinking about knowledge and reality. We saw that in transferring our allegiance from the faith-based to the science-based world view we vastly increased our understanding of the world in which we live, leading to a welcome rise in collective prosperity and individual opportunity; and yet that the price we have paid for that is that we have, as a society, lost our ability to explore the spiritual dimension of life. We can't go back: can we go forwards? Or, to pick up on our previous metaphor, are we destined to remain between Scylla and Charybdis, or can we sail on into clearer waters?

An unfashionable faith

A. N. Wilson is a well-known novelist, biographer, and journalist. For many years an atheist, in April 2009, at Easter, Wilson wrote the unexpected story of his conversion to Christ in both the *New Statesman* and the *Daily Mail*. His article in the *Mail* included the following words:

> *Like most educated people in Britain and Northern Europe, I have grown up in a culture that is overwhelmingly secular and anti-religious. The universities, broadcasters, and media generally are not merely non-religious, they are positively anti. To my shame, I believe it was this that made me lose faith and heart in my youth. It felt so uncool to be religious. With the mentality of a child in the playground, I felt at some visceral level that being religious was unsexy, like having spots or wearing specs.*
>
> *For ten or 15 of my middle years, I, too, was one of the mockers. But, as time passed, I found myself going back to church, although at first only as a fellow traveller with the believers, not as one who shared the faith that Jesus had truly risen from the grave. Some time over the past five or six years — I could not tell you*

exactly when – I found that I had changed. When I took part in the procession last Sunday and heard the Gospel being chanted, I assented to it with complete simplicity. My own return to faith has surprised no one more than myself. Why did I return to it? Partially, perhaps it is no more than the confidence I have gained with age. Rather than being cowed by them, I relish the notion that, by asserting a belief in the risen Christ, I am defying all the liberal clever-clogs on the block: cutting-edge novelists such as Martin Amis; foul-mouthed, self-satisfied TV presenters such as Jonathan Ross and Jo Brand; and the smug, tieless architects of so much television output.

But there is more to it than that. My belief has come about in large measure because of the lives and examples of people I have known – not the famous, not saints, but friends and relations who have lived, and faced death, in the light of the Resurrection story, or in the quiet acceptance that they have a future after they die. The Easter story answers their questions about the spiritual aspects of humanity. It changes people's lives because it helps us understand that we, like Jesus, are born as spiritual beings. Every inner prompting of conscience, every glimmering sense of beauty, every response we make to music, every experience we have of love – whether of physical love, sexual love, family love or the love of friends – and every experience of bereavement, reminds us of this fact about ourselves.[1]

Something missing

A. N. Wilson's article perfectly illustrates the way in which our complex cultural environment leads people away from faith; to hold fast to Christian belief in the face of so many dismissive voices requires a strength and autonomy that not many people possess. But his story also illustrates the way in which our collective abandonment of faith leaves a whole aspect of our lives unexplained and under-developed. In his parallel *New Statesman* article Wilson reflects that when he thinks about his atheist friends, they now seem to him 'like people who have no ear for music, or who have never been in love. It is not that (as they believe) they have rumbled the tremendous fraud of religion… Rather, these unbelievers are simply missing out on something that is not difficult to grasp. Perhaps it is too obvious to understand; obvious, as lovers feel it was obvious that they should have come together, or obvious as the final resolution of a fugue.' Atheists are wrong about God, he suggests; but that isn't really where their big mistake lies. Their big mistake is that they are also wrong about people. Men and women, as we read in the first chapter of the book of Genesis, are spiritual beings, alive because filled with the breath (or spirit; it's the same word, *ruach*, in the Hebrew) of God. It's something we've always known, and which many of us seem increasingly unwilling to deny: we have a soul. Materialism, says Wilson, will never explain that.[2]

A. N. Wilson is highly articulate, but his gut feeling that there is more to life than the material is common to many people. In 2006 Professor David Hay published the results of a research study conducted in Nottingham, interviewing non-churchgoers on issues to do with church and faith. One participant, Matthew, said this: "It's probably just a nagging instinct, that while all the material evidence is telling me, this is ludicrous, you know, this is all complete chaos, nonsense, it's arbitrary, you know, we're a rock in a vacuum just spinning through nothingness and, you know, the consequence of impersonal cosmic forces, nothing beyond it. Whilst my sort of intellectual faculty can tell me that, there is this other, and I'm not going to use the word 'soul', but there's this other bit of me which is just sort of going, 'hang on', you know, 'What if, pal?'."

Matthew suspects there's more to life than the physical, but he doesn't know how to evaluate it or find out about it, and he struggles to find the vocabulary to express his questions. Hay comments that Matthew was clearly frustrated that while science could tell him the atoms in his body were once part of a star, it did not answer his deepest questions about meaning. And although he was attracted by the thought that the Christian faith might have answers to such questions, Matthew did not feel those answers were available to him. Indeed, when asked about church he said this: "I think they get a lot out [of it]; this is probably envy in me, but why don't they invent one that I can go to?"[3]

Another participant, Tom, said he felt a 'need' to walk into churches, and reflected: "Maybe there's a sense of I want to believe in something definite and concrete and maybe I've got the idea that if I go in at that moment, I might see something." Sharon had gone further than Matthew or Tom and had actually tried going to church, but had come out more mystified than when she went in:

"I think they ought to do like a church for beginners really, because if you're not used to going, because they always have communion here. [She goes on to explain how she was encouraged to go forward for communion.] It was a really awkward situation, do you know what I mean? And he was giving us the sip of the wine, and the um, and he beckoned us to bring the children up as well, and they give you, whatever it is they give you to eat. Is it rice paper?"[4] No wonder Lisa (Chapter 1) had felt she needed an invitation before she could go to church. For many people today, church doesn't seem so much to answer questions as to create them. As the Church of England's report *Mission-Shaped Church* puts it, 'the reality is that for most people across England the Church as it is is peripheral, obscure, confusing or irrelevant.'[5]

Looking for a new world view

And yet the problem remains. Taking a broad brush view, neither a purely faith-based nor a purely science-based approach to reality will do. We need a third model, one which combines the strengths of the Hebrew and the Greek approaches, and in which the gospel acts as the cornerstone – a model which is capable of answering not one but *both* of the two fundamental questions we have to face as human beings: 'how do we know things?' and 'how do we make sense of them?'. Despite the 'rice paper', the Church has in fact lost neither its human focus nor its spiritual expertise. It is open to us as Christians, more fully now than it has been for centuries, to offer a coherent life philosophy, a way of reuniting the disparate parts of the human person which now float in disconnected and often unlabelled compartments.

Telling a different story

Everybody needs to be part of a story, to have a purpose and identity which goes beyond personal gratification. One of the results of our collective loss of faith is that we now live in a society with no story. Douglas Copeland, the novelist who first came up with the expression 'Generation X', remarks that losing our sense of story means that we no longer know where we have come from, where we are heading and, as a consequence, who we are. 'Either our lives become stories, or there's no way to get through them,' he says.[6] It's a problem not just for us as individuals, as we strive to make sense of our lives in a society which substitutes choice for meaning, but also for us as a nation. It is hard, as we saw in Chapter 3, for an individual to find an identity and a purpose in a society which itself does not have an identity or a purpose.[7]

Social philosopher Ivan Illich once said that if you want to change society you have to tell a different story.[8] It cannot escape our notice that, as Christians, we have one. It's a story about Jesus. Jesus invited one person after another to walk out of a failing story into a new story, one which would change their lives.[9] This new story is still available to us; not based on the ideology of one particular society but overarching them all, it takes us beyond the iron cage of our rational world view into the invisible, eternal world of spiritual reality. And this is what we have to share, the answer we have to offer, the meaning we can articulate into a broken world. Lesslie Newbigin expresses it well: 'The logic of mission is this: the true meaning of the human story has been disclosed. Because it is the truth, it must be shared universally. When we share it with all peoples, we give them the opportunity to know the truth about themselves, to know who they are because they can know the true story of which their lives are a part.'[10]

The problem for many people is not that they are reluctant to find their part in a story. Indeed, we live in a society which has devised many ways of doing just that. We can feed our spiritual yearnings through films like *Avatar*. We can immerse ourselves in soap operas, or log onto a virtual world website and forge a new identity in a fictitious but realistically complex online society. Or we can insert ourselves into the big picture by blogging, twittering, or appearing on TV. As I write, thousands of people are stranded all over the world due to a closure of European airspace; the BBC website interweaves their stories with the meteorological reports of the Met Office and the rulings of the Civil Aviation Authority. The individual story is now part of any major news item; 'have your say!', the invitation runs. Weaving ourselves into stories is what we have always done. The problem is not that we can't tell a story; the problem is that for the story to do its job properly, it has to be true.

How we know things – building a fiduciary framework

Modern society is built on human reason. We have assumed truth can be accessed only by reason, and that as boundaries were pushed back through scientific investigation we would get, as physicist Stephen Hawking put it, ever nearer to 'the mind of God'. But it turns out that it doesn't work like that, and that the question is bigger than we had thought. It's not so much 'how do we get at truth?' as 'what is truth?' And that of course is the question Pilate asked of Jesus. For a contemporary, western culture, it's the most helpful question in the Bible. Reality is not measurable after all. Reality is God, and God expresses himself in Jesus. Truth turns out to be a person.

For us, the inhabitants of a scientific age, this is hard to take in. We have tried to access truth by chopping everything up into little bits. The result is that we have come to hold a unique and peculiar view of truth. We've reduced truth to facts, cut it down to a size we can understand, expressed it in formulae and looked inside its smallest parts – only to find we are none the wiser about what makes the world work. Truth has become so small, so shrunken, that we have been forced to create a web of values and experiences to fill the vacuum its demise has created: truth now inhabits the movements of strings inside particles inside atoms, or molecules inside strands inside genes, and all I am left to replace it with is my own consumer driven choices and experiences.

Even in the Church, we have gone along with this. While scientists dissected the world, theologians dissected the Bible, taking it apart and then wondering why it seemed to lose its power. Even now, when Christians talk about the Bible as the word of God, we tend to understand that in rationalistic terms and reduce truth to black and white marks on a page, so that we end up with what's been called 'a spirituality of print'.[11] And so truth becomes a manuscript tradition, a moral code to live by, a series of creeds and canons. These things may be important, but they are not, let's face it, immediately exciting. Not, perhaps, likely to strike Matthew, Tom, and Sharon as instant and obvious good news.

Perhaps it is time to stand back, to worry less about the trees and to look afresh at the wood. Truth is much bigger than facts. The Bible is not the truth. *Jesus* is the truth. Truth is not just a fact but an encounter – an encounter with reality, in the person of the one who made both it and me.[12] This is very different from the reduced way scientific modernism has taught us to think about truth. And it has an enormous implication. If we put God back into the equation, as the ultimate reality which underlies everything we see and do, it becomes possible to answer both our fundamental questions – how do we know things, and how do we make sense of them – within a single framework. We know things as we explore them, using our reason; but we build our understanding of them on a foundation of faith, taking account of the fact that they have a creator and a meaning. And we make sense of things not by following our desires or seeking the pre-packaged answers of a secular society, but in the context of a relationship with Jesus, a relationship which enables us to find our own place and purpose within that of the world as a whole.

This is a message which may not be as scornfully dismissed as we sometimes fear. In 2005 Nick Spencer published the results of a study conducted in Coventry by Yvonne Richmond into the spirituality of people outside the Church. Their response to the Church was not encouraging: one summed it up like this – "I think the established Church could be tried in a court of justice and could be found guilty of killing off spirituality." Their response to Jesus, though, was quite different. Spencer comments: 'Jesus emerged from the interviews with a good reputation.'[13] I have tried to show, by including in this book the stories of people who have embraced the good news that God is interested in them and found a whole new sense of meaning and purpose to their lives as a result, that this is a message which many people – sometimes the most apparently unlikely people – are ready to hear. "The Son of Man," said Jesus as he offered new choices to a corrupt tax collector, "came to find and to restore the lost."[14] That's us.

But is all this a legitimate and credible way to make sense of reality? Will it do as the basis for a world view which will satisfy not just the ordinary people whose stories I have told, but also leading scientists and philosophers? The first person to call for a post-critical, post-rational and postmodern philosophy was Michael Polanyi. Polanyi argued that all knowing of reality involves the personal commitment of the knower as a whole person. Knowledge comes not in a vacuum but as a hypothesis; and you have to commit yourself to a hypothesis in order to test it out, see whether it holds up. Polanyi came to the conclusion that 'we must now recognise belief once more as the source of all knowledge. No intelligence can operate outside a fiduciary framework.'[15] That is, the assumption that knowledge can be seized objectively, without some prior assumption which acts as a foundation, is false; the onion model of knowledge is in fact deeply flawed. As Augustine put it, 'I (have to) believe in order that I may know' – not the other way round.[16]

This is not difficult to grasp. Is the chair beside my desk real? Is it solid? Will it hold my weight? There is one immediate way for me to find out: I have to sit on it. We cannot access ultimate reality by reducing it to its component parts; the reality of the chair does not lie in the wood where its timber was grown, the field where the cotton for its cover was picked, the factory where the alloy of the nuts and bolts which hold it together was poured into moulds. The chair only finds its true meaning, and it certainly only becomes useful to me, when I sit on it. People the world over will read the words of atheistic scientists such as Dawkins and, most recently, Stephen Hawking, and marvel, Ruth Gledhill comments; and 'then they will pray, not because faith is logical, but because it works.'[17]

We therefore have a choice. The illusion of objectivity has

long since gone from science, and so it should from the Church. We have to build our knowledge on an assumption, and then experience will tell us whether this assumption forms a solid foundation; whether we are, as Jesus would have said, building on rock or on sand. When I became a Christian I spent months trying to work out if it was all true. The best I could do, as like A. N. Wilson I watched those who lived and died by it, was to say that it was coherent. But even that didn't put me in touch with God. "Suck it and see," an immensely practical friend said to me. So I did. I committed myself to Jesus, and it worked. It's been working better and better ever since. It works, as Jesus said it would, because it turns truth from fact into experience. And it's experience that people are looking for.[18]

Seeking meaning in relationship

A few years ago I found myself in a small village on the shores of Lake Niassa, in Mozambique. We were working with the Anglican Church, at the invitation of Bishop Mark Van Koevering and his wife Helen, to train leaders in the use of the *Rooted in Jesus* discipleship course, and this was our second visit. Some sixty priests, catechists, and evangelists crowded into the small church to listen, pray, and sing, while waves thudded on the shore and clouds of insects rose in twisting black columns far out above the water. Boys threaded small fish onto reeds as their fathers sat on the sand mending their nets, and women and girls laughed at the water's edge, naked from the waist up, as together they washed enormous cooking pots and bundles of clothes. I slept at night in a small wooden hut, slightly disconcerted by the presence of an old man who lay on the sand against its wall, until it was explained to me that he was the local chief, acting as night watchman and guaranteeing my safety with his presence. Just behind the church was the village, a jumble of clay huts each surrounded by a neatly swept earth garden and enclosed by a flowering hedge. From this village came the cooks; local women who had offered to look after both the conference participants and the visiting team. They fed us separately, and each evening we were served, at a table beside the lakeshore, fresh caught fish which we had watched being hauled out of the water by lines of men pulling on a single shelf net stretched between two dugout canoes. One evening the cooks lingered as they cleared away. They were not really part of the church, they said, but they had noticed that great and wonderful things seemed to be happening inside it, with singing and prayer and rejoicing; and they wondered whether we would be willing to pray with them too? We said we would, and one by one they told their stories.

The first was Lydia. Her brother had died suddenly a year earlier. She had been very close to him, and she'd been devastated by his death. Since then, she would settle each night to sleep, only to wake in the early hours and toss and turn until the morning. Could we help? We asked Lydia if she was a Christian; did she have a relationship with Jesus? No, she said. We explained that we ourselves could not help her, but that Jesus could, if she would like to ask him. Lydia said she would. She asked him, aloud, in her own words, committing her life to him and explaining her problem. We were then able to pray for her. A beautiful smile spread over her face. She said she felt wonderful, thanked us, and went home. The next morning we woke to find sixty hungry conference delegates, and no breakfast. Lydia, they complained, hadn't come. It turned out she was fast asleep.

The next to ask for prayer was Thomas, our driver. Thomas wanted to be freed from the waves of unprovoked anger which swept over him whenever he was alone. Thomas was not a Christian, either. We explained that if he committed his life to Jesus, we would pray for him to be filled with the Holy Spirit, so that he would experience not anger but love. Thomas said he would like to do that. As we prayed, he began to experience waves not of anger but of amazing peace. That night, Thomas had a dream. In his dream he was caught up in a great flood in which all the houses but his were swept away, and all the people but him drowned; Thomas remained safe inside his home. He woke, still alone, but at peace; assured that the waves of anger would never overcome him again.

Thomas was followed by Elena and Alicia, handsome, well-dressed women who did go to church but found themselves unable to pray or worship. They would open their mouths to join in with the prayers and the creed, and no words would come out. They couldn't understand why this was; they knew the words, they moved their lips, but there was something blocking their speech. There was obviously nothing wrong with them physically, so we asked if they had ever been to a witchdoctor – Mozambique is well known for its witchdoctors, and in the absence of proper medical care many people seek their services. There are two main kinds: *feiticeiros*, sorcerers who effectively do black magic; and *curandeiros*, spiritual practitioners who consult spirits and prepare herbal medicines which they believe carry spiritual power for healing.[19] These women had been to see a *curandeiro*. Alicia, who seemed tormented, dull eyed, dead inside, said she'd often taken her husband when he was sick. Had he been cured? No, he'd died, and she'd not been again. Elena said she'd been once or twice with her son. When I asked her to look at me she couldn't; her eyes flickered violently, and she said she felt a cold constriction in her chest. We invited them to answer the baptism questions, 'Do you turn to Christ?', 'Do you repent of your sins?', 'Do you renounce evil?'; and then prayed for them to be filled with the Holy Spirit. They themselves were then both able to pray aloud. They left, singing, and the next morning appeared with a spring in their step and a glow of confidence in their eyes.

Lydia, Thomas, Elena, and Alicia had never considered the nature of truth or the merits of the Church. They simply knew that they had a problem, and when the opportunity presented itself they were willing to bring their difficulties to Jesus in prayer. Kevin, Lisa, Tony, Nicky, Fran, Dawn, and Paul were also willing to respond to Jesus when they first met him. After all these years, Jesus still seems to offer something which the most sophisticated and wealthy society in the history of the world finds itself unable even to talk about. He offers life.

Confidence in the gospel

This book is about confidence in the gospel. Confidence that our faith makes it possible for us to explore both of humanity's fundamental questions, 'how do we know things?' and 'how do we make sense of them?' Confidence too that Jesus is not just a concept or a habit, but that he is the answer to the increasingly sharp-edged spiritual searching of our times.

The word 'confidence' is an interesting one. Usually we think of confidence as an emotional state, an inner awareness that all is and will be well, that we have what it takes, that things are going in the right direction. To give confidence is to encourage, to bolster morale, to reassure. But the word confidence isn't about human activity or emotion at all. It actually means 'with faith' – con-fid-ence. The true basis of confidence is, as every African knows, relationship. True confidence comes from relationship with God. Everything that we know, and everything that we do, ultimately traces its origin back to a conversation which each one of us must have with the man who said he was God, with the one who is the writer of the story which began with the creation of the universe. Jesus stands outside both the world views we have inherited, offering us not only a part in the history of a people and an understanding of the created world, but a personal relationship which will draw us into a completely new place. This is indeed good news.

Perhaps this is why Jesus didn't write a book, but got stuck into people. Perhaps it's why he didn't so much offer explanations as ask questions and tell crazy stories. Lesslie Newbigin comments, 'If it is the case that the ultimate reality which lies behind all our experience is, in some sense, personal… then it will follow that personal knowledge of that reality will only be available in the way in which we come to know another person.'[20] People are not only still interested in Jesus, they are becoming more informed about him. In a *Guardian* poll conducted in 2005, 57% knew what Easter celebrates; by 2008 *The Sunday Times* found that the proportion had risen to 90%. One man explained why: "Well, it's just been on the telly this week, hasn't it?" In recent years the BBC has screened series on the miracles of Jesus, the passion of Jesus, and the nativity of Jesus – presumably because they think people want to watch them rather than because they think they couldn't care less. *The Sunday Times* reporter remarked that he had expected people to be evasive and embarrassed to talk about Jesus – but that this had not been the case.[21] 'If ever there was a time to rediscover Jesus the Messiah, it is now,' Michael Frost and Alan Hirsch have suggested. 'It is possible that the story of Jesus may find a hearing once more, if it can be cleansed of its institutional accretions and retold in simplicity and honesty,' Michael Riddell writes.[22] If we can do that, we will have a new platform on which to build our lives in a confused world, and a new confidence in the gospel. For the first time in centuries we have the opportunity not just to react to the culture, but to lead it, to offer a basis for life which is as compelling to our confused society as the Christian response to the plague was to the panic-stricken Roman empire.[23]

Simplicity in the midst of complexity

Will that do for a postmodern philosophy? It has been said that 'there is a simplicity on the near side of complexity which is worthless, and a simplicity on the far side of complexity which is priceless.'[24] In every period of cultural change, it is imperative that Christians think insightfully about the obstacles and opportunities people will encounter in their search for faith. That is a complex and necessary undertaking; but the main task lies beyond it – the main task is that we help them to meet Jesus; and for this we do not need to be articulate philosophers or well-equipped theological experts. To return to the image we used in Chapter 1: if we are to grow healthy trees we need both to understand the nature of the polluted environment in which they are planted and then to provide access to the appropriate nutrients. Is it possible for us to move beyond the complexities of cultural analysis and return to the simplicity of our message – to tell them about Jesus?

We began this chapter with Paul's words to the Corinthians: 'For I decided to know nothing among you except Jesus Christ, and him crucified. I came to you in weakness and in fear and in much trembling. My speech and my proclamation were not with plausible words of wisdom, but with a demonstration of the Spirit and of power, so that your faith might rest not on human wisdom but on the power of God.'[25] If confidence in the gospel begins with an understanding of why it is still needed in our sophisticated but confused society, it continues with a reliance not on knowledge but on the resources that are made available to us through our relationship with Jesus. What those are and how we can use them will be the topic of Part II of this book. For the moment, let us remind ourselves, with Eugene Peterson, what it is that we are doing when we embrace the good news that such a relationship is open to us: 'Following Jesus is a unique way of life. It is like nothing else. There is nothing and no one comparable… Following Jesus takes us right out of this world's assumptions and goes to a place where a lever can be inserted that turns the world upside down and inside out. Following Jesus has everything to do with this world, but almost nothing in common with the world.'[26]

Jesus is not a leisure activity for the retired.

Good news for Richard

Richard was a drug addict on remand in Swansea prison for aggravated burglary. This is his story.

> *To help me cope with my feelings of guilt I began to*
> *attend the chapel in the prison. I felt really good when*
> *I was in Chapel. Whenever they served communion*
> *I felt somehow clean. As I took the bread and wine*
> *a strange warm feeling went through my body and I*
> *didn't understand it. A Methodist local preacher visited*
> *me. He began to tell me about Jesus and how He loved*

me. He offered me a Bible, but I told him I had one already in my cell. The Bibles in our cells had nice thin pages, so if we were out of cigarette paper we would tear out pages and use them to roll our cigarettes. One day I needed some paper for my cigarette. I tore out a page and struck the match, but suddenly, I heard an inner voice that said I should be reading this. I unrolled the page, and began to read it. It was the Gospel of John. I found it captivating. I then fell asleep, and slept the deepest and most peaceful sleep that I could remember. It was as if the weariness of years of turmoil, crime, drugs, aggression and fighting was being rolled away. The next day I read more, and the more I read the more I wanted to know about this man called Jesus.

I began to think about Jesus. I thought, I don't know what He looks like. At this point, the only image of Jesus I had ever seen came powerfully to my mind. Opposite Llanelli Police Station there is a Catholic church. Outside the church there is a cross with a representation of Jesus on it. As I stood with my eyes tight shut, that image of Jesus on the cross came alive in a vision, and it was as if I was actually there, at the cross, as Jesus was crucified. I saw His wounds, the blood, the darkened sky. Then Jesus lifted His head and looked at me. I saw His eyes and they seemed to pierce my soul. He simply spoke one sentence: 'Richard, I did this for you.' I just broke. The tears began to flow. I just said. 'Lord, I give my life to You.'

Technically I was still a drug addict. I needed a regular fix or I was a mess. But one day went by, then another, and I wasn't experiencing any withdrawal or *craving. I was amazed; I no longer wanted drugs. It came as a beautiful breaking dawn. Both mentally and physically, I was absolutely free.*[27]

Richard is now a pastor in South Wales.

For reflection and discussion

THE UNINVITED GUEST

He seems to come in like the leaves –
Blown in at the open window,
And always on a light and airy day.
Never in stormy weather.
And always, I've noticed,
At an inconvenient time –
Right in the middle of the washing.
He looks at me and shows me these holes in his hands.
And, well, I can see them in his feet.
'Not again,' I say.
'Please don't stand there bleeding
All over the kitchen floor.'
Sometimes he comes softly, sadly,
At night – close, by the side of my bed –
Sometimes I latch the door –
But he never goes away.

THELMA LAYCOCK

Read the poem by Thelma Laycock. Have you experienced such moments of awareness, times when you have felt the presence of God particularly strongly?

'The glory of God is a human being fully alive' – Irenaeus. What do you think he meant?

Do you think it is time for Christians to reclaim the intellectual ascendancy? Are we ready to say not just that our faith is a helpful personal thing, but a coherent way of making sense of the whole of reality?

'Then Jesus went about all the cities and villages, teaching in their synagogues, and proclaiming the good news of the kingdom…' (Matthew 9.35.) Should we be doing that today?

Chapter 6

The Response of the Church

How not to do it

Imagine you have just moved to a small English town. My work with ReSource takes me to a lot of small English towns; peaceful, beautiful places, a mix of old and new, with twisting streets and modern supermarkets, small primary schools and perhaps a secondary school, a variety of housing, daisy covered parks, a weekly market. Somewhere near the middle is a parish church, surrounded by its graveyard; on the periphery of the town one or two smaller Anglican churches; dotted in between them a Methodist chapel, a Baptist, URC or Roman Catholic church, maybe an Elim centre.

Perhaps you are a Christian; perhaps you are just thinking that now as you readjust your life it might be good to take a wander into one of the churches. You pick the big one in the middle, you read the time of the service on the board outside, and you turn up. Unfamiliar with the parking, you arrive a few minutes late, and find yourself being greeted with a look of slight disapproval by someone who hands you two books and two leaflets, unclips the rope with its notice 'No entry – service only' and ushers you into the chapel where the congregation has gathered. You sit down. Most of the people seem to be elderly, but there's a woman with a baby and a toddler at the front. The service isn't too bad, although you don't know the hymns and there's a lot of prominence given to a choir in blue gowns and starched collars. You muddle your way through with the books and the leaflets. After the service there's coffee at the back, so you stay on and nervously try to engage some people in conversation. Most of them look slightly irritated at the interruption, but they talk to you politely for a few minutes before turning back to their friends. You feel a bit discouraged, but you think you'll give it another go next week. Next week it's the same, and the one after; so after a bit you try the other churches. Most of them have small congregations of retired people – the age at which people naturally become interested in faith issues, one minister tells you with a smile at the door as you share your hesitation. One or two have a younger membership, but although there's more of a buzz about the place and they do seem pleased to see you, there still doesn't seem to be an easy way of actually getting to know them, and as you have a busy job you haven't the time to try out the midweek Bible study or the coffee morning. In all these churches you feel you are having to make all the running; and after a few more weeks you decide it's not going to work. If you are not a Christian you may reflect that church is a bit too much of a spectator sport, or at best a social club for people with different tastes and life circumstances from yours; if you are a believer, you may sadly add yourself to the 1500 people in Britain who decide to leave the Church each week. It is now estimated that one million Christians no longer belong to churches; it's the fastest growing sector of the Christian community.[1]

About a year ago I was invited to a boarding school in just such a small English town, to launch the Christian Union programme for the coming academic year. Numbers of those attending the midweek meetings had dwindled to a core of four; the hope was that through a punchy relaunch more people might be attracted to join. And so it was that I found myself in an upper room speaking with about twenty students, some Christian, some not, on 'The meaning of life – does Christianity work?' After I'd shared something of my own journey, I was bombarded with questions, mostly from students with little Christian background who struggled to find the right words to express their thoughts; a continuous forest of hands vied for the chance to ask about everything from Islam to spiritualism. At the end one girl came up to me and said that she used to be a Christian and that she really wanted the kind of spiritual life I was talking about. But where, she asked imploringly, could she find it? If she went to church she didn't find relationship, she found herself sitting in rows and singing hymns. She said if you aren't very careful you come out exactly the same as you went in – and she obviously didn't want to do that. What should she do? "Find a church with some people like you in it," I suggested lamely, struggling inwardly with the knowledge that in most places, outside city centres, there is no such thing. The same hunger was there in many of the students. One asked what he should read. The member of staff who had invited me told me a few days later that another, a German girl with no church background, had spent the rest of the evening lying on a sofa saying "Oh, Mrs Bentley, now I know!!" Regular attendance at the Christian Union rose to seventeen.

Not all our churches, of course, offer the experiences described above; many, both traditional forms of church and the increasing number of fresh expressions of church, look and feel radically different from this. And yet it remains true that most church services are little more than remnants of a habit; the earth does not tremble, the heart does not rise. And whilst the majority of churches regard themselves as friendly and welcoming, often this means that their members are (human nature being what it is) friendly and welcoming primarily to one another.[2] It also remains true that even when churches bite the bullet and decide to do things differently, it's often the doing rather than the being which is different – coffee in the middle of the service, or chairs arranged round tables, or meetings at a different time of day. The teenagers described above, and all the people whose stories are told in this book, are not looking for a slightly more accessible kind of meeting; they are looking for a whole new way of living – for an encounter with something real.[3]

Often it seems that even as the world is embarking on a new spiritual searching, the Church has been moving the other way. In many places it seems that we have largely lost touch with the dynamism of what is available to us. We have developed ways of doing and explaining things which may have served us well in the past, but don't cut the mustard for people today. One visitor to a traditional church wrote despairingly afterwards, 'It made me feel like the church has made up its own version of reality which doesn't have much to do with the world outside its walls.'[4]

It was to a church that Jesus said, "I stand at the door and knock."[5] I often wonder what would happen if he really did turn up one Sunday in a small English town?

Shrinking the gospel

One of the things which has always mystified me is how you put any woollen garment through the washing machine. Every so often I will wash a jersey belonging to a member of my family, following the care instructions to the letter – only to find it shrinks. I tug on the sleeves and stretch it from end to end, and nervously return it, looking just the same, to its owner; and yet I rarely get a good response – for it no longer fits. I think that this is all too often what happens to us as, with the best will in the world, we try to sustain our faith. All too often we turn the stupendous life-changing glory of a living relationship with God into a set of routines which look much more like a remembrance service for a dearly beloved and clearly departed figure from history than a living reality. Faith is only any use if it fits us today.

And yet it doesn't need to be that way, and in fact we

already have all the resources we need to ensure that it is not. We have over the last half century got back in touch with a whole host of things which have enriched our faith, and we have poured our energy into developing all sorts of new approaches to ministry. The problem is that somehow we have managed to compartmentalise these insights within different segments of the church community, with the result that instead of enriching our shared faith they have effectively served to shrink it. Is there a way of drawing on the new insights we have had, of joining together the strengths of our different denominations and traditions, in order to offer something which recaptures the breadth and excitement of the vision offered by Jesus – something which will clothe us completely, something which will not shrink with every successive wash but rather which we can fashion into a beautiful new garment, a garment for a new age?

Four tribes

I once watched a meeting between a Tanzanian bishop and a group of Masai elders – would they like to lend a couple of cows to pull a watercart belonging to the local church, most of whose members were from the Gogo tribe (and therefore agriculturalists rather than pastoralists)? In return they would be able to use the cart to bring water to their own village, located several miles from the nearest well, thus sparing their women the daily trek laden with plastic drums to fetch it – surely a win-win solution? "No," said the elders; "We are Masai. Masai do not share their cattle." And that was the end of that.

Things are not so very different in the Church. There are, remarked the Bishop of Peterborough twenty-five years ago, four tribes in the Church of England (and more widely, in the

Church as a whole). As distinct as the Gogo and the Masai, these ecclesiastical tribes have different priorities and different ways of doing things – and the danger is that whilst one has the cart, another has the oxen needed to pull it. The question for us is how to pool our different resources and experiences so that we actually get the water. What insights have we gained that we can share with one another in order to enhance our ability to share the good news of the kingdom of God?

The liberal tribe: learning to use our hands

Over the last generation or so we have learned to use our hands. This has been the insight of the liberal wing of the church. Liberals learnt to minister within the world view of modernism, embracing the humanist values of our society and working to bring about social change. This has had the advantage of getting us back on the streets and to the places where the pain is, and it's enabled us to recover a key dimension of the ministry of Jesus, a concern for the poor. Martin Luther King articulated this approach as follows: 'The gospel at its best deals with the whole man, not only his soul but his body, not only his spiritual well-being, but his material well-being. Any religion that professes to be concerned about the souls of men and is not concerned about the slums that damn them, the economic conditions that strangle them and the social conditions that cripple them is a spiritually moribund religion awaiting burial.'[6] Another early figure was William Booth, founder of the Salvation Army; but perhaps the best known exponent has been Mother Teresa, whose simple but assertive care for the poor of Calcutta earned her not only the admiration of the world but also the Nobel Peace Prize.[7]

As a result of these and other examples it is now clear to us all, in theory if not in practice, that we can live our faith credibly only if we are prepared to love and serve those for whom life is tough. And yet this is not the whole message, but only part of the message, and all too often we have loved and served them as if that in itself was the good news. It isn't. The good news is not that we care but that God cares; our caring is merely a sign and an expression of his care. If we fail to explain that, we sell God's love very short indeed. This was staunchly pointed out to me by Stanley Hotay of the Diocese of Mount Kilimanjaro in Tanzania. "You people," he said, referring to an English mission agency, "come to build us wells. This is very helpful for us. But why when you dig the wells are you not willing to talk to our people about the living water which is available to them through Jesus Christ? To be sure, they need fresh water. They will die if they do not get it. But fresh water is only for this life. One day they will die anyway. You should not hesitate to explain to them that this fresh water is just a sign of the living water which will prevent them from being thirsty for all eternity." All this time, money and effort, he was saying, and you are missing the main issue. As the apostle Paul wrote to the Romans, faith comes from what is heard; it is our privilege, once we have earned a hearing through our willingness to obey the commandment of Jesus to love our neighbour, to make sure that he hears and understands the immensity of what is on offer.[8]

The evangelical tribe: learning to use our heads

Whilst liberals have focussed on social action, the evangelical wing of the Church has showed us how to use our heads. We live in a scientific age which places great stress on thinking, on the search for objectively verifiable truth. Evangelicals have responded to this by seeking to restate the gospel as truth. Evangelical scholars have offered a reasoned advocacy for the truth of the gospel, looking at everything from the manuscript tradition of the New Testament documents to the historical, forensic, and circumstantial evidence for the resurrection of Jesus.[9] This scriptural approach presents the gospel as a credible choice in a rationalistic age, and offers a clear way forward for those who wish to build a firm foundation for their lives based on eternal truth rather than on contemporary secular values. This is how I found faith; I wanted to know whether the Christian faith had any basis in fact. Through the evangelical movement the church has found a new and effective focus, and rediscovered what it means to articulate the good news of the gospel and invite a personal and life-changing response. Many people did respond; many still do.

However, it's possible to have too much of a good thing, and sometimes this approach, if disconnected from the others, can lead into a cul-de-sac. It is all too easy to reject the materialist values of modernity but to accept its basic premise, which is that knowledge is based on fact and certainty is available. We simply find ourselves investing this certainty in a different place – in scripture. Scripture becomes literally true, and a guide for everything from whether women should speak in church to how many days the world was made in; and believing the right things becomes more important than loving people. I wrote in Chapter 4 about a talk I gave to church members and their guests on the subject of Science and Faith. The next day, along with the email from Adrian, I received one from a member of the church who wanted to say how disappointed he was with my doctrinal position, and in particular with my failure to affirm the literal historicity of the book of Genesis. After a short and fruitless exchange, I asked how his non-Christian guests had responded to the event. It turned out that he had not brought any guests; most of his friends belong to a small circle of people who have signed the same carefully worded statement of faith that he has signed. This is a classic way to shrink the gospel, a way of turning what should be a living, outward-looking relationship with God into a spirituality of print. "You know neither the scriptures nor the power of God," Jesus said to the legally minded Sadducees; "he is God not of the dead, but of the living."[10]

Because of this one-sided emphasis on a propositional gospel, it seems that sometimes our attempts to share it, though well meaning and courageous, in fact miss the mark. In 2004 I spent a couple of days as part of a SOMA team in a slum area in Nairobi called Kamakunji. The Anglican Church was holding a crusade, preaching the gospel and hoping to offer new life to the people whose lot it was to live there. This they did by putting on a staged appeal – an immaculately dressed choir, a bishop in purple shirt and expensive suit explaining the gospel in clear, amplified words over the litter-strewn ground and the fetid river which ran between the shanty houses and the piles of smoking rubbish, and an invitation to come forwards in response. Sensing the inadequacies of this approach, we wanted to help clear the place up, but it was feared too dangerous – we had no gloves, and the ground was littered with used syringes. So some of us played football with ragged teenagers, glue bottles in hand, and others of us wandered around praying. I sat down amongst the litter by a drinking booth, and got talking to a man named Sam. Sam was drunk. He said he got drunk every day; it helped him to cope. Why had I come to this place? We began to talk about Jesus. When the appeal was made to go forward and make a commitment to Jesus, Sam rose unsteadily to his feet. "I want to do that," he said. "I've heard this message many times before. But this time I am going to do something about it. I'm going up there today because of you: you are the first person ever to sit down and actually talk to me." Sam went forward, committed his life to Christ, and was prayed for. We went to congratulate him. Sam, drunk only a moment before, was clear-eyed and steady on this feet. It is not enough to state the truth – we must live it.

The charismatic tribe: learning to use our hearts

Both the hand and the head approaches have great strengths. But we live now in an age where people are more interested in their hearts. The question now is not 'is this true', but rather 'does it work? Does it change the way I feel?' The new measure of authenticity is not belief or action so much as connection – people don't want to do things or believe things, they want to experience them.

The most powerful response to this new dynamic has come from the charismatic wing of the Church. Commenting on the evangelical emphasis on the letters of Paul, Pentecostal scholar Gordon Fee points out that 'one reads Paul poorly who does not recognise that for him the presence of the Spirit, as an experienced and living reality, was the crucial matter for Christian life, from beginning to end.'[11] The charismatic movement had done just that. The fastest-growing movement in the Church worldwide, it has brought a spiritual refreshment, an immediacy of relationship with God, that has revitalised the ministry of the Church. My faith began when I signed up to the idea that the gospel was true; it took off when I discovered that it would change me. Our faith is more than service, more than belief:

Paul wrote that we are to be 'letters of Christ, written not with ink but with the Spirit of the living God, not on tablets of stone but on tablets of human hearts.'[12] Relationship with Jesus is not just about doing, or believing, but also about becoming.

And yet the charismatic movement, taken on its own, is as likely to lead to shrinkage of our faith as the liberal and evangelical approaches. For a start, it often fails to take scripture seriously – as if, Tom Smail once suggested, now we have rediscovered the Spirit we feel we have grown out of the need to do theology.[13] In particular, charismatic Christians have tended to focus on certain aspects of scripture at the expense of others; it has been justly remarked that 'our experience of the Holy Spirit cannot be reduced to the charismatic manifestations so highly prized by the Corinthians.'[14] Secondly, the charismatic movement has become increasingly monochrome: charismatic churches are likely to be middle class and suburban in lifestyle and outlook, with a branded subculture characterised by a particular musical style and approach to ministry. I notice with some puzzlement that at some gatherings, charismatic leaders can now be identified by their uniform dress code, a combination of blue denim jeans and a crisply ironed long-sleeved shirt. As we travel round the country it is becoming increasingly clear that whilst many churches do wish to move into the things of the Spirit, they do not necessarily wish to become, in the words of one church leader, 'culturally charismatic' in this branded sense.[15] Finally, the charismatic movement has often been inward looking, as if spiritual renewal were an end in itself rather than a means to an end. The result is that many charismatic churches are now wondering what all the excitement was about – what was the renewal movement actually *for*? It's not enough to focus on our experience, however real and life-changing it may be.

The Anglo-Catholic tribe: remaining faithful to our history

Finally, we have at our disposal the insights of the Roman Catholic and Anglo-Catholic parts of the Church. Often regarded as the least dynamic of all the tribes, many Catholic Christians are traditionalists, committed to protecting the tried and tested patterns of faith developed by previous generations. It may seem, in a fast-moving society, that tradition is the last thing we need. And yet history suggests otherwise. Chris Szejnmann is Professor of Modern History at Loughborough University, and he is currently working on a book on the rise of the Nazis. Chris's research on German voting patterns reveals that it was the Protestant areas, influenced by the new liberal theologians, who voted the Nazis in. The Catholic areas of Germany, less inclined to follow the latest theological trends, voted solidly against Nazism.[16] Traditionalists within the Church watch unmoved as attractively dressed bandwagons rattle down what all too often turn out to be dead end streets. In their insistence on the value of our heritage, they prevent us from the uncritical embracing of the latest ecclesiastical fashion; or at least they keep us safely together until the new ideas have been filtered by the passing of time.

I found a living example of both the strength and the weakness of a traditional Anglo-Catholic approach when working in Mozambique. For over thirty years Mozambique lived through war, first the armed struggle for independence from Portugal and then a protracted and bloody civil war. For much of that time the Church was a proscribed organisation. Since then, despite facing both flood and famine, Mozambique has begun a remarkable programme of reconstruction. As we talked with the clergy, we discovered that for a whole generation they had had no input, no training, no theological education; they had continued to do things the way they'd always done them, but with the memory of why fading with every passing year. They explained that they faithfully follow a complex Anglo-Catholic liturgical pattern, and we saw that their churches have the stations of the cross marked on the walls in Roman numerals; and yet they had never prayed for their own personal needs. They asked us to explain why churches meet on Sundays rather than Saturdays, why they use incense, and whether it's idol worship to have pictures on the walls. A complex recent case of child abduction in which both witchcraft and murder played a part had divided the clergy between those who felt the guilty parties should be put to death, and those who did not. They had a whole scaffolding of tradition, but not much inside it; in terms of living discipleship they had little to offer to a hungry people. And yet they were still there, having lived through some of the most horrendous experiences of modern times, still faithful to their calling. It was as if we were looking at a tree encased in strong bark, still standing despite the ravages of a violent and long lasting storm; but with only a trickle of life inside it, only the faintest trace of sap rising up towards the leaves.

Tradition is like the bark of a tree; it protects what lies within. It is not itself the life; merely the carrier of the life. And yet because the bark was still there, the Church in Niassa has been able under new leadership to enter into a period of steady spiritual and numerical growth. In the last five years the number of clergy and congregations has doubled, eighty new churches have been built, church membership has increased by 60% and Mothers' Union membership has tripled. Whereas once people were confirmed knowing nothing more about the

Christian faith than the Lord's Prayer, learnt by rote, now they must offer evidence of active discipleship through membership of a small faith-building *Rooted in Jesus* group; and in addition to deepening their relationship with God in this way, each group member offers practical support to ten families in their community, offering services as varied as care for orphans, water provision, health and HIV education and support for the long-term sick. 'The excitement of being church is palpable,' Helen Van Koevering writes.[17]

So tradition keeps us going in difficult times. And yet it is all too easy to forget that the visible bark is not what our faith is actually about. I think of the teenager asking in despair where she could find a church experience that wouldn't just be about sitting in rows and singing hymns. I think of Sharon, trying to find out about Jesus and ending up wondering what the rice paper was for. I think of the young mother in Carlisle explaining she wanted her baby baptised but didn't know anything about God. It's all too easy to cling to what we are used to, to a set of words and rituals which we persist in offering to people who no longer understand them, so that the local church becomes little more than what Rosemary Ruether has called a 'drab, dull, mediocre sacramental service station.'[18] 'Eleven in the congregation,' commented one mystery worshipper at a healing service in a historic church in a university town, 'so a fairly empty church – but it suited the style of the service.'[19]

Pooling our strengths

Each of these church traditions has grasped something really important; but none is complete in itself. I actually think we have a tremendous opportunity to put them together – as they are doing in the Diocese of Niassa, where their next target is to develop confidence in the healing ministry. It is open to us now as never before to draw on hands, heads, hearts and history; to learn afresh to be the body of Christ. Jesus ministered to the poor, talked about truth to his disciples, depended on the Holy Spirit in everything he did, and firmly upheld tradition as laid down in the law and the prophets. To do anything less is to shrink the gospel. We have learnt many things; between us we have all the resources we need to offer a powerful, dynamic and holistic faith, one which embraces all we are and reflects both the diversity of human experience and the nature of the Creator God. If we use both the oxen and the cart, we will be able to share living water more effectively than we have done for generations. In many places, we already are.[20]

Good news for the church

Holy Trinity Leicester is a charismatic evangelical church. It does not follow the lectionary; sermons are planned in termly series which follow either topics or books of the Bible. One spring we were working our way through a series on the psalms, and it fell to me to preach from Psalm 141. 'Let my prayer be counted as incense before you,' I read. I remembered John's vision of heaven in Revelation chapter 5, in which he saw golden bowls full of incense, representing the prayers of the saints; and I remembered the question asked by the Mozambicans. As far as I know Holy Trinity had never used incense; but it occurred to me that incense would be a powerful way of helping people to feel and see what happens when we pray – that it would be a sensual representation of a spiritual truth, reminding us that prayer is an offering we make to God, that it is fragrant and beautiful both to him and to us, and that just as the smoke ascends before our eyes to heaven, so our prayers rise from this world to the next.

And so I went to see David Cawley, rector of St Mary de Castro, one of Leicester's oldest churches – and in fact the one from which Trinity was founded as a church plant in the mid-nineteenth century. I asked him if I could borrow a censer and some incense, and if he would be so kind as to teach me how to use it. David was both astonished and delighted, and that Sunday as I preached Kim walked up and down the church swinging the censer. Apart from the worship leader, who spluttered that she couldn't breathe let alone sing, it caught people's imaginations. Several cell group leaders went out and bought incense sticks so that they could use them that week as they studied the psalm. A couple of weeks later those planning a day of prayer for the ministry of the church decided to call it an Incense Day. Six years later, Trinity is still holding termly Incense Days, characterised by the determination to model and enable prayer in as many different and creative ways as possible. Old, simple, and new.

For reflection and discussion

GUESTS

Oh, the trouble we've had
with this building over the years!
Heavens, the unwanted guests!

Rats, do you remember,
after the Dustbin Men's strike,
getting, somehow, into the wafers?
And trying to get the Council round
before Harvest Festival
to flush them out?

And then pigeons constantly
blocking up the drains
with those stupid bunches of twigs
they call nests.

And then for years, and years and years,
Death-Watch
(for those of us who can still hear)
Tap-tap-tapping in quiet bits of the service …
Lord! When the man told us
what it would cost to sort that out
well, it nearly broke our spirit
but we managed.
We managed.

And squirrels in the roof
several years running.
They had to be gassed, eventually.
Yes, it's certainly been a labour of love.

And now, I hate to say it but:
We, The Committee,
are pretty sure someone has been
SLEEPING IN THE CHURCH.
I can't imagine where they're getting in.

But they'll have to go.
Absolutely the last straw.

As I remind my committee,
when you take on a building of this size,
you take on a huge responsibility.

LUCY BERRY

How do you respond to Lucy's poem? Does it ring any bells?

Are the ways we do things as a church accessible to those who come from non-church backgrounds? How can we hold fast to the essentials of our faith without diluting our message of good news?

Which 'tribe' does your church belong to? Can you think of any ways in which you could strengthen your life and witness by drawing on the insights of the other tribes?

"Forget what happened long ago! Don't think about the past. I am creating something new: There it is! Do you see it? I provide roads in deserts, streams in thirsty lands... for my chosen people" (Isaiah 43.18–20, CEV). Do you think this was a promise for the past, or could it apply to our age too?

Chapter 7

Thinking a new world

The time is now ripe for what I have called a redefinition of the faith. This will not be a redefinition that devalues and discards all that has gone before. Rather it will be motivated by asking what are the elements of Christian belief that we now need to rediscover and emphasize in new ways in order to call people into effective discipleship in the cultural circumstances in which we find ourselves.

John Drane[1]

Tomorrow afternoon I am due to meet with four clergy from the Diocese of Nandyal, India. Anxious for their predominantly Anglo-Catholic diocese to become more effective in evangelism, they have come on a fact-finding mission to England. Whilst I'd like to think that England is a model of dynamic evangelism, it may be that they will find not so much answers to follow and patterns to embrace as the challenge to a way of thinking which inevitably comes from stepping outside one's own culture. Putting it the other way round, if the poem at the end of the last chapter describes your experience of church, a trip to southern India would probably provide you with considerable food for thought.

We may not be able to go to India, but we need nonetheless to find ways of stepping outside our own assumptions if we are to express the gospel creatively into our changing circumstances. Confidence is not to be found by retreating into a huddle of like-minded people, or by devouring the miracle-studded stories of individuals you've never met. Confidence comes from faith; from the inner, experienced conviction that there is a world we do not see, a world prepared for us by God which has been inhabited and celebrated by generations of Christians from many different cultures and which remains accessible to us today.[2] Our task is not to cheer ourselves up in the face of declining church attendance, or to try harder to make our services attractive to people who aren't really interested in them. Our task begins with the realisation that as Christians we have access to more substantial and meaningful answers to the big questions of life than those commonly on offer – that it is intellectually perfectly respectable to invite people to step outside a world view which increasingly leaves them feeling trapped, and entirely appropriate to offer them the opportunity to place their faith not in material possessions or dubious spiritual practices but in Jesus. It is open to us, for the first time in generations, not just to react to the culture in which we live but to transcend it, to offer a basis for life which is as compelling to our confused society as it is proving to be, for example, for the spiritually starved people of China.[3] It is time to build a new plausibility structure, to tell a different story, one which isn't about what you do on a Sunday morning but rather about how you live your life. And between us we have the resources to do it.

It is said that nothing can be done which has not first been imagined. Imagination, Einstein recognised, is more important than knowledge; for 'knowledge is limited, but imagination encircles the world.'[4] From Genesis to Revelation, the Bible bears witness to the power of imagination. God thought the world before he created it; he has already rethought it, and promised that he will therefore in the fulness of time recreate it. In between, he guides his people into a continuously unfolding future formed not through the careful communication of methodology but through the visions and dreams of poets and prophets. Perhaps, despite our utilitarian backgrounds, we still instinctively understand this: the last Pope and the current Archbishop of Canterbury have both been poets, men with a leaning towards the mystical. Karol Wojtyła, with his insistence on the 'poetry of resistance', saw ordinary people bring about the collapse of communism in Poland through the simple imagination of something different, something more alive, more vibrant. Rowan Williams has caught the imagination of the Church of England with his call for the creation of fresh expressions of church, a Spirit-dependent way of engaging creatively with a community, a way which comes through discernment rather than through strategic planning.[5] We should not be surprised at the appointment of such leaders; Jesus' major challenge was to the imagination, and today imagination remains part of the leadership task.[6] The implication is clear: before we can change what we do, we have to change how we think. 'The empires of the future are the empires of the mind,' Churchill once said.[7] If we do not learn to think creatively and prophetically, we will remain chained to the past.

Thinking in new ways – creating a climate of questions

Management consultant Ken Blanchard begins his book *Mission Possible* with a simple story. Imagine, he says, some children on a beach. They have built a complex and beautiful sandcastle near the seashore, but the tide is coming in and already the castle is beginning to crumble into the water. What do they do? The children react in different ways. Some shrug their shoulders and turn their attention to other things, abandoning the sandcastle to its fate. Others, more determined, move further up the beach and start again above the tideline, creating an improved, stronger castle. A third group of children, aware of the dangers of the rising sea, is intent on devising a new way of playing castles without building a permanent structure at all. These three groups of children, says Blanchard, represent the three possible responses of any organisation to the need for change: give up, improve, innovate.[8]

When ReSource meets with groups of church leaders, we often ask them a simple question: If you were to start again from scratch, would you do things the same way? Most say no, they would not. And that of course begs a second question: Why then are you not changing things now? Usually the answer is because the church in question has not succeeded in imagining anything radically different: most are like the first group of children, some are like the second, but very few are like the third. It's easier to tinker than to reinvent; but the situation we are in calls for something more radical than that. We always need to improve what we have, Blanchard suggests; but if we are to be sure of the future we also need to innovate – we need not just a 'today' approach but also a 'tomorrow' approach. For most of us this does not come naturally: we do not live in a reflective society, and our thinking is generally both purpose-driven and conducted at speed. Almost by definition, most church members are neither poets nor management gurus. So if we are to learn to think creatively, subversively and prophetically we will need to start by changing gear.

There are some tried and tested ways of doing this. First of all, instead of trying to persuade one another that all is going well, we can try to face together the reality that it is not. If you are a church leader, you might like to begin, as Michael Frost and Alan Hirsch suggest in their exceptionally helpful book *The Shaping of Things to Come*, by creating a sense of holy dissatisfaction.[9] Twenty people in your village live a life of committed discipleship and mutual caring – but the other 280 have no connection with the church. Eight hundred attend your city centre services – but the remaining 300,000 have never had any real exposure to the gospel. Your worship is beautiful, but unfortunately nobody under the age of thirty seems to connect with it. You are working hard on various local projects, but few people seem to find faith as a result. You've been doing things faithfully and consistently for a long time – but it has all begun to feel just a little bit stale. We cannot imagine a better future until we can see an inadequate present; so find those among your number for whom the glass is always half empty, and learn to look for the 'buts'. It may be painful, but it is also necessary.

Secondly, we can start asking provocative questions. Questions are powerful – and it is notable that Jesus asked far more questions than he gave answers.[10] So ask one another, what difference would it make to your life together if the building fell down tomorrow? If you could no longer meet on Sundays? How would you explain who you are and what you stand for if you were not allowed to use the word 'church' at all? What can the church learn from al-Qaeda? What did Jesus mean when he said he came to set us free – free from what (no religious words allowed)? Most leaders are chosen for their gifting as pastors and teachers; they are expected to be the people with the correct answers and the right advice. Learn to ask questions instead of relying on the expertise of leaders, and you may find prophets lurking in your midst.

Thirdly, it can be helpful to invite people to discard their secular expertise – it's surprising what a handicap secular expertise can be – and learn to think like children. Reading books can be a good way of jolting people out of their certainties; get stuck together into novels like William Young's *The Shack*, or Nick Page's *The Church Invisible*. Try Rob Bell's book *Velvet Elvis*, or his twelve-minute *Nooma* DVD series. For the more conceptually minded, offer *The Wild Gospel*, or Stuart Murray's *Church after Christendom*, Michael Frost's *Exiles*, Michael Riddell's *Threshold of the Future*, or Alan Hirsch's *The Forgotten Ways*.[11] Discuss films together – what did you make of *Chocolat*, or *Avatar*, or *Chicken Run*, and what do they tell us about people's hopes and dreams? Finally, look at ways of getting outside your comfort zone – spend a night with some Street Pastors or get involved in an inner city project; get to know people with a different world view – talk to asylum seekers, or go to a mind body spirit fair and pray for those you meet there; take a 'retreat on the streets', or try something new by joining a local association of some kind.[12] Finally, encourage people to volunteer for short-term cross-cultural mission with an organisation such as SOMA. New experiences enable us to evaluate old ones in new ways. All these things force us to become learners, and as American social writer Eric Hoffer observed, 'in a time of drastic change, it is the learners who inherit the future. The learned usually find themselves equipped to live in a world that no longer exists'.

Fourthly, we can take risks – which means that we must give one another permission to fail. John Keats remarked that failure is the highway to success; as all he did of note in his short life was write poetry, we can assume that he had a large waste paper basket. C. S. Lewis, an Oxford academic and popular theologian, observed that failures are finger posts on the road to achievement. Both men seem to suggest that success is not a fortuitous event but the end point of a long journey. Today we know that no organisation can flourish if it is not prepared to embrace failure. This is the advice given by Thomas Watson, chairman of IBM: 'Would you like me to give you a formula for success? It's quite simple, really. Double your rate of failure.' It's reasonably obvious – you only find out whether something works by trying it, and learning from your mistakes. But there's a deeper reason too for taking risks. My experience is that it is only when I am prepared to go out of my depth that I see God most fully at work; only when I reach the end of my own expertise and plunge into the unknown that the Holy Spirit is able to step in and take the initiative. If we stick to the predictable and the familiar, then we limit God. We need to be prepared to take risks, to make space for him to act. I find that it's in the gap between my vision and my competence that things happen.

Finally, we can welcome and celebrate change. At one time we used to alter the programme in our church every eighteen months, simply on the grounds that we wanted change to become normal. So mix people up. Get them to try new roles. Hold brainstorming sessions. Get the creative juices flowing by experimenting with new ways of doing things. In one African diocese the bishop asked us to run an extra session on law and grace, as he felt this was a key issue for the clergy. The most powerful moment came not in the course of my colleague's careful theological exposition, but in a discussion of Psalm 139 in which he asked participants to draw a picture of their relationship with God. This caused a certain amount of consternation – they were not used to drawing – but they applied themselves tentatively to the task. One priest produced a two-part picture which showed himself in his house on the left of the paper, and himself in church on the right; he explained that this was an illustration of when God was pleased with him and when he was not. This led to an animated discussion of what it is that God expects of us, and then later to a profound time of ministry in which we invited people to enter more deeply into God's love. The bishop's objective had been met – but not in quite the way we expected.

Thinking in new ways – harnessing the tools of the culture

Every human culture is based on a set of shared beliefs and values, and these beliefs and values vary widely from one culture to another. It is very hard to assess our own cultural matrix, for it has formed the way we think since babyhood. But two terms can help us. The first is the 'ideavirus', a term coined by Seth Godin to describe the way marketing ideas travel through a target audience; the second is the 'meme', a term coined by Richard Dawkins (and likened by him to the gene) to express the way beliefs and concepts are passed on from one person to another without ever having been consciously adopted.[13] Neither should be taken literally, but both helpfully emphasise the way in which what seem to us to be individually held ideas and values are in fact embedded in the intellectual fabric of a whole society – they are as much 'caught' as they are taught.

As Christians, or 'resident aliens' living in a world to which we no longer belong, as Paul and Peter put it long ago, our first task is to try and prise ourselves free from this unconscious matrix of beliefs and values, so that we can evaluate them from the standpoint of the eternal truth of the gospel.[14] Our second task is to begin to find ways of helping others to do the same; and one of the simplest ways of doing that is to use the same media through which the memes or ideaviruses spread most naturally. In 2005 the Bible Society embarked on a series of advertising campaigns, starting in Nottingham with posters asking questions about soaps and inviting text replies, and following them with more posters suggesting that the Bible has something constructive to say about common life issues. A series of events in public venues supported the campaign – a telling of Mark's gospel in a theatre, a film festival on the theme of spirituality, public discussions in a council chamber, a café, a bookshop and a pub. Many people got involved, and polls taken before and afterwards suggested that awareness of the relevance of the Bible had risen.[15]

One of the strongest advocates of the need for Christians to make full use of the opportunities provided by the media is Charles Colson, formerly known as the 'evil genius' in the Richard Nixon administration and eventually imprisoned for his role in the Watergate scandal. Colson became a Christian after reading C. S. Lewis, and following his release founded a national prison ministry. He has written many books, the best known of which is *How Now Shall We Live?*[16] Colson is convinced that the pain in Western society is deeply rooted in the pseudo-scientific, consumerist world view on which it is founded, and that it is our task to present the Christian faith not simply as a personal choice to be exercised within that flawed world view, but as a wholesome, viable and God-given alternative. This means, to go back to our previous image, that if we are to offer people a part in a different story, we need to find ways of explaining not just the part but the whole story. And that, Colson argues, is best done using precisely the tools which currently serve to reinforce and disseminate the flawed story: television, advertising, film, music and art. Mel Gibson's film *The Passion* is a striking example of what can be achieved, as are the recent BBC programmes *The Miracles of Jesus*, *The Monastery* and others. The internet is a powerful medium of communication, and the ReJesus site caters for both Christians and non-Christians – current posts include a happiness e-course, interviews with leading scientists who are also Christians, and a free music album called *Jesus is for Losers*.[17] In 2009 the Church of England ran an innovative Christmas radio campaign featuring a nativity horse race, a chart run down, a football match, and a police chase. It all helps; every exposure is a seed for a different way of thinking.

Some of these things can be done at local level too. How exciting is your church website? Does it offer anything to those who may be exploring faith? At ReSource we were taken aback by the Abbey church which invited us out of the blue to work with them – why us? we asked. Because, they said, you have poetry on your website. What untapped artistic talent do you have in your congregation or community? In Leicester we ran a creative arts day which we called 'Art and Soul', inviting people to exhibit paintings, photographs, and installations representing their own spiritual journeys, and opening the church to visitors. The day ended with an evening of music and dance. We were astonished and delighted both by the quality of the contributions from people who had previously played no active role in the life of the church, and by the numbers of visitors who came. For several years we began each of our 'Questions' guest evenings with a provocative topical film made by Nick Hamer, a member of the church. 'Questions' continues today, offering drama, music, and dance as well as film. It's a format which can be used as a one-off event in a school or community centre, or as part of a mission programme. Meanwhile minsters, civic churches, and cathedrals all over the country are now exploring the use of installations to help visitors engage with the building at greater spiritual depth: prayer trees, candles, post-it boards, water, world maps, stress pebbles, doodle sheets, bubbles, images of Christ, and works of art are just some of the things that have been tried. A focus on the arts enables a church to express its faith in fresh new ways, to connect with the fast-moving vibes of the culture and speak God's word into it in creative and inviting ways. It seems godly; I am always struck by the fact that the first person said in scripture to have received the gift of the Spirit was not priest or prophet but the craftsman Bezalel, appointed to work on the Ark of the Lord.[18]

Thinking in new ways – moving into the public arena

We have already seen that after many years of increasing secularisation, there seems to be a rising interest in the spiritual dimension of life, and that this presents the church with a new opportunity to speak about the gospel. This means that in addition to ensuring that as Christians we are both constantly extending our own horizons and learning how to connect with people in new ways, we also have the opportunity to speak more widely and generally about our faith. Nick Spencer, of the public theology think tank, Theos, and author of its first report *Doing God: A Future for Faith in the Public Square*, suggests that as it increasingly orients itself around the question of human well-being, society is effectively moving back towards God of its own accord; for long seen as a private matter, faith is now moving into the public arena. John Micklethwait, editor-in-chief of *The Economist*, has summed up the new situation in the simple three word title of his best-selling book: 'God is back'.[19]

This opens up a number of possibilities for us. Despite the drive towards secularism in the workplace, there is an increasing recognition of the role faith-based organisations can play in the public arena. There are new opportunities for Christians to partner with government agencies in offering local care and services, and to do so from a confident and explicit faith base; in North East England alone there are over 5,000 faith-run social projects involving more than 45,000 volunteers.[20] Campaigning atheists such as Richard Dawkins have given an enormous boost to public and private debate about the relationship between science and faith, with the result that many people are now interested in coming to locally organised events which provide a forum for discussion of these issues. The growing debate about the place of religion in society and its relationship to secular equality legislation enables individuals and churches to speak out for religious freedom, and provides an excellent opportunity for public discussion of the nature of Christian belief. Organisations such as the Christian Legal Centre are taking a public stand on behalf of persecuted employees such as those whose stories are told in Chapter 1. Everywhere, faith is on the agenda. Meanwhile many local issues, correctly handled, offer an opportunity to share the gospel – a Somerset museum has just decided, after local consultation, to cancel a booking from a group of spirit-seeking ghost busters to run a horror evening in their premises, involving mediums, spiritists, and 'calling up the dead.'

Finally, there is an increasing public shift from a focus on economic growth to a focus on personal happiness. In 2006 David Cameron called for a measure not just of GDP but also of GWB – 'general well-being', and measuring and promoting happiness is now government policy. Research by economist Richard Layard demonstrates that people who believe in God are happier than those who do not, and the Prime Minister's Strategy Unit itself found a similar correlation between life satisfaction and religious belief.[21] In all these areas we have something valuable and life-changing to offer.

So it seems that it is increasingly open to us both privately and publicly to assert that a Christian world view is not just a personal lifestyle choice but a way of making sense of life for society as a whole. The implications for the Church are clear, and who better to articulate them than Shakespeare: 'There is a tide in the affairs of men which, taken at the flood, leads on to fortune; omitted, all the voyage of their life is bound in shallows and in miseries. On such a full sea are we now afloat, and we must take the current when it serves, or lose our ventures.'[22] It's time to stop apologising.

Looking ahead

One of the most powerful and effective ministers of the gospel the world has ever known was St Paul. He told the Corinthians his secret: to focus on Christ alone, and to rely in everything he said and did on the Holy Spirit. In this way, he said, he would be sure that his hearers were not simply assenting to human teaching but experiencing the power of God at first hand.[23] It would seem therefore that if we are to minister effectively, we too must find ways of depending not on our own resources but on those which God makes available to us. History teaches us that periods of successful ministry in the life of the church have been characterised by a renewed focus on two things: the power of the Word and the gifts of the Spirit. Perhaps alone of all organisations, the church has the tools of ministry built into its DNA; and we can all use them. What that means in practice is the subject of Part II.

Good news in Keynsham

Keynsham is a town of some 15,000 people located between Bristol and Bath. In 2008 the churches, working together, launched 'More to Life', a community initiative which aimed to draw people together through a range of events organised around a monthly theme chosen after a process of community consultation – travel, relationships, music and arts, the environment, sport, community, and others. Beer mats, sweatshirts, a banner, and a prayer card helped to publicise the events, which took place in schools, clubs, churches, and community venues with the full support and involvement of local businesses and the town council. Taking its inspiration from Jesus' statement "I have come that you may have life, and have it to the full," 'More to Life' aimed to demonstrate the living truth of these words in Keynsham and its surrounding villages. Church members were encouraged to perform 'acts of kindness' and to meditate on relevant passages of scripture and other writings in small groups; visiting speakers and facilitators led events, local projects were set up, and outings and performances were laid on with the aim of drawing as many people into contact with one another and with the church as possible. The profits from these events were dedicated to 'sowing goodness' into the local community, and it was generally felt that 'nothing has ever touched the whole of the community in such a positive way.' Looking back on the events, vicar John Samways observes that the Alpha courses offered during the year were well attended both by seekers from the wider community and by church members wanting to refresh their faith, and concludes that 'the shared enterprise delivered more than we could have imagined. It has begun to transform the nature of the spiritual landscape in the town and surrounding villages, it has energized the church community and it has opened doors and brought life to dry bones (Ezekiel 37).' 'More to Life' continues today as the outreach arm of Churches Together in Keynsham.[24]

For reflection and discussion

IN BROKEN IMAGES

He is quick, thinking in clear images;
I am slow, thinking in broken images.

He becomes dull, trusting to his clear images;
I become sharp, mistrusting my broken images.

Trusting his images, he assumes their relevance;
Mistrusting my images, I question their relevance.

Assuming their relevance, he assumes the fact;
Questioning their relevance, I question the fact.

When the fact fails him, he questions his senses;
When the fact fails me, I approve my senses.

He continues quick and dull in his clear images;
I continue slow and sharp in my broken images.

He in a new confusion of his understanding;
I in a new understanding of my confusion.

ROBERT GRAVES

Read the poem by Robert Graves. How can we help people to face uncertainty, ask questions, embrace ambiguity?

'I had a college professor who said "All around you, people will be tiptoeing through life, just to arrive at death safely. But dear children, do not tiptoe. Run, hop, skip, or dance, just don't tiptoe"' – Shane Claiborne.[25] How willing are you to take risks?

Think about your church. If you could start again from scratch, would you do things the same way? If not, then why are you not changing things now?

'Do not be conformed to this world, but be transformed by the renewing of your minds, so that you may discern what is the will of God...' (Romans 12.2). What can you do together to try and open yourself up to new ways of thinking?

Part II

The Tools of Our Trade

Chapter 8

The Word of God

*Man does not live on bread alone, but on every word
that comes from the mouth of the Lord.*

Deuteronomy 8.3 (RSV)

We are verbivores, a species that lives on words.

Steven Pinker[1]

Words in context

When I was eight years old my teacher Mrs Garrard went into
hospital and, things being as they then were, her mother-in-law
came to teach us for a term instead. Mrs Garrard senior was half
Australian and half French. Both these factors were important;
I learned to draw brightly coloured fish, and I acquired a few
words of French. With the French came the unexpected, life-
changing realisation that words were not the same as thoughts,
for I suddenly found I could imagine thinking in a language
which as yet I could not speak. By the end of the year I'd decided
that I wanted to study languages at university. And so it was that
eventually I became a linguist, a university lecturer in Italian,
and began to acquire smatterings of something like a dozen
modern and medieval languages.

Since that time with Mrs Garrard, words have been a constant source of fascination for me. What are they for, I began to wonder as life carried me from primary to secondary school. I concluded that at the simplest level they are the carriers of meaning. And so when at the age of about sixteen I began to wonder what life was all about, it seemed obvious to look for the answer in words. I took myself to the local bookshop, and there I picked up, for the first time in my life, a Bible. I opened it, and this is what I read: 'In the beginning was the Word, and the Word was with God, and the Word was God. He was in the beginning with God. All things came into being through him, and without him not one thing came into being. What has come into being in him was life, and the life was the light of all people' (John 1.1–4). These words didn't actually tell me anything, because I couldn't make head or tail of them. But they tantalised me. It took me another eight years to begin to understand them and to join in with them.[2] And yet that experience served only to deepen the fascination; words truly are the most remarkable and astonishing things.

As Christians we are people of the Word. In a way that sounds reassuringly straightforward – we have a book of words, the Bible, and so it seems obvious that all we have to do is read it in order to grow in our faith, and then share it with others so that they can grow in theirs. But there's more to it than that. We've already talked about how easy it is to shrink things without really noticing – and I think that often we shrink the Word of God. We shrink it sometimes because of the flattened way our society conditions us to think about words, sometimes because of the pseudo-scientific expectations we tend to bring to it, and sometimes simply because so much of it gets lost in translation. The Word of God is tantalising both because it stretches our brains over the normal boundaries, and because of the way it moves beyond the conceptual and becomes active – it has an alarming tendency to spring off the page and come to life. This too is key to our understanding of it – we need to take on board that Word and Spirit cannot be separated, any more than matter and energy can be separated. Word and Spirit together are the two means by which God communicates with us, the primary tools of our trade and the major source of our confidence as we seek to minister to others.

What is a word?

Words are chameleons, which reflect the colour of their environment.

Billings Learned Hand[3]

If we are to understand the power that is available to us through the Word of God, we must begin by examining our own understanding of words. Words are very familiar things; we live surrounded by them and spend our lives acquiring them. It is estimated that a two-year-old learns a new word every two hours, and that a literate adult has mastered 120,000 of them.[4] Without words we cannot be who we are. And yet words don't always feel like friends: we live in a world which is drenched in words – words bombard us through televisions, radio waves, hoardings and computers, through text and instant messaging and email and junk mail. It's been said that one of our most necessary skills is to know how to filter out words. And yet words are the key to everything.

Let's start by asking ourselves the simple question: what is a word? Most of us would probably say a word is a black and white unit printed on a page; and so when we talk about the Word of God we tend to think primarily of a printed book – the Bible. But before the invention of the printing press in the fifteenth century most people must have understood a word not as something printed but as a sound in the air, so it cannot strictly be said that a word resides in its written form. Is a word then determined by its meaning? Medieval philosophers thought that it was: 'Words are the consequences of things,' the saying went. But Plato had suggested otherwise – 'Nothing has its name by nature, but only by usage and custom' – and we tend to go with Plato. Lewis Carroll unpacks him for us: "When I use a word," Humpty Dumpty said, "it means just what I choose it to mean – neither more nor less."[5] Humpty knew that there is no actual correspondence between a word and the thing it describes, and he knew too that there is no guarantee that when I use a word my understanding of it is the same as yours. Words are not chiselled in stone, like little statues each carrying its own message; they are simply associations, overlapping like clouds caught in the web of a spider. If it were not so it would be very hard to think at all; there is a limit to the number of ways we can arrange statues, but no limit to the overlapping of clouds.

What effect do words have on our thinking?

The relationship between thought and language is a fascinating one. Can we think without words? Probably not, or at least not very well. Try and formulate the thought that you are going to open the door, without using words, and you will very likely succeed. But try a more complex task, like planning what you are going to do tomorrow, and you probably won't; most people find that as soon as they try to do this, words creep into their heads. Words are necessary even for mathematical thought: the Piraha people of Brazil, who have words only for 'one', 'two', and 'many', apparently find keeping track of the precise number of more than three objects impossible. The Eveny people of Siberia, on the other hand, who have 1,500 words to describe the shape, body parts, and moods of reindeer, can engage in a complexity of thinking about these animals of which English speakers are incapable. For our part we are able, after generations of literacy, to pursue abstract thinking in a way which non-literate peoples are not; it's not just what the words are, but whether we can write them down or not which influences the way in which we use them.[6] Finally, it is worth noting that words do not just enable our thinking objectively but also colour it emotionally. The Italian word *prego* has no direct English equivalent – it means please, or don't mention it, or after you, or here you are. The Swahili word *pole* means I'm sorry, or I feel for you, or even – when repeated twice and in the appropriate context – please go slower on this bumpy road. The words available to us affect not just what we do or who we are but also how we feel; words are as much about relationships as they are about concepts and events.

After years of careful consideration I have concluded that words can perhaps most easily be regarded simply as the clothes that thoughts wear. They have no independent existence and no meaning apart from the thoughts they clothe; and yet without them our thoughts can scarcely get going of a morning – they may stagger out of bed, but they won't look very sophisticated, and they certainly won't travel very far.

God's thoughts and our thoughts

For my thoughts are not your thoughts, neither are your ways my ways, says the Lord. For as the heavens are higher than the earth, so are my ways higher than your ways and my thoughts than your thoughts. For as the rain and the snow come down from heaven, and do not return to it without watering the earth and making it bring forth and sprout... so shall my word be that goes out from my mouth; it shall not return to me empty, but it shall accomplish that which I purpose, and succeed in the thing for which I sent it.

Isaiah 55.8–11

As human beings, we use words in many different ways. And just as we wear different clothes for different occasions, so we use different words for different purposes. We use them for information, as when we read a newspaper. We use them for description, as in a novel, and for persuasion, as in advertisements. We use them for instruction, as in car manuals; and for discussion, to share our ideas and opinions. Finally, we use them for relationships, communicating with one another through conversation, email, poetry. And because we use words in these particular ways, we tend to assume that God does the same. At first sight this seems correct: his written word, the Bible, contains plenty of examples of words being used in all these ways – the genealogy of Christ (information), the decoration of the temple (description), the exhortations of St Paul to the young churches (persuasion), the Ten Commandments (instruction), the conversations between Jesus and his disciples (discussion), the poetry of the Song of Solomon (relationship). And yet it's more complex than that:

for if words are the clothes that thoughts wear, surely we should expect the words of God to do more than our words do – for his thoughts are more complex than ours.

For many years our family had a pet rabbit. Floppy was a lovely rabbit, tame and affectionate. But it must be confessed that Floppy was not bright. His thinking was fuzzy, and I often used to reflect that it must be rather like being drunk all the time. He had enormous difficulty working out simple cause and effect things like whether if he ran into that corner we would be able to pick him up and put him away, or not; and he never did grasp that you can't, if you are a rabbit, get through a closed kitchen door by digging through the lino.

Our thought processes must be just as limited, from God's point of view. 'My thoughts are higher than your thoughts,' God had said to Isaiah; it would seem that his thoughts are considerably more complex and more powerful than ours. Perhaps we are like the rabbit when we compare our use of words to God's; perhaps God uses words in ways we know nothing about. If we think in one dimension, perhaps he thinks in three – if string theorists are right, it's actually at least eleven.[7] If our words describe the world, God's words create it; if ours smooth relationships, his determine events. If we reduce the word of God to the categories of thought we use words for, we strip it of its power. And, like most things, this matters most when we don't know we are doing it; for we run the risk of making God in our own linguistic image.[8]

How does God use words?

In the Bible we find that there are at least three different words which are translated by the single English term 'word'. If we do not understand the differences between these three words, we will be limited, rabbit-like, to a flattened understanding of what God means by a word, and how he uses it.

The Word of God: dabar – *being and becoming*

> *The word is a distinct reality charged with power. It has power because it emerges from a source of power which, in releasing it, must in a way release itself.*
>
> John McKenzie[9]

When the Old Testament talks about the word of God it uses the word *dabar*. This word *dabar* has two meanings. First of all, it means 'word'. But it also means 'deed'. So for the Old Testament writers, the word of God is both a word and an action. God's words actually *do* something; they make things happen. We may assume that this is why people were so afraid of the Old Testament prophets – they knew that their words were not empty, but carried within themselves the power to bring about that which they foretold.

The first mention of God speaking in the Bible comes in the third verse of the book of Genesis: 'Then God said, "Let there be light"; and there was light.' And so begins the story of creation. For six days, God spoke; and a universe came into being. God thought light and darkness, sky and land and sea, sun and moon, birds and animals, grass and trees, man and woman; and as he spoke they became. 'By the word of the Lord the heavens were made; he spoke, and it came to be; he commanded, and it stood firm,' the psalmist writes, years later. 'We understand,' summarises the writer to the Hebrews, 'that the worlds were prepared by the word of God, so that what is seen was made from things that are not visible.'[10] Furthermore, it seems that the word of God has the power not only to create but also to destroy, for Peter explains that the same word which created the heavens and the earth has also reserved them for destruction by fire – an echo of Isaiah's more urgent warning that with a word of rebuke God can dry up the sea, turn rivers to desert, and reclothe the heavens in their primordial darkness.[11] Psalm 102 picks up the idea of words as clothes, and remarks that one day, when the heavens and the earth wear out like a garment, God will change them like clothing, rethink the universe and speak it in different words – words which for now we can imagine only in the poetic and visionary language of the Book of Revelation.[12] In the meantime, God continues to think and speak, for his speaking is not just an event in history but also a continuous process in time. Psalm 147 describes how God sends out his word and clothes the earth in snow, scatters it with frost, hurls down hail from heaven; Psalm 104 praises him for the way in which he continues to sustain with his breath that which he first created with his words.[13] The word which made things happen still has to be spoken so that they may not unhappen, for it contains the energy which keeps them alive. Reflecting on Sir James Jeans' suggestion that the universe looks more like a great thought than a great machine, Annie Dillard rightly observes that 'the question of who is thinking the thought is more fruitful than the question of who made the machine, for a machinist can of course wipe his hands and leave, and his simple machine still hums; but if the thinker's attention strays for a minute, his simplest thought ceases altogether.'[14]

Nobel Prize-winning scientist Alexis Carrell once said that the most powerful form of energy that we can generate is prayer, for it seems that as we pray, God is still willing to speak creatively into reality even today.[15] We are not used to thinking about energy in this way – we hold that the universe traces its history to a particular event in time which we refer to as the Big Bang, an explosion of energy which began the process which led to life. Energy is about physics, not about vocabulary. And yet in 1970 a curiously biblical article in the *Scientific American* suggested that the share of that primordial energy which the earth receives daily from the sun (some 5×10^7 megawatt hours of power per second) could alternatively be expressed as a continuous gift of 10^{37} words of information per second.[16] Words are about more than print.

If the word of God, *dabar*, contains locked within itself a powerful energy which changes things, it follows that in order to minister effectively to others we will need to learn to release that energy. This will not happen if we hold a flattened understanding of the Word of God as a series of black and white marks written on the pages of our Bibles. If we are to speak the word of God into the human condition and expect things to happen, we must begin by restoring our understanding of it to a multi-dimensional one. We must expect that when we speak to God in prayer, our words will acquire something of the power of his.

My colleague Martin was preaching one day in Holy Trinity, Hounslow. Sensing the strong presence of the Holy Spirit, he asked the vicar, Oliver Ross, how long it had been like that. "About thirty years," Oliver said, "it had started on the day that Lottie died." Lottie, then sixty-three, was a faithful church member, and she was sitting one Sunday in the front row. During the service, a Eucharist, Lottie died in her seat. Her body was carried out to a table behind the screen at the back, and a doctor and two nurses pronounced her clinically dead. But the vicar (who had never done such a thing before) took her by the hand and said, "Lottie, you can't go – in the name of Jesus, come back!" – and she did. "Lottie," Oliver continued, "is now 93, and she's sitting over there – why don't you ask her yourself?" Lottie confirmed the story, in all its parts, to Martin, adding only one thing, which was that when she returned to life she found that every ache and pain in her body, including all her arthritis, was healed. "The last thirty years," she said, "have been the best of my life!" Lottie finally died at Easter 2008.

Living life on a more modest scale, I once prayed with my distraught eight-year-old son over his cold, stiff and to all intents and purposes thoroughly dead hamster – apart from the evident rigor mortis it was not breathing and had no heartbeat. As we prayed, my hands became hot as radiators, and Edward gasped "his whiskers are moving!" We watched astonished as life crept down the hamster's motionless body from whiskers to nose, to mouth and ears, torso, front and then back legs, until finally the hamster, eyes bulging, rose with an air of faint surprise to its feet. Hamsters live a charmed life, and this one escaped six months later never to be seen again; but Edward's faith in God has remained unshaken to this day. What had happened? A small boy and his compassionate mother had spoken some words.

Events such as these remain rare; but instances of physical healing in response to words of supplication or command are increasingly common. At ReSource we often speak to churches and other gatherings about the power of the word, and we finish by inviting people to enter into the presence of God and to listen for a word from God which they themselves can speak, then and there. Listening to God in threes one evening in Carlisle, Clare thought she'd heard him say, "Encouragement. Use us." Jill, who came from another town, then shared that she'd been asking God to say something to her about her sick daughter's baby, just put up for involuntary adoption – something which might alleviate the pain and distress she was feeling. Clare, suddenly understanding what God had meant, was then able to tell the success story of her own two adopted children, and Jill embraced this as a direct message of encouragement from God. "I felt such a strong urge to come tonight," she said, "but I didn't know why!"

One woman at the Tubestation church in Polzeath, Cornwall, said that as she prayed, she had heard the words "In Jesus' name, be healed!" This, she felt, was clearly not for her but for the elderly stranger sitting next to her. In a rush of obedience she turned to her and spoke out the words she had heard. Her pain disappearing, the elderly lady was healed in that moment of her arthritis.

The Word of God: a framework for living

> *He declares his word to Jacob, his statutes and ordinances to Israel.*

Psalm 147.19

The word of God, *dabar*, not only speaks life into being, it creates a framework within which that life can be lived. For the created world, this happens as God sustains the natural processes on which life depends; not only is he 'before all things', Paul says, but 'in him all things hold together.'[17] Our daily life as human beings is sustained in this way too; but for us there is an additional, moral framework – a framework of commandments.

On the sixth day, we read that God created man and woman. Having spoken them, he began to speak *to* them, a speaking which like creation itself continues to this day. He set them a framework of words within which they could safely live in relation with one another and with him. This framework, expressed in the commandments given to Moses (the *debarim* or, in Greek, the 'decalogue' – that is, the 'ten words') and set down at greater length in the covenant ('the words of the Lord'), was upheld by Jesus, who stated himself, the living Word, to be its fulfilment.[18] It is a framework of law, and its words form the political and social order within which human beings are designed to live. Observe these words, Moses said, and life will go well for you: you will live in harmony with your environment, and its fruits will be your fruits, its blessings your blessings. Ignore these words, and your land will turn to desert, your social order disintegrate and your relationship with God will be severed.[19] The Word of God creates our physical environment, but it also forms our social environment; and the two are linked.

This has profound implications for our relationship with scripture. All too often we have adopted what we have referred to as a 'spirituality of print', paying our respects to a holy book which we locate in history, reduce to the printed word, and study carefully in its proper context.[20] It is good to do this: Psalm 119 famously urges us to treasure the word of the Lord, to delight in it, be revived by it, keep it, hope in it, welcome it as a lamp to our feet and a light to our path. And yet I suspect that when the psalmist urges us to delight in the word, he is not simply trying to say that Bible study is helpful, or fun. He is urging us not merely to study the word as a source of information, but to absorb it – to consume it as the prophets consumed the scrolls presented to them in their visions. It is not enough to know it; it must become part of who we are.

For many years I sat Saturday by Saturday in a riding school as my daughter Katy learned to ride a horse, and it seemed to me then that the horse offers a helpful picture of what it means to live by the Word of God. The horse is a living creature, and to ride it successfully you need to know more than how to climb on and how to hold the reins: you have to work out how to ride in rhythm with its natural motion, how to allow your own body to enter into harmony with the power and energy of the horse. If you don't succeed in doing that, your movement remains awkward and even painful; you may be carried forwards, but it will not be an easy ride – you will jolt and bump most awfully. And I think that's what the psalmist means when he talks about living by the Word of God. The words of God are not intended as a set of instructions or a straitjacket of rules; to live by the Word of God means to live in harmony with reality itself. It's the difference between connecting with the rhythm of the horse and being jolted along like a sack of potatoes. In absorbing the Word of God, we learn how to survive and flourish in a complex world. In practice this means that just as the Word of God is spoken creatively and powerfully into the physical world, so it speaks into our inner lives, healing the bruises suffered by those who have not managed to live by his rhythms, and providing direction for each person who is willing to be open to his purposes.

I have prayed with countless people who have failed to live within the framework offered by God, or who have been damaged by the failure of others to do so, and I have seen many released from pain and guilt as they have confessed their hurts and their failings to God in prayer. One was Sandra. Deprived of love in her childhood, Sandra had sought it through sex. She wasn't sure how many men she had slept with, but thought perhaps it was about fifty. The men had failed to meet her needs, and she was on powerful anti-depressants. "I don't want anything religious," she said firmly as she came to talk things through. I said I had nothing else to offer her. As we prayed, Sandra decided to commit her life to God. Filled with unexpected peace, she was able to forgive her parents and grandparents and to ask for healing from her own failures. Within a year Sandra felt she had become a different person. The nightmares, the party lifestyle and the compulsive desire for sex had been replaced by a new sense of wholeness, a new rhythm of life.

Another was Kathy. Unlike Sandra, Kathy had been brought up in a loving family, but money had been tight, and most of her clothes and toys were hand-me-downs from her sister. Kathy had always suffered from low self-esteem, and this was now compounded by the fact that many of her work colleagues were no longer speaking to her. As we prayed, Kathy began to realise that her childhood experiences had caused her to believe that not just her clothes and toys but she herself was 'second best'. God drew our attention to Isaiah 43.4: 'you are precious in my sight, and honoured, and I love you.' As we shared the words with Kathy, they seemed to her to come alive – almost as if they had been written for her personally. At that point Kathy did what few people do. She wrote the words down on a piece of card, put the card in her handbag and began to meditate on them daily, reading them again each time she heard the insistent whisper 'second best'. Over the next few weeks we watched Kathy grow in confidence and self-assurance. As she absorbed the truth of who she was in Christ, she began in fact to be that person in the circumstances of her daily life. Her colleagues began to treat her differently, and her relationships were transformed.

The Word of God: logos

> *Long ago God spoke to our ancestors in many and*
> *various ways by the prophets, but in these last days he*
> *has spoken to us by a Son.*

Hebrews 1.1–2

If the Old Testament called a word *dabar*, the New Testament calls it *logos*. That's the word John uses to begin his gospel. 'In the beginning was the Word, and the Word was with God, and the Word was God. All things came into being through him.' We're going back to the beginning, back to creation – but this time the angle is different. Like the Hebrew *dabar*, the Greek word *logos* has two meanings. Firstly, it means a 'word', and specifically a spoken word. Secondly, it means 'reason', the rational principle which governs the universe. The philosopher Seneca had said that *logos* was what put meaning into the universe and into man – *logos* was the mind of God. So when John sat down to explain the gospel to the Greek-speaking world, *logos* was the way he described Jesus. Jesus, he was saying, is the mind of God become a man. The Bible is God's word spoken and written, but Jesus is God's Word living. The Word became flesh and lived among us. The Word of God became a person.

It's not hard to see that our rather flat term 'word' doesn't do justice to any of that. Perhaps the best translation of *logos* is to be found not in our English Bibles, but in Jerome's fourth-century Latin. Jerome caught the meaning of *dabar* into his translation of *logos* and wrote 'in the beginning was the verb'. 'The word is the Verb, and the Verb is God,' said poet Victor Hugo some 1,500 years later.[21] What is a verb? We learn that at school: a verb is a 'doing' word. So here we are again: the Word of God *does* things.

And so it was that in the year 4 BC, or thereabouts, the conversation took a new turn. The prophets of the Old Testament had received, and passed on, the Word of God. We are told not that Jesus received the Word but that Jesus *was* the Word. Jesus' whole life was to be a human utterance of the word, will, purpose and intent of God.[22] The people of God, by and large, had failed to absorb and live by the Word of God; now it was time for the word to step out of the pages and insist on a hearing.

As we follow the story of his life, we find that when Jesus spoke, his words carried the same power that God's words carry in the Old Testament. The word-events spoken by the prophets became a Word-person, and everything moved up a gear.[23] Like his Father before him, Jesus spoke order into chaos: "Be still!", he said to the wind and the waves on the Sea of Galilee; the storm subsided. He spoke forgiveness into sin: "Your sins are forgiven," he said to a paralysed man; and, "so that you may know that the Son of Man has authority on earth to forgive sins… stand up and take your mat and go to your home." He spoke life into death: "Come out!" he said to Lazarus, and Lazarus staggered out from his tomb, still wrapped in grave cloths. Similarly, Jesus spoke healing into sickness even at a distance by the simple use of words: "Just speak the word, and I know it will be done," said the centurion whose servant at home was paralysed; it was. And finally, Jesus spoke deliverance into bondage: "Come out of him," he said to an unclean spirit in a man of Capernaum; and it did.[24]

All these utterances of Jesus were marked by visible physical consequences. But the changes which came about in the mental and emotional lives of those who listened to his words were equally remarkable. His sentences were like nutcrackers, breaking open the assumptions of those to whom he spoke and releasing the kernel of life within. He never seemed to speak in straight sentences, but in parable and metaphor, telling subversive stories which sprouted like seeds in the lives of those who heard them. He cut down the rule-mongers with unerringly accurate exposés, offered insults to the uncooperative, and argued with the difficult. He had a habit of replying to questions with more questions, and on one occasion he just bent down and wrote in the sand. Jesus' words were wild, untamed things, far from the tidy precision of so many of ours. "You search the scriptures, because you think that in them you have eternal life," he thundered, "yet you refuse to come to me to have life." It became increasingly clear that the Word of God cannot be confined to the printed page. People noticed: women wandered off in a daze; men crept back at night with questions. Many left their homes and livelihoods to follow him. This Word certainly knew how to use words.[25]

Now all this goes way beyond anything in our own human experience. Jesus' words were the living expression of the thoughts of God; they made things happen. He turned physical reality upside down and mental worlds inside out. This is a long way from the way we use words, for information, description, instruction, persuasion, discussion, and relationship. If words are the clothes that thoughts wear, we can be in no doubt that Jesus, as the *logos*, the mind of God made man, does the multi-dimensional thinking of the creator and not the one-dimensional thinking of the creature. If we think and speak in black and white, Jesus thought and spoke in colour.

The question, then, is this: are we destined just to continue with our powerless human use of words, or can we, once we have entered into relationship with this Jesus, expect more than that? Are we doomed just to watch in awe, as my intellectually challenged rabbit used to watch me, or can we join in? The astonishing discovery made by many Christians is that we can: Jesus still speaks in all these ways today, and he does so through us. "Wait," he had told the disciples, "until the Spirit comes upon you." They waited; and when the Spirit came, their words acquired the same power that they had seen in his; the book of Acts, as its name suggests, tells the story.[26] We have a tremendous opportunity today to assist Jesus in his continued desire to speak into people's lives: not interested in verbal straitjackets, and clearly disillusioned by the glossy words of a spin-driven society, all the evidence is that people are increasingly open to the kind of word which works.

When we pray in the name of Jesus, we find that our words have the same power that his did. People are regularly healed in churches, at conferences such as New Wine, and in the many Healing on the Streets initiatives now taking place around the country as people pray in teams in shopping centres and market squares. I have prayed over the years with many people, both in the UK and in Africa, who have needed healing or deliverance from evil; healing comes often, but I cannot think of a single instance in which a person requesting deliverance has not received it.[27]

Can such things happen in ordinary, daily life? A few months ago a young mother was backing the car out of her drive in the village of Thurnby, Leicestershire when, tragically, she knocked down her little boy. An ambulance was summoned and the paramedics examined the boy. They said he was critically injured. The family was not Christian, but a member of the local church happened to be passing by. She stopped and offered to pray for the child. The offer was accepted, and the boy was then taken to Leicester Royal Infirmary. On arrival he was examined by the doctors staffing the Accident and Emergency department, who to their surprise found him to have suffered only minor injuries. The family responded to this experience by beginning to attend church.[28]

That's all very well, perhaps you are thinking; but I've not had any kind of training for this. I'm not sure you need it. Dorisia Chende is an illiterate woman of advanced years, and she lives in a remote part of rural Tanzania. Dorisia is part of a *Rooted in Jesus* group, and when the leader prayed for people to receive the Holy Spirit, Dorisia received the gift of tongues. The next Sunday she stood up in the middle of the church service and said, "I have to say that there is a woman here with a problem in her abdomen. I want to pray for her." The pastor, to his great credit (it is not usual for elderly women to interrupt the service), asked the congregation if there was anybody present who had such a problem. Another woman stood. She said she had been suffering from almost continuous bleeding – fourteen, twenty-one days each month. Together they prayed for her, and she was healed. Dorisia continues to receive words of knowledge and to pray for people in her village. Where does she get the confidence to do this? I suspect it's just that no one has told her it might not work.

The Word of God: rhema

> *You have been born anew, not of perishable but of*
> *imperishable seed, through the living and enduring*
> *word of God. For "All flesh is like grass, and all its glory*
> *like the flower of grass. The grass withers, and the flower*
> *falls, but the word of the Lord endures forever." That*
> *word is the good news that was announced to you.*

1 Peter 1.23–25

The first Christians didn't understand a word primarily as a thing written, nor yet as a thing living. Most of them, like Dorisia, probably couldn't read or write. For them, it was a thing spoken. It was a message. And this brings us to the third biblical term, which we simply translate 'word'. Jesus spoke, and the *logos* became a *rhema*, a statement. 'You have been born again through the word [*logos*] of God,' Peter wrote to the Christians in Asia; 'this word [*rhema*] is the good news that was announced to you.'[29] In other words, after Jesus had returned to his Father, the word lived on amongst those who had experienced it. It was passed on from one to another as a message, a piece of good news. This means that the word of God is no longer just something which we, awestruck, watch the Creator do. It is no longer just something which we, as hearers or readers of Jesus, receive and are challenged by. As we enter into a living relationship with Jesus, the word is something which becomes active within us; we are required not just to hear it but to pass it on.[30]

And this is indeed how the first Christians understood the word that they had heard. In the book of Acts, the Word of God is presented as a living reality which grows, spreads, and gains influence as people respond to it. Paul says it 'sounds forth like a shout' as it is carried from one place to another by those who have accepted it. Peter and James, echoing Jesus' words to Nicodemus, say that people are 'born again' when they hear it – that they begin to live in a newly awakened way, once they are placed in direct contact with this mysterious force which is the Word.[31] We receive a word as more than information, and we pass it on as more than instruction. It is a thing of power, a thing which brings physical, emotional, and spiritual transformation. We do not need to be articulate to do this; we just need to be willing. We do not even need to get the words right. We have already seen how Rob's simple words, "Let's let in some light" broke into Tim's darkness in Leicester. It's a common pattern. Liesl, sectioned for schizophrenia, escaped one day from the secure psychiatric unit where she was being held, and walked into a local church where a man was talking about healing. An old lady came up to her and said: "Would you like a cup of tea? You're in a bit of a state, dear, but Jesus knows, he cares, he loves you." For Liesl it was the first step on a journey which led to her complete healing; she now speaks powerful words of healing into the distress of others.[32] Stephanie, attending a talk I gave at Leicester High School, said afterwards to my daughter Katy, "Your Mum's talk was great – I was really helped by what she said about forgiveness." Surprised – for my topic was evolution – I went through my notes, and found that I had indeed said nothing about forgiveness; but God, it seemed, had. He may have poor material to work with; but if we are willing to open our mouths, he can speak through our words.

Where is the Word of God today?

When God first gave the Ten Commandments, or Ten Words, Moses felt it necessary to offer some reassurance to the people. This is what he told them: 'This commandment ... is not too hard for you, nor is it too far away. It is not in heaven, that you should say, "Who will go up to heaven for us, and get it for us so that we may hear it and observe it?" Neither is it beyond the sea, that you should say, "Who will cross to the other side of the sea for us, and get it for us so that we may hear it and observe it?" No, the word is very near to you; it is in your mouth and in your heart for you to observe.'[33] It is not a complicated, difficult thing to obey the word of God, Moses said. This word actually lives inside you. Some 1,500 years later, Paul repeated Moses' words, reinterpreting them in the light of the resurrection of Jesus. This is what he said: 'The word is on your lips and in your heart, because you confess with your lips that Jesus is Lord and believe in your heart that God raised him from the dead.'[34]

And so once we have heard this word, this message of good news, it takes up residence within us. Jesus had said that the word of God is like a seed.[35] It isn't a head thing at all. It isn't information, it isn't instruction, it's life itself. And like a seed, it grows. It produces shoots and roots, leaves and buds, flowers and fruits. It is, like all seeds, organic. As the seed grows within us, we change: we grow into the people that God means us to be, living the life he has planned for us, ministering with the power he promised us. Once we have received it, the word of God lives within us – and that changes things.

One man who knows this better than most is Robert Hicks. Born tongue-tied and dyslexic, in and out of children's homes, abandoned by his mother and beaten by his father, Robert was generally regarded, in the words of his headmaster, as 'a waste'. He left school functionally illiterate and still unable to speak properly, but managed to get a job as an errand boy for a local grocery. One of the staff, an ex-nurse, realised that Robert was physically tongue-tied, and sent him to see a doctor. The doctor recommended surgery, and after the operation the surgeon advised Robert to copy words out from a book and practise reading them aloud as he did so. The only book Robert could find at home was a battered King James Bible lying at the back of a cupboard full of rubbish. Slowly, painfully, he began to copy and read it. It took him two years, and it was an exercise that changed his life. Robert found a church, a second-hand bookshop – and a new determination to succeed. Now a firm Christian, the errand boy became a shop manager, then a chain manager. He joined a rising new company called Tesco. He became marketing director for the Co-op and opened Britain's first hypermarket. Then, fired by his experience of the Word of God, he moved to Scripture Union, then losing £1,000 a week, and within a year turned it round. He joined forces with Ladybird and produced the Ladybird Children's Bible. He founded his own Christian publishing company, and applied his energy to sponsoring and supporting Bible initiatives all over the world – New Testaments into Eastern Germany, Millennium Gospels into millions of British homes, Gospels to students through UCCF. One of Robert's best-known initiatives is Back to Church Sunday. He was once interviewed by Esther Rantzen, who said afterwards, "During all the years I've spent making programmes, I've been particularly interested in the stories of people who've had very tough childhoods; deprived childhoods, sometimes painful ones filled with abuse; and yet have managed to turn their lives around. But of all these stories, the most extraordinary, the most inspirational was the story of Robert Hicks."[36]

Robert's story is remarkable for the independence of the dialogue between a teenage boy and a King James Bible. But his story of transformation is not unique; it is shared by many people who have submitted their lives to God in prayer and taken the time to meditate on the words they have received. This is what we were made for: for a life lived in conversation with God. It may be surprising, but it's never boring. 'Life with God,' Richard Foster remarks, 'is an ongoing, ever-changing, relational adventure. It is not a matter of being driven through life, stopping every now and then to get out of the car and see the surroundings. God invites us to climb into the landscape of our journey, to breathe deeply with full lungs, to feel blood pulsing through muscles doing what they were made to do, to experience the wonder of having a body with which to see and hear and smell and taste and touch this astonishing world.'[37] It's a world created, sustained and made accessible through words.

I think that deep down, we already know this. It seems that the average Christian owns nine Bibles and is looking for more.[38] It is certainly useful to be able to compare different translations; but I suspect that the average Christian is not regularly to be found poring over parallel texts. Perhaps it is more to do with the nagging suspicion that there is more power, more life, locked up in these written words than we have yet been able to access – and the tentative hope that maybe a different translation would somehow make it easier to get at. Not so; the missing ingredient is not to be found in the words themselves but in the Spirit who breathes them – as we shall see in the next chapter.

Good news for Gary

Gary was a young man who enjoyed life and had a clear idea of what he expected from it: he wanted to be a millionaire businessman, to marry a beautiful wife, and to cheat on her. One evening Gary pulled into the car park of a local pub with his friend Colin; up his sleeve was some pornography he'd stolen earlier in the day. To Gary's dismay, instead of going into the pub Colin followed a couple of attractive young women over the road – and into the chapel opposite. Furious, Gary followed. The preacher began to speak: "So you came to church for the first time. You have been lying, stealing and looking at your pornography." Gary nervously checked his sleeve, thinking perhaps the porn had fallen out, and protesting to himself that there was nothing wrong with that. The preacher continued: "You are thinking, what is wrong with that? There is something wrong with it!" "Perhaps there's something in this Jesus thing," thought Gary. The preacher went on to explain the gospel, and Gary made three decisions: to buy a Bible and read it, to go to another church and listen some more (but to a quiet one, with old ladies, not this one), and to never become a Christian.

A few months later, on New Year's Eve, Gary invited his friends round to share a few beers. The conversation turned to Christianity. "What a load of bollocks," they said. Then Gary heard a voice. "Speak for me," it said. "No," said Gary. The voice came again: "Just say, 'That's not fair'." Reluctantly, Gary began, "That's…" – at which point he felt himself being filled with a power as sharp and strong as electricity, like nothing he'd ever encountered. He fell to the floor and cried; his friends, to his shame, went home. Eventually Gary decided to talk to someone about it. He knew of a local scaffolder named Jonathan, a Christian. He told Jonathan that a power from God had filled him one evening, and that he'd told God to go away. The answer was unexpected: "Can I ask, was this on New Year's Eve? Between *Match of the Day* and *Parkinson*?" "Yes," said Gary, puzzled. "I was praying for you then; and the same thing happened to me." It took Gary a long time, but eventually he gave his life to Jesus. He did become a successful businessman and marry a beautiful wife; but he has never cheated on her. Gary eventually went to Bible College, and now uses the profits from his business to fund a remarkable youth ministry in his local Methodist chapel.[39]

For reflection and discussion

> Jesus did not give us dead words
> for us to salt away in little tins
> (or big ones),
> for us to preserve in rancid oil.
> Jesus Christ, my girl,
> did not give us word-pickles to keep.
> No, he gave us living words…
> The words of life, …
> On us, weak creatures of flesh, it depends
> to keep these words uttered in time alive,
> to feed them and keep them alive in time.

CHARLES PÉGUY[40]

What do you think is the difference between a pickled word and a living one?

Would you say that your relationship with the word of God is like that of a rider moving in rhythm with the horse, or like a novice jolting along like a sack of potatoes? What could you do to improve your riding?

'God is not silent, has never been silent... He is by nature continuously articulate' (A. W. Tozer).[41] How do you most clearly hear or see him speaking?

'We also constantly give thanks to God for this, that when you received the word of God that you heard from us, you accepted it not as a human word but as what it really is, God's word, which is also at work in you believers.' 1 Thessalonians 2.13. In what ways has the word or words of God changed you?

Chapter 9

Entering into conversation

Jesus... stood up to read, and the scroll of the prophet Isaiah was given to him. He unrolled the scroll and found the place where it was written: "The Spirit of the Lord is upon me, because he has anointed me to bring good news to the poor. He has sent me to proclaim release to the captives and recovery of sight to the blind, to let the oppressed go free, to proclaim the year of the Lord's favour." And he rolled up the scroll, gave it back to the attendant, and sat down. The eyes of all in the synagogue were fixed on him. Then he began to say to them, "Today this scripture has been fulfilled in your hearing."

Luke 4.16–21

Over the last ten years I've been working to enable the development of Christian discipleship in Africa through a practical, interactive course called *Rooted in Jesus*, of which I am the editor. First written at the request of the Diocese of Mount Kilimanjaro in Tanzania, *Rooted in Jesus* is now in use in some thirty dioceses or denominations in thirteen African countries, where it has so far been translated into twenty-five languages. This has been something we neither planned nor expected;

it seems to have spread from one place to another, gathering momentum as it travels.[1] 'I have no doubt,' Bishop Martin Breytenbach wrote recently from South Africa, 'that God has commissioned and anointed this course for Africa in much the same way as he is using Alpha in more urban and "western" settings.'

Rooted in Jesus began, rather unexpectedly, in conversation with God. "These are my people, and I love them; I have plans and purposes for them, and I want you to be part of those plans," God seemed to be saying to me as I stood one morning on a hillside in Zambia watching the trickles of smoke rising from the houses below. Baffled, I waited. The following year, God said to Stanley Hotay, diocesan missioner and regional director of the Jesus Film in Tanzania, "Look at Matthew 28.18–20. It is not enough for you to be making converts. I want you to make disciples." But how, thought Stanley; we have no resources with which to teach discipleship, and in any case many of our people are illiterate. A conversation among the bluebells of Rutland Water a few weeks later led to the birth of *Rooted in Jesus* or, as it was called in Swahili, *Kuwa na mizizi katika Yesu*. Directing its development over the last ten years has been akin to finding myself swept like a train speeding over unsuspected points and towards an entirely unplanned destination; and yet if I were God I can see that I might start by sending Mrs Garrard to an eight-year-old, and continue by depositing her at fifteen with a dialect-speaking family in the Solognot region of France, and then send her to university in Italy to learn how to live in a culture that speaks with its hands and thrives on the unexpected. And then I might, at a conference in England years later, whisper to her that I had a job for her, which would include not just work in the UK but also in Africa; and respect her terrified plea to reveal it only one step at a time. In following God's word, we become his word; in becoming his word, we release his word.

Africa is a beautiful continent. It's an ancient land, a place of glorious sunsets, snow-topped volcanic peaks, immense valleys, deep lakes, and coral coastlines. It's the cradle of humanity and one of the most popular tourist destinations in the world – truly a land of superlatives. For thirteen years now it has been my privilege to visit it annually, usually as the guest of an Anglican diocese, to work, worship, laugh, and pray with fellow Christians there. African hospitality is superb. I have been served fresh-caught bream from Lake Malawi and little, red-tailed river fish from the Luangwa in Zambia, carefully presented by men who sold them with wide smiles and morning greetings. I have walked through dark, rickety markets lit with splashes of coloured cloth and piled with precarious pyramids of oranges and tomatoes, and stopped to laugh with curious stall holders who wished to ask me questions about my children. I have been caught up into bounding, guttural Masai dances, and welcomed among steaming black pots bubbling with thick maize porridge by women who greet me as their sister. I have listened dumbfounded to the harmonies of village choirs; I have slept in comfortable beds whose owners lay graciously on the floor beside me; I have exchanged greetings with more people in Africa than in a lifetime in England. I've been given chickens, bananas, kangas, and a great deal of love. I have learnt to laugh in different ways; I have learnt to feel at home.

And yet Africa is a land of need, and behind the smiles lurks a great deal of pain. It's a place of poverty; in most African countries GDP is going not up, but down. Climate change is bringing increasing pressure on an already precarious subsistence lifestyle. I have seen people digging two-metre holes in sandy riverbeds to find water, and met children for whom daily reality is a ten-kilometre walk to the nearest well. I have worked with leaders whose own children have died of malaria or malnutrition, and with others trying to support families abandoned in shame and despair by a father no longer able to provide for them. I have been to ghost villages populated by grandparents and orphans struggling together to make a living, and to whole areas where the wind sweeps plastic bags across a dusty landscape and rival tribes kill one another for water. A cow must drink daily, a goat every three days; for pastoralist peoples cattle represent both their savings and their income, and a crash in the water table makes the collapse of a Western bank seem a very slight thing indeed.

Africa is, for millions of its inhabitants, a place of low educational opportunity. We worked recently in Angola, where the oil industry pushes the cost of living up to ludicrous levels, and yet 60% of the population remains illiterate. In one diocese in DR Congo we discovered that of eleven archdeacons, eight had received no secondary education. In south-west Kenya we found that whilst some children go to primary school, many are required to look after the family animals; "I was one of the lucky ones," one pastor said to us, "I went to school."[2] For some tribes, schooling is not seen as an advantage; it does not equip young people to care for the cows on which the livelihood of the family depends, but rather draws them away to the cities, where in practice they join the ranks of the unemployed. Meanwhile the government is putting land into private ownership, drought alternates with flooding, and finding pasture becomes ever more difficult.

Then there are health issues. In northern Mozambique, in the year 2007, 75% of the population sought treatment for malaria. In one small diocese in Zambia, two young priests were dead within a year of our visit; another two have died in the five years since – representing a fifth of the diocesan staff. It takes a minimum of three years to train a priest. In Malawi it's hard to find a functioning clinic because all the nurses have been recruited by the NHS and are working here. So people go to traditional healers and witchdoctors or diviners, some of whom use herbs but many of whom depend on spirit guides, spells and incantations. Spells don't make you better, and often we find ourselves praying for individuals who are experiencing nightmares and suffering from spiritual oppression and mental instability in addition to the illness they had to start with. Life expectancy is going down in many places, mostly because of AIDS. In the UK it is now 81 years; in Zambia it's 38. In some African tribes women are not permitted to refuse sex to any man; in others if your brother dies you are expected to marry his wife – and if he died of AIDS then you and your other wives get that too. In parts of East Africa up to a third of people are infected; I was in a village in Zambia recently where 60% of the inhabitants were estimated to be HIV positive. In many places there is a belief that having sex with a virgin cures you of AIDS, so men molest little girls.

Tradition is observed in other ways too. I once spent a night in a small tent in rural Tanzania, thoughtfully guarded by a night watchman with a machete, but unable to sleep because of the insistent beating of drums. In desperation we got up to enquire. There's a circumcision tomorrow, we were told; they play the drums to keep the children awake so that they do not feel the pain so keenly. Ah, we said; boys, or girls? Both, came the reply. It's illegal; but it is still practised all over the continent. The young girl is offered to her future husband with the guarantee of virginity and a greatly reduced risk of promiscuity; she also comes deprived of the pleasure of sex and with a strong likelihood of permanent disability.

Finally, there is what Nelson Mandela has called 'the tragic failure of leadership', which afflicts many African states. Democracy isn't in Africa's history, and superimposed on existing tribal loyalties it doesn't work very well. Corruption is widespread, and is related to the fact that those with more status or wealth are by custom obliged to provide for members of their family, clan, or tribe who have less. If your only hope of food, education, and employment is in the hands of a 'big man', you will in practice vote for the corrupt guy who turns up in a limo, the guy who has wealth, and not for the honest idealist on a pushbike. And so big men get power on the backs of promises to their supporters, usually members of their own tribe, and then it's in everyone's interest to keep them there. Kenyan politicians recently awarded themselves the second highest parliamentary salary in the world, arguing they need it because the cost of supporting needy constituents is so great, and that this is the basis on which people vote for them. And so the system is self-perpetuating. The long-term results can be summarised in images of bodies dumped like sandbags on country roadsides, of mothers fleeing with their children, rags in one hand, cooking pot in the other; or of boy soldiers, burnt out buildings, abandoned villages. Or just, if you prefer, in the single words 'Rwanda' or 'Mugabe'.[3]

Invisible solutions to visible problems?

So what has all this got to do with the Word of God? It would seem obvious that these problems are best solved in practical ways. Surely as Christians we should be working alongside governmental and charitable organisations to provide clean water supplies and cheap drugs, support malaria prevention schemes, run education programmes, offer aid and debt relief, promote fair trade, and tackle corruption? These are the tried and tested – and, it has to be said, mostly unsuccessful – ways in which wealthier nations have supported African countries for several generations now. The problem is that, well meaning as we are, it is becoming increasingly clear that our interference is not only not helping, it is in many ways making things worse. We are discovering in Africa something which we so carefully conceal from ourselves at home: that money is not the answer. To put it in biblical terms, man does not, and cannot, live on bread alone. Our deepest problems lie not in the world we inhabit – DR Congo is, due to its deposits of minerals and metals, potentially one of the richest countries in the world – but in the reality of our hearts.[4] And yet it still seems hard to believe that the secret to Africa's pain might lie in Christian mission, or that it is Christian discipleship which will remove the thorns from the African rose. Is it really going to help, while people are dying, to stand there, muttering prayers and wittering on about God?

In December 2008 *The Times* printed an interesting article by Matthew Parris. This was the headline: 'As an atheist, I truly believe Africa needs God. Missionaries, not aid money, are the solution to Africa's biggest problem.' This is how he goes on:

> *Travelling in Malawi refreshed … an observation I've been unable to avoid since my African childhood. It confounds my ideological beliefs, stubbornly refuses to fit my world view, and has embarrassed my growing belief that there is no God. Now a confirmed atheist, I've*

become convinced of the enormous contribution that
Christian evangelism makes in Africa: sharply distinct
from the work of secular NGOs, government projects
and international aid efforts. These alone will not do.
Education and training alone will not do. In Africa
Christianity changes people's hearts. It brings a spiritual
transformation. The rebirth is real. The change is good.
I used to avoid this truth by applauding … the practical
work of mission churches in Africa. … I would allow
that if faith was needed to motivate missionaries to
help, then, fine: but what counted was the help, not the
faith. But this doesn't fit the facts. Faith does more than
support the missionary; it is also transferred to his flock.
This is the effect that matters so immensely, and which I
cannot help observing.

Wherever he was in Africa, Parris continues, he found that 'the Christians were always different. Far from having cowed or confined its converts, their faith appeared to have liberated and relaxed them. There was a liveliness, a curiosity, an engagement with the world … that seemed to be missing in traditional African life. They stood tall.' He attributes all this to the powerful release which the gospel brings from an oppressive framework of belief which puts big men in power and keeps them there, fills people with fear and anxiety, prevents progress and stifles creativity. The Christian gospel, he concludes reluctantly, sets people free. He ends with a warning: 'Removing Christian evangelism from the African equation may leave the continent at the mercy of a malign fusion of Nike, the witch doctor, the mobile phone and the machete.'[5]

Christian evangelism of the kind Matthew Parris has

observed is not just a single announcement of good news, but the planting of a seed which will continue to grow until it bears the kind of fruit he has seen on his travels. Or, to change the metaphor, Christian evangelism marks the beginning of a journey from one way of being to another – which is why the first Christians were referred to as 'followers of the Way'.[6] Journeys require maps, resources, companions on the road, and in this respect the Christian journey is no different from any other. And yet these things are singularly hard to come by. Missionaries do a sterling job, but there aren't many of them. Clergy too are thin on the ground, and most congregations are in practice led by catechists or evangelists, who may have only primary education and may not possess a Bible. Those who are well-pastored become strong; but as the church grows it is easy, in Africa as elsewhere, for the Christian life to cast itself as a Sunday habit which, when subjected to the simmering pressures of famine, tribal conflict, disease and poverty, proves to be little more than a veneer. Hence Stanley Hotay's request for something that would help young African Christians learn to pray, to depend upon God, to live their lives in a way which pleases him, and to bring healing to one another and to their communities. The result was *Rooted in Jesus*, a course in practical discipleship written in the conviction that humanity's problems, there as here, start not in our circumstances but in our hearts – and that the long-term answers to Africa's problems are therefore to be found within, through enabling ordinary people to develop a life-changing relationship with God and equipping them to share their experience effectively with others. It takes its inspiration from Jesus' final command, recorded in Matthew 28.18–20 ('go and make disciples'), and from Paul's advice to Timothy in 2 Timothy 2.2 ('who will teach others also'); and is named after the biblical comparison of a person in relationship with God to a tree with its roots in water – a vivid image in Africa where the land is dry for months at a time.[7] Based on scripture memory, it is not a study course but an interactive programme which invites participants to enter together into a living and growing practical relationship with Jesus.

Over the years we have heard some extraordinary stories of the difference it has made to people to enter into conversation with God through these small discipleship groups. Like the boy learning to keep his Scalextric car on the tracks, or like the girl learning to move in harmony with the natural rhythm of a horse, many participants find that their lives change radically and permanently when exposed to the word and Word of God. As they complete each book together, group members speak out the memory verses and give a short testimony; many tell of personal growth and transformation as they have absorbed the word and prayed it into life. This is Simon Msonde, speaking to Michael Samuel, the *Rooted in Jesus* coordinator in the Diocese of Kiteto, Tanzania: "Before to receive my life to Jesus I had one big problem, my problem was anger. Every day I was quarrelling with others and my wives, but since I started to learn the Word of God and to repent this sin I feel free. Now I have peace and joy to all, and my friends they wonder as well and my wives trust that real Jesus has power and all of them are in the group." Simon, once known for his anger, is now known for his leadership within the local church.

Some tell stories of inner peace, some of deliverance from fear, nightmares and the pressing forces of evil; some of miraculous answers to prayer – and some of deep personal repentance and renewal.[8] This is Jacob Lihhima, group coordinator in the Diocese of Mount Kilimanjaro:

*I cannot forget the testimony of one brother from a
group in the parish of Logoeti. His testimony is that he
had bad habits, but now he really thanks God. Before
he started hearing the teachings of the group he left his
wife to be with another woman. He really tormented
his wife and gave her no money and abandoned his
children so that they were no longer able to go to school.
But after learning about the word of God he cried and
decided to return to them and to take back his wife
and to totally leave the other woman behind. Now they
live with great joy because Jesus has turned their lives
around and he reigns and is the shepherd in their lives.*

Sometimes their stories are painful to read, witness to a past way
of life based not on truth but on lies. We tend to think of the
benefits of living by the word of God in personal terms, but in
fact the word brings release not just to individuals, but to whole
communities. This is Elizabeth Hudati:

*These lessons help me to understand the word of God.
In the beginning I don't understand the word of God.
Several time I was fall in sin with servants of God that
have bad character. One day the servants of God came
to our Boma. After praying the servant of God told me
to make sex with him. I told him that this is sin and
every time you preach why you convince me to do it? He
told me that this is not sin because the Bible says 'Do
not deny yourselves to each other' (1 Corinthians 7.5).
I agreed to make sex because who was telling me is the
servant of God who knows, as well about Bible – but*

*now I can't do that because I know that verse is special
for people who married.*

Michael adds, "When she explained this she was crying continuously." Elizabeth's release will affect not just her own life, but that of her entire village. Are the commandments, the *debarim*, there to restrict our freedom, as so often we conclude in the West – or are they really there, as Jesus suggested, in order to set us more truly free than we have ever been before?

Changing society

*You are a letter of Christ, written not with ink but with
the Spirit of the living God, not on tablets of stone but
on tablets of human hearts.*

2 Corinthians 3.3

When the first generation of groups in Tanzania completed the course, we went back to ask them how they had got on. We hoped to hear they'd found it very helpful. What we actually did hear took us completely by surprise. Talking with the group leaders was like talking with a completely different bunch of people from the nervous and deferential ones we'd met with a few years earlier. They did indeed stand taller, seem stronger and more determined. One after another they said they now had great confidence in God, that he was with them and powerful to work through them. Many said they used to read the Bible 'like a newspaper or magazine', but that they now pray over it daily and find that it speaks to them. Some said that they had lost their fear, some that they feel a new power in their preaching, and some that they feel an unexpected love for their group members. Several said that their churches are now full; one said his whole village had been transformed. All agreed that their churches had stopped being impersonal Sunday gatherings and become active fellowships of people committed to God and to one another.

Secondly, they told us story after story of the changing lives of group members. One said that on the fourth lesson he had taught his group the memory verse John 1.12, which says 'to all who received him he gave power to become children of God.' He said they hadn't known that. They were churchgoers, but they'd not heard of the Holy Spirit or realised any act of commitment was necessary. He explained the verse, and the whole group was filled with the Holy Spirit. Other leaders said their people had stopped worshipping 'the wrong God', had begun to pray for the sick and see healings, had given up drugs and cigarettes, and were no longer getting drunk or beating their wives.[9] Prayer was becoming normal in the villages; in one Masai village the elders were still meeting under the tree to take decisions, but now they were praying over those decisions. Group members were sharing their faith with others, and many were coming to Christ; illiterate people were teaching others from the memory verses, and some had been inspired to learn to read and write so that they could read the Bible for themselves. One group leader said that the members of his group who had grown the fastest were in fact the illiterate ones, because the memory verses had for the first time enabled them to receive and absorb the word of God. Everywhere group members were speaking out against witchcraft and had stopped putting 'medicines' on crops. A woman who had been bitten by a snake had come to the group for prayer instead of visiting the witchdoctor, and had been healed. A child who 'used to fall down all the time' was prayed for until he too was healed, with the result that his whole family came to Christ and joined the group. One of the most remarkable stories was told to us by an evangelist named Japhet, who said his group had been meeting one day in the church when a Muslim came in. As he walked past the church his feet had begun to burn as if they were on fire. "I don't know what you are doing in here,' he said, 'but I think I need to join you!" He too came to faith in Christ.

Perhaps one of the most moving responses came in answer to a question about the memory verses – had they been hard to learn? Yes, came the reply. My heart sank; I had hoped that in an essentially oral society it would be an easier thing to involve people in than it is here. I asked them to tell me about it. One woman said that she had been particularly challenged by James 1.2–4, 'whenever you face trials of any kind, consider it nothing but joy, because you know that the testing of your faith produces endurance; and let endurance have its full effect, so that you may be mature and complete, lacking in nothing.' She said that the problem had been not that they couldn't remember the words, but that whilst they were learning them they were also facing severe drought and famine; most were living on just one meal a day. But, she continued, she had found that the more she had meditated on the passage, the more she had been filled with an extraordinary peace. I was so overwhelmed by all this that I cried.

Speaking a living language – the role of the Holy Spirit

All scripture is inspired by God and useful for teaching, for reproof, for correction, and for training in righteousness, so that everyone who belongs to God may be proficient, equipped for every good work.

2 Timothy 3.16–17

When I first began to think about the Christian faith, it was suggested I read John's gospel. I remembered reading the first chapter in the bookshop eight years earlier and having my mind blown by John's concept of the Word, so I thought that was a great idea. At the time I was a student. I don't have a good memory, and I'd got into the habit, which I still have, of making a summary of each book I read to help me remember it. So I read John's gospel, wrote a summary, and gave it to the man who is now my husband. He read it. "It's amazing," he said, "really good. So clear! But did you leave out the Holy Spirit on purpose?" "The what?" I said. "The who?" I hadn't really noticed any Holy Spirit, and in so far as I had, I hadn't been able to work out what John was talking about. The world I'd grown up in had no room for the Holy Spirit; there isn't much scope for the Holy Spirit in a rational secular world view.

And yet when God spoke the world so dynamically in the beginning, he did it through the power of the Holy Spirit, who was there, hovering over the waters. When he created man it was the same: 'And the Lord God formed man from the dust of the ground, and breathed into his nostrils the breath of life, and the man became a living being' (Genesis 2.7). The Hebrew word *ruach*, as we saw in Chapter 5, means both breath and Spirit.

The Holy Spirit is the breath of God.

When Jesus began his ministry on this earth, he was reliant on the same Holy Spirit, who had descended on him in the shape of a dove at his baptism. When he left his disciples, he promised that the Holy Spirit would come to them, and give them too the power to speak words which were not just information, description, or instruction, but words which did things, words which would do works and wonders greater than those he had done himself. And as God breathed life into Adam, so Jesus breathed on them with the breath which first brought life to the world, and gave them the Holy Spirit: "'Peace be with you. As the Father has sent me, so I send you." When he had said this, he breathed on them and said to them, "Receive the Holy Spirit. If you forgive the sins of any, they are forgiven them'" (John 20.21–23). And so they go, filled with the power and presence they need to speak the words of God in the way that God meant them to be spoken, ready to pass them on to others and so ultimately to us.

It follows that the Holy Spirit is the bridge not just between us and God, but between our use of language and God's use of language. Through the agency of the Holy Spirit, our words can do what Jesus' words did. They have the power to act. They become words which can express not just our thoughts but the thoughts of God. This role of the Holy Spirit makes sense; it is not possible, Irenaeus remarked long ago, to speak a word unless you also breathe.[10]

And so it's proved to be for me. I can explain the gospel to someone. My human words have no power whatsoever. And yet by the power of the Holy Spirit my words can land like a seed in another person's heart, and begin to grow. I've watched a drunken man receive those words and become instantly sober.

I've watched a woman who never smiled receive those words and begin to smile all the time. It isn't information that brings about transformation, it's the Spirit of life who inhabits the words, the message, and who makes them grow and bud and bear fruit. The Word of God does not bring about change in the lives and communities of those who hear it merely because it offers information, instruction or persuasion; its power does not lie in the accuracy of its advice or in the truth of the concepts it conveys. When Paul told Timothy that 'all scripture is inspired by God,' the word he used was *theopneustos*, a combination of the words for God and for Spirit. Like *ruach*, *pneuma* is both spirit and breath – the power in the word comes from the fact that it is not only inspired by God but also breathed by God. This is how the Word of God, breathed by the Spirit of God, remains as potentially active now as it was in the beginning.[11]

The Holy Spirit has always been something of a mystery. Already by the fourth century Gregory of Nazianzus was describing him as 'the God whom nobody writes about'; he is poorly understood not only in Africa but also in England.[12] I was talking recently to Keith Powell, the Renewal Advisor for the diocese of Bath and Wells. Keith had just run a day on spiritual renewal for three Somerset villages, and he had asked the thirty-six people present how many of them had ever received any direct teaching about the Holy Spirit. Only two raised their hands. This is the faith the first missionaries took to Africa; even to this day, and despite the fact that most Africans have a naturally spiritual world view, there is considerable insecurity amongst Anglicans in this area – the Holy Spirit, they will often say, is for Pentecostals. In Mozambique we found that the only experience of prayer the clergy had had was the formal liturgical prayer of a church service; they had never prayed for healing, for peace, or for guidance – they had never seen the Word at work. In one area of Uganda the first missionaries did try to teach about the Spirit – but it seems translators used the wrong word for 'wind', describing the Spirit instead as 'fart'. This apparently did not lead to a surge of interest.[13]

It seems therefore that it is essential to talk not just about the Word but also about the way in which it is brought to life by the Holy Spirit; to tell people that in engaging with God through scripture and through prayer, they will find that they are entering into a dynamic process – planting a seed, embarking on a journey, beginning a conversation. For many, the conversation begins straight away as we come together into the presence of Jesus. In the Diocese of Niassa, Mozambique, the seminars were being organised by Amorim Rocha. In one of the sessions Martin Cavender told the story of a woman he had met in Rwanda. This woman had lost forty members of her family in the genocide, including her husband and all her five children. The two oldest children had been on the phone to her while men came through the door to murder them, and she had heard them die. She had been able to forgive the killers. As he listened to the story, Amorim burst into tears. He told us that when he was seventeen years old he had seen his father shot by government forces on a false accusation. Now thirty-four, he had struggled with anger ever since. He asked us to pray with him, and he too was able to forgive. The next morning he was a different man. Within weeks he was expressing his astonishment as he watched the Holy Spirit transform the lives of those to whom he ministered. A year later he wrote this:

Thanks to God I am again in Lichinga after seeing the miracles produced by the Holy Spirit in the Zambezi

Ecclesiastical District. The meetings went well; with the help of the Holy Spirit I trained eighty leaders. It really was a big spiritual renewal in those areas and I also grew and was blessed. In Mocuba many participants were touched, being delivered as Christ cut all cords uniting them with Satan. Some had problems with their neighbours, not speaking with each other but being catechists; many brought themselves to Christ, renouncing drunkenness, smoking tobacco and their involvement in black magic. We had cries and tears, but finished by all being renewed and strengthened through the Holy Spirit. In Morrumbala even more remarkable things happened: one catechist who had led a congregation for three years revealed that he had been a witchdoctor and presented all his instruments of divination, superstitious healing and black magic (three tails of wild animals, three earthenware pots with drugs, six gourds and a kind of small cushion). All this he brought to be burnt, and he remained liberated, receiving Jesus Christ as his Saviour. Other catechists from Morrumbala brought their problems with drink, smoking, worship of ancestors, involvement with magic ceremonies and other superstitious things; these studies are a blessing and the Holy Spirit is working. Since I began my ministry, I have never seen such marvels that I have seen during this seminar journey. I am sure that God is doing, and will do, his work, and a spiritual renewal in the Diocese is happening.

In 2008 Amorim joined a team to Zambia. How were things going at home? "Now we speak a different language," he said simply. The word of God changes things in a way that nothing else can.

Jesus began his public ministry with an announcement in the synagogue at Nazareth, in which he promised to bring release, healing and freedom to those who were bound and oppressed. In the days that followed he was tempted by Satan, to whom he declared that we live by every word, *rhema*, that comes from the mouth of God. He cited specific words from scripture to defend himself, and the words did the job.[14] They still do. I have prayed for many people, both in England and in Africa, who have needed deliverance from evil spirits. It's an astonishing experience to listen to an evil spirit which has been afflicting a person speak to you in words of defiance. "Who are you?", one asked me once. "No one at all," I said, "but I stand here in the name of Jesus Christ. Get out." It did, and a woman who five minutes before would have been sectioned under the Mental Health Act by any doctor who saw her was instantly clothed in her right mind. Just because of some words.

The Word of God is a powerful thing. This is what Isaiah Chambala wrote from the Diocese of Mount Kilimanjaro, where he had established over a hundred *Rooted in Jesus* groups:

> *There has been an eruption of spiritual growth and strong faith amongst many Christians in the parishes I visited which have been practising the* Rooted in Jesus *course. I discovered that the Bible has started to be sweet to some of the members of these groups. The fear that it is a supernatural book that has to be dealt carefully only by those who are skilled in how to deal with such kind of supernatural powers is now getting to be eliminated. They read the Bible not only as a book; they have*

> *discovered that this book teaches them the way of "how*
> *to live" and the way of "how to be right with God".*
> *The verses they have put in their hearts have started*
> *to speak to them, such that now, "we hear the voice of*
> *God talking to us", one of them commented. They say*
> *that the Bible has transformed their lives. They confess*
> *that the word of God contains powers that give them*
> *confidence in the Holy Spirit to share with others about*
> *their new experience in the Lord. They have the courage*
> *to say verses from the Bible to prove what they believe.*
> *Church growth in some parishes is a good sign that there*
> *have been fruits from the course.*

Rooted in Jesus, Isaiah wrote later, is 'the idea that has reshaped my ministry.' He is now bishop of the Diocese of Kiteto.

Is this what happens here – where, although we do not routinely visit witchdoctors or put medicines on crops, we do engage in all sorts of dubious alternative spiritualities and seek to dull our pain through other, more materialistic, devices and substitutes? Are we willing to find life through the living Word of God, or would we in our heart of hearts rather keep it sitting quietly on the page whilst we devote our attention to the pressing issues of daily life? John Wimber used to say that the Bible is meant to be the menu, and yet we treat it as if it were the meal – as if the written marks on the page were themselves the reality it contains. Just imagine, he says, going into a restaurant and settling down at your table. The waiter brings the menu. You pore over it. Mm, yes, look. Roast duck in orange sauce. Pan-fried baby squid with wild mushrooms and peppers. Lemon syllabub. Fresh raspberry tart. Mmm… You spend a happy half hour or so browsing, savouring the various possibilities. Then you stand up, hand the menu back to the waiter with a smile of thanks, and leave. Often, Wimber says, that's what we do with the Bible. We don't really take it seriously; we fail to recognise that it is the outward expression of something which is embedded in our hearts and minds, something which relates intimately to who we are and where we are going – that it contains words of life and power, words which offer us the opportunity to enter into a creative conversation with the God who makes reality, and to be drawn into his purposes. Instead we read it, admire it, and close it.[15] The result is that many of us are not so much 'culturally charismatic' as 'theoretically charismatic' – we believe in the life of the Spirit and the power of the Word, but we don't in practice experience these things.

How do people change? They change from within. They change because you tell them a different story, and because you tell it in words that are alive. Those words are found in scripture, and they are spoken by Jesus both then and now. But for the words to take root we need an ingredient which is all too often missing – the Holy Spirit. Walter Brueggemann comments: 'People do not change because of moral appeal. People in fact change by the offer of new models, images, and pictures of how the pieces of life fit together.' If we want to bring transformation to the lives of ordinary people, we need to realise that it will be done only 'through a process of inviting each other into a counter-story about God, world, neighbour, and self… through what we take to be the live word of God.'[16]

Looking to the future

We stand at a turning point in the life of the Church. For 300 years we read the Word through scientific spectacles. We dissected it, analysed it, reduced it to human dimensions, and occasionally wondered why it didn't seem to do what it had done before – rather as if we'd disconnected it from the mains and taken it apart, and then got used to the idea that it doesn't really work. Our churches began to empty.

But over the last generation or so all that has begun to change, and perhaps in the nick of time. We now live in a different world, one which places less emphasis on facts, more on personal experience, and is willing to explore the spiritual dimension which had been neglected for so long. We are learning that there is more to heaven and earth than is dreamt of in our secular philosophy – that advances in scientific understanding, enthusiastic use of modern management theories, and painstaking textual criticism, important though they all are, don't put the smiles back on people's faces. We are learning that it's great for something to be true; but that it also has to *work*. It has to make a difference.

I came across a story recently of a pilot who'd been practising high-speed manoeuvres in a jet fighter. He turned the controls for what he thought was a steep ascent – and flew straight into the ground. He was unaware that he had been flying upside down. It's a picture of our Western society. We have, in comparison with our fellow human beings in Africa and many other parts of the world, vast amounts of money, an astonishing array of technological resources, and a fast-moving lifestyle. But, like the pilot, we've no real idea whether we're upside down or the right way up. We can't quite work out why we aren't happier, when we've believed for so long that these things would make us happier; and it is beginning to dawn on us that somehow we aren't in sync with reality.

For me the answer to the problems of our age lies in the

relationship between the Word and the Spirit. We need to learn to live by the Word of God, the word as God's kind of word – that is, the word brought alive by the Spirit. We are sent to speak, not human words of explanation, but spiritual words of life: 'words plus', Eugene Peterson has called them. It's the Spirit who brings the Plus, who brings life to the Word – to the word written, to the word living, and to the word which is at work in us and through us. Word and Spirit are not meant to be separate. We need to remember this as people who are sent, as the first disciples were sent. We are sent not as human beings with answers, but as people who breathe and speak in the presence of the Holy Spirit.

A couple of years ago I came across a prophecy attributed to Smith Wigglesworth and said to have been given in 1947. It's hard, over sixty years later, to be sure whether – or why – he said it – but it's not a bad thing to keep in our prayers:

> *During the next few decades there will be two distinct*
> *moves of the Holy Spirit across the church in Great*
> *Britain. The first move will affect every church that*
> *is open to receive it and will be characterised by a*
> *restoration of the baptism and gifts of the Holy Spirit.*
> *The second move of the Holy Spirit will result in people*
> *leaving historic churches and planting new churches*
> *… When the new church phase is on the wane, there*
> *will be evidenced in the churches something that has*
> *not been seen before: a coming together of those with*
> *an emphasis on the Word and those with an emphasis*
> *on the Spirit – when the Word and the Spirit come*
> *together, there will be the biggest movement of the Holy*
> *Spirit that the nation, and indeed the world, has ever*

seen. It will mark the beginning of a revival that will
eclipse anything that has been witnessed within these
shores, even the Wesleyan and the Welsh revivals of
former years. The outpouring of God's Spirit will flow
from the UK to the mainland of Europe, and from there
will begin a missionary move to the ends of the earth.[17]

We can identify the first two of these moves over the last forty years; are we ready to experience the third?

The Word at work – a scary thought

One of the most alarming – but also exciting – verses of scripture is this saying of Jesus:

I tell you, on the day of judgement you will have to give
an account for every careless word you utter; for by your
words you will be justified, and by your words you will
be condemned.

Matthew 12.36–37

The word 'careless', or 'idle' as it is rendered in some translations, does not do justice to the word Jesus actually used. The word he used was *argon*, which actually means 'ineffective', or 'not working'. Jesus didn't mean that we are not to waste our words in idle chatter or sloppy imprecision, or that we are not to thoughtlessly upset people by what we say. He meant that our words are meant to *work*. They are meant to *do* something. Our words are intended to be *dabar* words. They are meant to be words which, breathed with the help of the Spirit within us, bring about change in the lives of those who hear them.

This to me is an enormous challenge. It means that when I teach a group of people, my task is not to offer thoughtfully crafted pleasantries or helpfully articulated explanations; that when I pray with someone, my contribution is not to reassure, or to express shared concerns in a godly way. It means that I am to remain constantly aware that the words I utter, if uttered in submission to the Spirit of God and in the context of a relationship with the Son of God, are supposed to bring about change in the hearts and minds of those into whose lives they are spoken. "Is my word not like fire, and like a hammer that breaks a rock in pieces?", the Lord demanded of Jeremiah; "Let the one who has my word speak my word faithfully!". "The Spirit of the Lord is upon me," said Jesus, quoting Isaiah; "he has anointed me to bring good news to the poor; he has sent me to proclaim release to the captives and recovery of sight to the blind." Three years later he bid farewell to his disciples: "As the Father has sent me, so I send you." When he had said this, he breathed on them and said to them, "Receive the Holy Spirit." The implication is that as we speak the word of God, our words too will become active, will express the thoughts of God and carry the power of God; that we too, as Jesus promised, will by our Spirit-filled words do the works that he himself had done.[18]

We live in a world of words, endlessly humming, swat-away words. Is there still a place, in that world of intrusive, devalued words, for the Word of God? Can we with any confidence continue to offer our word into the midst of all these other words? I think we can; for our words are living words, words filled with the breath of the Spirit who is within us. The word of God is living, active, powerful, and available to us; it is the kind of word that makes things happen.[19] Our words can be his words. And there's one good thing about that – this is what the Lord said to Jeremiah: "I am watching over my word to perform it."[20]

Good news for a member of the KGB

John Sentamu is now Archbishop of York, but at the time of this event he was a student flying from the United States to his home in Uganda. At the airport he found himself sitting next to a Russian. Undeterred by their lack of a common language, he did his best to tell him about Jesus. On the plane, he found himself seated next to this same man, so he kept going, using the New Testament and adding signs and gestures to his English words. At Heathrow, as they waited together for their connecting flights, John continued to speak about Jesus. When the time came for them to part, he gave the Russian his New Testament, but they did not keep in touch. Some years later John, now a bishop, arrived in Moscow for a meeting with members of the Russian Orthodox Church. A man approached him, his hand extended in greeting, and explained in broken English that he had been the man on the plane. "You talked with me about Jesus," he said, "for twenty hours. Twenty hours!", he repeated, punching stiff fingers into his palm. "I didn't understand a word you said, but when I got home I took the book you gave me and asked a priest about it. He led me to faith in Christ, and now I'm a lay leader in the Orthodox Church. What you didn't know as you were speaking to me was that I was then a senior officer in the KGB." Such is the power of the living *rhema* of God, spoken into a man's heart. John told this story in York Minster at the 2009 Commissioning Service for the Archbishops' College of Evangelists.

For reflection and discussion

The Spirit must scream
plummet down
like a bird of prey
and sit fierce
talons clenched
in your bleeding lips
and your words become
his Word
and his Word become
your words
that your speech
dead in the agony of self
might be resurrected
In self-extinction.

JOHN LEAX

How do you respond to John Leax's poem?

It's been said that we tend to adopt a 'spirituality of print,' whereas Jesus said that our words should be working words, which bring about change in people's lives. Is this your experience?

'Christians don't simply learn or study or use Scripture; we assimilate it, take it into our lives in such a way that it gets metabolized into acts of love, cups of cold water, missions into all the world, healing and evangelism and justice' – Eugene Peterson.[21] Do you think that the word of God could bring about the same changes in people's lives here as it is doing in Tanzania and Mozambique?

'Is not my word like fire, says the Lord, and like a hammer that breaks a rock in pieces?' (Jeremiah 23.29). Meditate on this verse.

Chapter 10

The Spirit of God

The most confident Christian who has ever lived was probably St Paul. Paul travelled all over the Roman empire sharing the gospel – in synagogues and market places, in people's homes, on river banks, in lecture halls, at court, on ships, and in jail. Had he been able, like John Sentamu, to travel by plane we can be sure that he would have shared it there too. What was the basis of his confidence? We glimpse it from the three descriptions of his evangelistic ministry, which we find in his letters. To the Thessalonians he writes that his gospel message came to them 'not in word only, but also in power and in the Holy Spirit.' To the Corinthians he says 'my speech and my proclamation were not with plausible words of wisdom, but with a demonstration of the Spirit and of power.' And to the Romans he remarks that he has fully proclaimed the gospel of Christ, 'by word and deed, by the power of signs and wonders, by the power of the Spirit of God.'[1]

There are two common factors in all three passages: Word and Spirit. Even for Jesus, the living Word, the anointing of the Spirit had been essential. His own ministry did not begin until the Spirit descended on him at his baptism. Driven out into the wilderness for a time of testing, he had returned 'filled with the power of the Spirit' to make this announcement: "The Spirit of the Lord is upon me, because he has anointed me to bring good news to the poor. He has sent me to proclaim release to the captives and recovery of sight to the blind, to let the oppressed go free, to proclaim the year of the Lord's favour." When, three years later, he left his disciples for the last time, he instructed them to do nothing until the Holy Spirit had come to them too. Then, and then only, would they be equipped to embark on the ministry which he had prepared for them.[2]

The Holy Spirit duly fell upon the disciples, enabling them instantly to speak gospel messages in foreign languages, and equipping them with the power which Jesus had promised. Once again the blind received their sight, the lame walked, the dead were raised, and the poor heard good news.[3] Groups of Christian believers sprang up all over the Roman empire. In Corinth the church welcomed the Holy Spirit with such unbridled enthusiasm that Paul had to write to them to urge restraint. Always there was the same emphasis on Word and Spirit: repeatedly in scripture, but perhaps most clearly in the Acts of the Apostles, we see the same pattern – the Spirit comes down and the Word goes out. It never starts with us.[4]

And yet as the centuries passed, the Church gradually moved further and further from the edgy, dangerous faith of these first believers.[5] While the Word flourished, translated into everyday language from the fourteenth century and studied with increased vigour in the universities of the nineteenth, the Spirit was marginalised. *Dabar*, *logos*, and *rhema* were gradually flattened into the pounded human shapes of information and description – as if a live flower had been plucked from the lush meadow in which it swayed gently in the breeze, and placed between the weighted pages of a collecting book, there to dry and fade into a memory. By the nineteenth century it was possible for Nietzsche to declare that God was dead, and a little later Lenin suggested that in a world powered by electricity there was no further need for prayer.[6] By the end of the Victorian era numerical decline had set in, and increasingly people began to look elsewhere for meaning. The Holy Spirit is now generally treated, as Italian theologian Raniero Cantalamessa notes, not so much as 'the invisible force permeating all from within' as 'an idea or a theme, which we scatter here and there in our addresses as one would sugar on a pudding.'[7] We have shrunk him indeed.

And yet all is not lost. The evidence is that there is, in many places, a new willingness to be open to the Spirit, not just among spiritual pilgrims outside the Church but also within it. There are now over 500 million 'charismatic' Christians worldwide, and their numbers are growing by an average of 3% per year.[8] Increasingly the Holy Spirit is coming into the foreground across the denominations and traditions of the Church – a good barometer is the new and widespread interest in the healing ministry. At ReSource we are finding that many churches, whilst not necessarily wishing to become 'culturally charismatic', are nonetheless looking for ways to open themselves up more fully to the person and presence of the Holy Spirit. It's a good time to be a Christian.

New possibilities

When my daughter Katy was five years old she drew a picture of the Holy Spirit. She drew him, with a silver pen on red card, in the shape of a human being. He had three jagged tongues of fire sticking out from his head 'because that is what it says in the Bible,' and a flask in his hand, 'because he has some special stuff he pours out.' Already Katy had understood more about the Holy Spirit than many people grasp in a lifetime: the Holy

Spirit is a person, and one with some unusual characteristics – characteristics which would enable him, as Jesus had promised, to teach, guide, counsel, comfort, encourage, and work in and through all those who welcomed him.[9] And yet simple though that seems as a starting point, the Spirit is not easy to get our minds around. In the seventeenth century John Owen, one of few theologians to study the Spirit, could remark 'I had not the advantage of any one author, ancient or modern, to beat the path before me'; and even in the twentieth the great theologian Karl Barth was left dreaming that someone 'might develop a theology of the Holy Spirit which now I can only envisage from afar.'[10] The Spirit, like the Word, cannot be reduced to something we can label and box; as Isaiah knew, not only God's thoughts, but also his ways, are higher than ours.

Within a few years of the coming of the Spirit at Pentecost, Paul was writing about him in a new way – a way which did not so much promise what was to come as describe what was already taking place. The Holy Spirit, Paul explained, is recognised and experienced in two main forms: through 'gifts', and through 'fruit'.[11] The 'fruit' is recognised not through the things that we do but in what we become: a person who has received the Holy Spirit gradually changes on the inside, until his or her behaviour is characterised not by the negative emotions which dominate our world but by love, joy, peace, patience, kindness, generosity, faithfulness, gentleness, and self-control.[12] The 'gifts', on the other hand, enable us to relate to other people in a way that transcends our own human limitations, so that we can continue to do the works that Jesus did. They give us the confidence to minister in the firm expectation that we are the body of Christ, doing the things that he intends us to do.[13]

The gifts of the Spirit have been exercised throughout history, but have rarely had the central place in the life of the Church which Paul seems to have anticipated. It is no different today. The excitement which accompanied our rediscovery of the gifts in the 1970s and 80s has often led us to forget how and why they are given. The focus on a single chapter of a single New Testament letter, 1 Corinthians 12, has left many people wondering whether in fact these so-called gifts are not something of a minority interest, an impression confirmed by the rather misleading use of the very word 'gifts' in our English translations. Paul does not talk about gifts in Greek, but rather adopts a whole string of different phrases all of which emphasise not those who receive these things but the Spirit himself who gives them – they are 'spiritual things', 'graces', 'ministries' or 'services', 'energisings' or 'manifestations'. Using the single word 'gifts' for all these phrases has often encouraged us to see them as personal benefits, presents, ends in themselves, provided in order to bring a frisson of faith-enhancing excitement to those who receive them, rather than as the ways in which the Spirit works through us for the benefit of others; and this too has inhibited our ability to use them.[14]

It's helpful to remember that there is nothing especially remarkable about 1 Corinthians 12 except this: it describes the ministry of Jesus. As a stand-alone passage it is of limited usefulness, but as a commentary on the gospels it is invaluable. The Holy Spirit and his gifts are given to us so that we might continue the ministry of Jesus – they are given, as Tom Wright has remarked, not to provide us with the spiritual equivalent of a trip to Alton Towers, but so that we might take the victory of the cross into the world. They are the tools of our trade; the tools of mission. John Owen did not beat about the bush: 'Nothing at all can be done without these spiritual gifts, and therefore a ministry devoid of them is a mock ministry, and no ordinance of Christ... To erect a ministry by virtue of outward order, rites, and ceremonies, without gifts for the edification of the church, is but to hew a block with axes, and smooth it with planes, and set it up for an image to be adored.'[15] You might as well, he says, fix a carcass to a post and expect it to minister. And he is surely right. Patriarch Athenagoras of the Greek Orthodox Church was of one mind both with Puritan Owen and with evangelical Anglican bishop and scholar Tom Wright: 'Without the Holy Spirit, God is far away, Christ remains a figure of the past, the Gospel a dead letter, the Church a mere organization, authority a means to exercise power, mission a propaganda machine; worship becomes outdated and morality the action of slaves.'[16] The Holy Spirit is not the property of any one part of the Church; he is the life within the whole. It is time for us to learn again to depend on him in all that we are and do.

The Holy Spirit in action

How can we escape if we neglect so great a salvation?
It was declared at first through the Lord and it was
attested to us by those who heard him, while God
added his testimony by signs and wonders and various
miracles, and by gifts of the Holy Spirit, distributed
according to his will.

Hebrews 2.3–4

Much ink has been spilt in the attempt to pin precise definitions on the gifts of the Spirit listed in 1 Corinthians 12. This is hard to do, for each is described in a single word or phrase which is formed at least in part by the context into which Paul was writing – 'wisdom', for example, meant something rather different to Jews and Corinthians, and it means something different again to us. And he talks not about 'miracles' (literally, 'things to be wondered at') but about 'energisings of power' – which gives a rather different perspective. I have examined all this in more depth elsewhere, and the main point for us to note here is that the emphasis is not on us but on the Spirit, not on what we do but on what we expect and permit him to do.[17] 1 Corinthians 12 is just one of the places in the New Testament where we catch a glimpse of some of the ways in which he works: the gifts of the Spirit are intended not as feathers in the caps of individuals but as shared resources given to enable the mission and ministry of the church. Scripture, history, and experience all suggest that they are intended to be a normal part of the Christian life; and it is as we use them that we will find within ourselves the confidence that we do indeed have something to offer to the world.

Wisdom

Each of the gifts listed by Paul can be seen in action in the ministry of Jesus. Luke tells us that people were constantly astonished at the authority with which he spoke, and as the gospels unfold we see him responding with wisdom to all manner of issues and questions: Why do you eat with tax collectors and sinners? Why do your disciples not wash their hands before meals? Should Jews pay taxes to Caesar? What should be done with this woman found committing adultery? In all cases the answer Jesus gives to these life questions is theological – that is, it's an answer that derives from the nature of the kingdom of God, and not from law or custom. 'Where did this man get this wisdom and these deeds of power?' people wonder in Nazareth; 'is this not the carpenter's son?' It makes no worldly sense.[18]

The same kind of wisdom begins to operate in his disciples after Jesus' death. He had promised that when brought to trial, they would be given the wisdom to know how to answer the accusations made against them, and we see this happening.[19] Not only that, we see them tackling one dilemma after another in a godly manner or, as we might say today, according to kingdom values – the appointment of wise, Spirit-filled men to help with food distribution, the decision not to require non-Jewish Christians to be circumcised, and Peter's realisation through a dream that he was to share the gospel with the Gentile centurion Cornelius. Paul's own letters are written not out of his human experience but 'according to the wisdom given him.'[20] This same wisdom is available to us today, to help us live in harmony with God's plans and purposes, and in particular with the message of Christ crucified. As individuals, our task is to live by the rhythms God has built into the world he has made, to become the word that he has spoken, to find our place in his story; and for this we need the wisdom that comes not from the world, which often has other priorities and invites us to listen to other voices, but from the Spirit.[21] And as members together of the body of Christ, our task is not to form plans and ask God to bless them, but to find out what God is already doing and then join in. Should we re-order the building? Employ a youth worker? Help in the school? Begin a ministry to young mothers, surfers, stressed executives? No church can plan its ministry without seeking and exercising the gift of wisdom.

Knowledge

Paul speaks next about how the Spirit brings 'words of knowledge'. Again, it is hard to be certain what he meant, for 'knowledge', like wisdom, had a specific meaning in Corinth. One way in is to ask ourselves what kind of knowledge Jesus seemed to have which was available to him only through the Spirit. He knows, for example, that the Samaritan woman he meets at a well has had five husbands. He knows who will betray him, and he knows where the fish are in the sea of Tiberius.[22] Similarly, Peter knows that Ananias has lied about the money received from the sale of his field, and Paul knows that the ship in which he is sailing to Rome will be lost but that all those on board will survive.[23] Such supernatural knowledge is common today. The Spirit is willing to reveal things to us as we pray for one another – words or images which relate to someone's personal circumstances but which are unknown to the individual receiving them. Dorisia Chende received a word about a woman who had a problem with her abdomen; the woman was healed. "There's a left-handed man coming this morning with an injury to his right arm," said a member of our healing prayer team, who as he prayed had seen an image of a man wearing a watch on his right wrist. This word was given out during the service, and a man named Rob nervously came for prayer and was healed of a longstanding repetitive strain injury.

"It's something to do with children, I saw you being bullied in a playground, and I think I was being given Proverbs 12.1," said Ann, praying in the kitchen for a friend meeting with two others in the next room, "but that must be wrong, because you were praying about issues in the church, weren't you?" They weren't, and the scripture spoke powerfully to a young stepmother who desperately needed to know that she was not responsible for the pain in her family – and for whom words of human compassion and encouragement would not have been enough. It all seems to work in a kind of loop – the Spirit whispers the word, and as the word is shared so the Spirit works through it to bring healing, often to people startled, as the woman who met Jesus at the well was startled, by the unexpected revelation of information they thought was known to no one else.

Faith

In the New Testament faith is often linked with healing. Jesus sees the faith of the men who let their paralysed friend down through the roof, and heals him; he praises the faith of the centurion who knows that Jesus has only to say the word and his servant will be cured; he tells the woman who touches his cloak that her faith has made her well.[24] Peter sees Jesus walking across the Sea of Galilee and is able through faith to walk towards him. Paul sees that a cripple in Lystra is responding with faith to the good news of Jesus, and prays for his healing.[25] Faith, it seems, is not about how passionately we believe or want something, but about trust – a trust born of the confidence which comes from a spiritual insight into the mind of God. The word 'confidence' just means 'with faith' – and it's perhaps as good a summary as any of this gift.

The gift of faith makes it possible to pray confidently for a particular outcome, not because we want it (though we may!) but because we have received the assurance that God wants it, for 'faith is the assurance of things hoped for, and the conviction of things not seen.'[26] When George Muller thought in the nineteenth century that God was asking him to set up orphanages in Bristol, he was able to do so by faith, despite the fact that he lacked the necessary resources; praying daily for the funds and provisions he needed, Muller housed and educated tens of thousands of children. When a member of our church gave up his job and set off for an uncertain future working with street children in Brazil, we supported him in his faith that this was God's plan. Andy and Claudia have now established a city centre house and a restoration farm for homeless children, and are seeing many of all ages turn to God.[27] The major reason we run *Rooted in Jesus* is that we have been given the faith to know that this is God's plan and that our part is simply to respond to his calling. Shouldn't I be planning my future career, I was often asked as I cared full time for my children – but I knew that God had a plan, even if it was not yet clear to me what it was – for the simple reason that in 1984 when I first gave my life to him, he had told me so. And so it has proved: I have been offered jobs I didn't apply for, provided with money I didn't ask for, and invited by people I'd never met to minister in places I'd never heard of. Faith is an essential gift in the locker of every Christian – whatever we do, we cannot do it if we do not receive the certain faith that God goes with us and indeed before us.

Healing

One of the most common ways in which God reaches out to those who do not know him is by healing them physically, and Paul lists 'gifts of cures' as one of the spiritual resources available to us today. Jesus stated from the outset that healing was to be a key part of his mission, and in sending his disciples to proclaim the good news of the kingdom his first instruction to them was to heal the sick.[28] There are many instances of healing in the gospels and Acts – 18 of the 24 chapters in Luke, for example, include healings. Healing did not stop with Jesus or with the apostles; we have reliable testimonies of healing from every century from the first to the twenty-first. One of my favourite stories is the detailed contemporary account of the healing of a paralysed girl in Trèves, France, through the prayers of Martin of Tours in the fourth century. Irenaeus in the second century, Augustine in the fourth, Bede in the seventh, Francis in the thirteenth, Luther in the fifteenth and Wesley in the eighteenth centuries all reported healing miracles.[29] In the twentieth century, John Lake and his associates apparently saw 100,000 medically documented healings in Illinois over a period of five years. In our own time Heidi and Rolland Baker have experienced the healing touch of the Spirit on many as they have ministered in Mozambique, and Bill Johnson has written of the healings experienced through the ministry of Bethel church in Redding, California. Such stories have a high profile; but in churches all over the world God is healing people today, in ways dramatic and undramatic, small and large, through the prayers of ordinary Christians.[30]

I have seen many instances of healing, and in many cases in people for whom it was their first real experience of God, and the gateway into a whole new world.[31] It can feel odd: "You didn't tell me about the electricity," said Steven, a ten-year-old who received prayer for post-viral fatigue syndrome; off school for a year, he was soon playing squash and badminton for Leicestershire. "There's no need to shout," said Ginny, a four-year-old who had just received prayer for her partial deafness in Corby, as her mother asked her about it in the car on the way home. "Sorry I'm late, sir," said Edward, trotting nimbly into his English lesson, "but I broke my foot." "Oh dear," said his teacher Mr Kidd – "but Edward, no limp, no cast?" "No sir, it was prayed for" – as indeed it had been, for Edward had returned from football in a great deal of pain, with a severely swollen foot on which he could put no weight. Icepacks and ibuprofen had had no effect, but it so happened that at his home five members of the church healing team were enjoying a meal together. Prayer had followed, and the pain and swelling had disappeared. "Ah!", said Mr Kidd, slightly sardonically – "a miracle!" "Yes, sir," said Edward happily, taking his place.

Praying for healing is an excellent way to introduce children to God; but it can speak into situations of great trauma too. Two years ago I was part of a team working in a small town called Mfuwe in Eastern Zambia. I spent a whole afternoon standing beneath a tree, praying for the sick alongside Susan Chulu, Canon Missioner of the diocese. One was a young woman called Rhoda, who told us with deep embarrassment that she was suffering from genital boils and AIDS. We prayed for her. I returned to Mfuwe recently. Did I remember Rhoda, Susan asked? The boils had gradually cleared up and her blood count had improved to the point where she was taken off her antiretroviral drugs. She had felt so much better and so much more confident in herself that she had applied for jobs in a government office and in the army. This had involved a battery of medical tests – which to her joy and astonishment had revealed that she was now HIV negative. Others were healed too on that day, and the small church in Mfuwe has been transformed by an outpouring of grace, to which its members have responded with an ambitious programme of rebuilding and outreach.

The healing ministry in Holy Trinity Leicester began with an accident. Liesl, a twelve-year-old member of the church, was knocked down by a car and went into a coma. She was on life support for some time, and was not responding to stimuli of any kind. A group of friends from the church prayed round her bedside. As they prayed, Liesl coughed – the first sign of life she'd shown since the accident. Her father, an anaesthetist, knew this meant that against all the odds she was not brain dead. Liesl made a totally unexpected full recovery, and a healing prayer team was established. Hundreds of people have been prayed for and received healing since then, and now, some thirty years later, a new generation of people has begun to offer healing in the city centre – not to members of the church and their friends, but to 'Muggles', as Hils, its young leader, puts it. Healing is one of the ways in which we proclaim the good news to those who have not heard it.[32]

Miracles

'Energisings of power' (*energemata dunameon*), to use Paul's phrase, are by definition unusual. The word for 'power' is the same word from which we get our word 'dynamite'. So in a miracle we should expect to see not just something remarkable, but something which requires a specific injection of energy. A miracle is an event which can be explained only by reference to the same Spirit who once brought the universe into being in an explosion of power.[33]

The Old Testament is full of miracles – the plagues sent upon the Egyptians, the parting of the Red Sea, the manna and quails provided each day in the desert, and the miracles performed through Elijah and Elisha. Jesus too performed many miracles – he turned water into wine, fed 5,000 people with the lunch of a single boy, calmed a storm, and restored at least three people to life. In all cases the miracles seem to come not out of a desire on Jesus' part to demonstrate his own anointing, but out of his compassion for people.[34]

Miracles were a defining part of the life of the early church. Peter raised a girl named Tabitha from the dead, and Paul restored to life a young man named Eutychus who, unable to stay awake in a meeting, had fallen out of a window. Paul and Silas were released from prison by an earthquake, and Philip was transported miraculously from the Gaza road to Azotus.[35] Further miracles seem to have taken place in all periods of history. The sixth-century Pope and saint Gregory the Great, who wrote the great prayer 'Come, Holy Spirit', records many in his *Dialogues*. In the thirteenth century, Bonaventure recorded more in his *Life of Francis*.[36] Accounts become more detailed once they could be recorded in printed books: in the seventeenth century, for example, the Scottish reformer John Welsh insisted on praying for the young heir to Lord Ochiltree of Edinburgh, to the irritation of his doctors who had demonstrated that after forty-eight hours in a coffin he was irredeemably dead; the young man lived to become Lord Castle Stuart of Ireland.[37]

Miracles continue today. I have seen a prison riot instantly quelled with a single prayer, and dry rot disappear from a church building following a service of repentance and communion. I have heard astonishing stories – a flat filled with light in every room and cupboard, prompting its occupants to give their lives to Christ; a boy walking with a paper bag of brand new Honda ball bearings not once but twice out of the Nigerian bush to rescue a broken down missionary; a man trapped for twenty-seven days beneath rubble after the recent Haiti earthquake, and kept alive by water brought to him by 'a man in white'.[38] My own experience of miraculous restoration of life after death is limited to the hamster in Chapter 8, but there are well-authenticated accounts from Nigeria, DR Congo, and Mozambique of people who have died, been issued with death certificates and in some cases partially embalmed, and then recovered after prayer – and of course there was Lottie.[39]

Prophecy

Prophecy is a strange and complex phenomenon. Whilst some people seem to have a 'big picture' role of prophetic ministry, prophetic words for specific situations are commonly received by those who have learned to listen for them.[40] The prophet Joel had said that one day God would pour out his Spirit on all people, and that from then onwards not just 'official' prophets but even teenagers, old men and servants would prophesy. When the Spirit came on the gathered believers at Pentecost, Paul had recognised that this was now happening, and he urges the Corinthians they should each seek the gift of prophecy.[41]

The gospel with the most references to prophecy is John. All the gospels include examples of prophetic speech – John the Baptist, Caiaphas, Zechariah, Simeon, and Anna are all said to prophesy.[42] On one remarkable occasion a Syrian woman speaks prophetically to Jesus himself, suggesting he should minister not just to Jews but also to Gentiles.[43] In Acts Luke talks both about those who hold a prophetic office broader than any one community, such as Agabus, Judas, and Silas, and also about people who speak prophetically on specific occasions, such as the daughters of Philip and the new believers in Ephesus.[44] Most prophetic words are concerned with the present, but on occasion they relate to the future, particularly when given by Jesus – he announces the coming of the Spirit, warns the disciples that persecution awaits them, and tells Peter he will be taken where he does not wish to go.[45] Paul too sometimes speaks prophetically about the future, to Elymas, to the Ephesians, to his shipmates.[46]

Prophetic words continued to dominate the life of the early church. In the third century Cyprian writes that many persons are called into the ministry of the church by means of a prophecy given by others; that visions and prophecies are received which offer comfort to those preparing for martyrdom; that prophecies give personal guidance and direction; and that the Lord speaks in this way in order to lead churches into unity at times of conflict.[47] In recent years prophecy has occupied a lower profile in the church, perhaps through our own dislike of disorder or fear of dominating personalities. But prophetic words continue to play a key part in the guiding of individuals, in the building up of church fellowships, and in the birth and growth of ministries. Linda, a young mother, was comforted after a diagnosis of cancer by the words "You will live to see your grandchildren" – which indeed she did. Often prophetic words are given to provide direction; I agreed to take responsibility for our healing prayer team after a prophetic dream in which a crippled girl hobbled up to me as I stood admiring wall paintings in a medieval church, asked "Are you Alison?" and then said "You are supposed to pray for me." Prophecy is one way in which God speaks directly and personally to individuals.

Prophetic words may also be given to whole groups. When a group of bishops praying together before the 1978 Lambeth Conference received a prophetic word to 'care for the nervous system of the body of Christ,' they founded the international missionary organisation SOMA, which has, over the last thirty years, ministered powerfully into many struggling and suffering Anglican dioceses. ReSource came into being after a seemingly unlikely prophetic word that Anglican Renewal Ministries and Springboard, then two independent organisations, would amalgamate; another prophecy spelled out ReSource's mandate to support and resource ordinary churches in this country.[48] Prophecy protects us from pursuing good ideas and helps us pursue God's ideas.

Discernment of spirits

One of the most useful ministry tools is the gift of discernment of spirits. When someone asks us to pray for them, how do we know what the real problem is? And in particular, how do we know whether the need is psychological, emotional, or spiritual? The answer often is that we don't – but we can ask the Holy Spirit to guide us, or to give us, in Paul's terms, the ability to discern between spirits (and not, as one well-meaning Zambian translator wrote, to manipulate spirits!).

In the New Testament we see discernment at work in diagnosing illness, in evaluating prophecy, in understanding people's hearts, and in recognising the presence of evil spirits.

Jesus knew when a person's affliction was purely physical in nature and when it had a spiritual cause – a woman with bleeding is healed by touch, but a woman with a bent back is healed when he casts a spirit out of her; a blind man is healed by anointing his eyes with mud, but a deaf man is healed by dismissing an evil presence.[49] Paul recognises the Cypriot magician Elymas as a demonic prophet whose words were leading people away from Jesus; and he discerned that the prophecies given by a slave girl in Philippi were inspired not by the Holy Spirit but by a python spirit, and silenced her by casting it out. Jesus had done the same with a man in the synagogue at Capernaum, and he also recognises when words spoken by Peter are not of God.[50]

We can ask God to give us spiritual discernment in many different situations. First, when we are praying for healing. In the West we are accustomed to look for medical solutions to physical, emotional, and even spiritual problems. So we may treat a depressed, addicted, or mentally disturbed person with drugs, which are often what is required, but which may not deal with the problem if in fact the primary issue is spiritual. Liesl (Chapter 8) was sectioned for schizophrenia and given both drugs and ECT – but the real problem turned out to be a spiritual ceremony she had undergone as a young child in India. Olive, a refugee struggling to forgive both her husband and those who had killed him, was released through prayer from a powerful spirit consulted by the witchdoctor to whom she had been taken as a teenager.[51] Iris, chronically weak and lacking in appetite, collapsed in church – the same church in which Rhoda was healed from AIDS. Carried out unconscious, Iris was restored by a simple prayer of deliverance, repented of her inappropriate sexual relationships and was filled with the Holy Spirit. She returned next day healed, strong, hungry, and able –

to her surprise – to read the Bible without the visual disturbances she had experienced up to that point. More mundanely, Angela's preoccupation with money ended when she discovered an ancestor had spent a lifetime chasing an elusive inheritance; a simple prayer brought release.

It can work the other way around as well, particularly in Africa where people tend to look for spiritual answers to physical or circumstantial problems. A thirteen-year-old girl brought for prayer in a remote Zambian village turned out to be not demonised, as her parents believed, but autistic. A young woman in Leicester hearing voices ordering her to kill herself was not, as she believed, possessed, but suffering from schizophrenia. Sheila, diagnosed with manic depression, was not, as she had thought, struggling with unresolved spiritual issues – she was simply not well, and with appropriate medication has successfully returned to a normal life.

Secondly, discernment enables us to gauge the spiritual temperature in a place. The dry rot in our church was healed after a spiritual problem was diagnosed and dealt with. The oppressive worship in a town in Kenya turned out to be due to the fact that it was being offered to the Kikuyu divinity Engai, who had not been clearly distinguished from God, Father Son and Holy Spirit. A renewal day held in a Somerset church was handicapped by the sensation of a blockage between earth and heaven; it turned out that the church had a history of commitment to Freemasonry. In many places renewal and revival has come after prayer and repentance in the spiritual realm – for often the problems lie not in people but in 'the spiritual forces of evil in the heavenly places.'[52]

Tongues and interpretation of tongues

The last manifestation of the Spirit mentioned by Paul in this part of his letter to the Corinthians is the gift of tongues – the only one not mentioned in the gospels, except by Mark, who relates a prophecy of Jesus that believers would speak in new tongues.[53] It's a complex and controversial gift, and Paul devotes a lot of space to it. He is clear that, as with the other gifts, it is given to some only, and when required; not all believers should expect to speak in tongues. And yet it's important; just as God speaks through prophecy to believers, so he may speak through tongues to unbelievers. This is what happened in Jerusalem when the Spirit first came to the new believers at Pentecost; they began instantly to proclaim the gospel aloud in the languages of the many foreign visitors present. But it seems that at other times the tongues spoken are not intelligible by natural means, and in this case Paul says we should pray for the ability to interpret them.

Whilst many Christians find that to pray in tongues is an uplifting experience in itself, there are some remarkable stories of the Spirit working in this way as a direct means of proclaiming the gospel, or even just out of compassion. There is an impressive account of this in the fifteenth-century autobiography of Margery Kempe, an illiterate housewife and fervent Christian who travelled as a pilgrim to Rome. Praying for someone to hear her confession, she found a priest who, himself speaking only German and Latin, was miraculously able to understand her and give the appropriate penance. Not surprisingly the story was doubted by her companions, who fixed up a dinner party to test it out – and found that it was as she said.[54]

Similar things occur today. During the civil war in

Mozambique, John Lowes travelled from South Africa to the Diocese of Lebombo as part of an exchange programme. John was a lay evangelist, and when invited to preach in a village one Sunday he offered the only sermon he knew – an evangelistic one. Speaking through a translator, he concluded with a prayer of commitment to Christ. As he prayed he became aware that the translator had fallen silent, but that people were nonetheless able to understand what he was saying, and to respond in their own language. About 300 people came to faith that day. Less than one week later, rebel forces came and massacred the entire village. God had prepared them for what was to come.[55]

Another remarkable story was confirmed to me by Revd Caz Dunk, who was present at a meeting of the Oak Tree Anglican Fellowship in north London. A single voice was heard rising above the sound of the hymn, and as the hymn ended the voice continued. It belonged to a quiet, unobtrusive member of the church, a secretary by occupation. When she stopped singing, an Iranian came forward, a visitor to the church, and said that she had been singing a beautiful song in High Persian to 'the prince of heaven'. "Who is the prince of heaven?", he asked. As the gospel was explained to him, the Iranian committed his life to Christ. Afterwards he asked the secretary, "Where did you learn my language?" He had been a university lecturer, and High Persian is used only amongst the highly educated. She of course had no knowledge of High Persian; she had been singing in tongues.[56]

In these ways and others, God resources us through the Holy Spirit to continue the ministry of Jesus: to proclaim the good news that the kingdom of heaven has come near, demonstrating through words, healings, miracles, deliverance, and other Spirit-led phenomena that this is indeed so.[57] We may lack the confidence to present the gospel to the people of England, but we do not, as the Archbishops' report feared, lack the resources.[58]

Good news for a poor community in Kiteto, Tanzania

One of the earliest *Rooted in Jesus* conferences, held in 2003 in a small and dusty Tanzanian town called Engusero, closed with a remarkable time of worship, marked by joy, fervour, and the distribution of new spiritual gifts. As the Spirit moved among the people, silence fell, and one person stepped forward with a prophecy: "I think God wants to say this to you: 'This is a beautiful place. But I know that life is hard here. In the eyes of the world, Kiteto is not an important place, and you are not important people. But I want you to know that in my eyes Kiteto is a very important place, and to me you are a special people. If you will seek me with all your heart, if you continue to praise and to pray as you have done today, then I will bless you'." Four years later we returned to a different people. Not only did they tell us the stories of spiritual growth outlined in Chapter 9, but their material circumstances had been transformed as well. This time we met not in a small brick church, but in a large, new cathedral in a compound containing a Christian college where people from the whole region could come to learn practical skills and deepen their understanding of God. In the same compound stood a new primary school and a complex of administrative buildings. Nearby was a hospital and a borehole providing fresh water. In the villages there were new pastors' houses, church nursery schools, water filters and carts, and a scheme for group leaders to receive milk goats to help support their families. What advice did they have for new leaders in other places, we asked? "Recognise that this is a call on your life," they said; "and depend on the Holy Spirit in everything you do."

For discussion and reflection

THE OTHER

There are nights that are so still
that I can hear the small owl calling
far off and a fox barking
miles away. It is then that I lie
in the lean hours awake listening
to the swell born somewhere in the Atlantic
rising and falling, rising and falling
wave on wave on the long shore
by the village, that is without light
and companionless. And the thought comes
of that other being who is awake, too,
letting our prayers break on him,
not like this for a few hours,
but for days, years, for eternity.

R. S. THOMAS

You are part of something big – bigger than your own experience, bigger than the world you can see. Read the poem by R. S. Thomas. When do you most feel connected to this otherness, this spiritual reality which is to be found not just outside the world but also within it, and not just outside you but also within you?

'The gifts of the Spirit are not given to provide us with the spiritual equivalent of a trip to Alton Towers, but so that we might take the victory of the cross into the world' – Bishop Tom Wright. What does that mean in practice? Refer to Hebrews 2.3–4.

'Many in the church today are content to live with only one parent. They live with the Word, and the Spirit only has limited visiting rights' – Jack Deere.[59] What can we do to ensure we are depending on both Word and Spirit in equal measure?

'Preach this message: "The kingdom of heaven is near." Heal the sick, raise the dead, cleanse those with leprosy, drive out demons. Freely you have received, freely give' (Matthew 10.7–8 NIV). Does that apply to us?

Chapter 11

The Word on the Wind –
confidence in creation

*Ever since the creation of the world, his eternal power
and divine nature, invisible though they are, have been
understood and seen through the things he has made.*

Romans 1.20

As we saw in Part I, one of the factors which most undermines
confidence in the gospel is the ongoing debate about the proper
relationship between science and faith, and our mistaken
tendency to choose either the one or the other as we seek to
answer the two fundamental questions which life asks us – how
do we know things, and how do we make sense of them? In
recent years this debate has stretched itself primarily between the
two opposing poles of evolution and creation: on the one hand
we find atheist geneticists brandishing Darwin and claiming
that evolution offers a complete and self-sufficient explanation
for the development of life, and on the other we see creationist
Christians waving Genesis and claiming that God created
the world and everything in it in a single six-day period less
than 10,000 years ago. Many churchgoers sit bemused in the
middle of all this, worried that somehow both sides are missing

something, and wondering if it's really necessary to choose between them. Outside the Church, the popular misconception that Christians don't accept the theory of evolution is a major stumbling block to the gospel.

The good news, of course, is that we do not have to choose between belief in God and the theory of evolution. Science and faith, often falsely represented to us as alternatives, are in fact partners in our attempt to understand the universe and our place within it. Science is a process, a methodology which seeks to explain the properties of the physical world – the word 'science' comes from the word for knowledge, and science, as we saw in Chapter 2, is about what we know. Faith, on the other hand, is a framework, an attempt to look at the big picture and to explore what it all means – the word 'faith' comes from the word for trust, and it's about how we make sense of what we know. Aristotle called them by the perhaps more helpful terms of 'physics' and 'metaphysics': metaphysics is that which goes 'beyond physics'. The vast majority of scientists and theologians affirm this distinction. Owen Gingerich, professor of astronomy and history of science at Harvard University, reminds us that 'science works within a constrained framework in creating its brilliant picture of nature', but that 'reality goes much deeper than this.' Theologian Wolfhart Pannenberg suggests that if we are properly to understand the natural world, we must bring our understanding of God to bear on what we discover through science.[1] For many people over the centuries accurate observation of the created world has been not an obstacle but a great stimulus to their faith, and this remains so today. Science and faith are not in competition: they have different remits.

Clearing the decks

We saw in Chapter 8 that the Bible is a complex text which, like God himself, uses language in many different ways. Written over a period of some 2,000 years, it contains a mix of different literary forms. Within its pages we find myth, law, history, poetry, prophecy, and plain ordinary correspondence. Consistent in its claim to offer truth, that truth is expressed now as fact, now as metaphor, now as dream or vision. It seems obvious that just as today we do not read an instruction manual with the same expectations that we bring to an advertisement or a love letter, so we should not read Genesis in the same way that we read Luke's account of the Acts of the Apostles or Paul's letters to the Corinthians. We, living in a scientific age which thinks of truth in scientific terms as something simple, objective and verifiable, can easily forget this; and it is this which lies at the source of the current confusion.[2]

The book of Genesis was written not as history or science but as theology; in Aristotle's terms, it's a work of metaphysics, not physics. Properly speaking, it is myth – not in the popular, myths-and-legends sense of fictional writing, but in the technical sense of truth expressed in narrative or poetic form. It does help us to understand what was happening as God created the world, but it does not aim to explain how he did it. To look to Genesis for a literal account of how the universe came into being is to impose on it a mindset completely alien to those who wrote it; it is to make what is properly termed a 'category mistake'.[3] Our task as Christians is to relate to the natural sciences as they actually exist; we cannot create our own sciences.

If creationism is indeed based on the uncritical acceptance of modern scientific assumptions about the nature of truth, we should expect to find that it is a relatively new approach to the attempt to understand how the world came into being; and this is exactly what we do find. Throughout history theologians have warned that the book of Genesis should not be taken as a literal account of how the world was created. In the first century, Jewish scholar Philo explained that its opening chapters were intended symbolically, being not literal explanations but 'modes of making ideas visible'. In the third, Origen pointed out that as there clearly could not have been morning and evening before there was a sun and a moon, the Genesis account is clearly intended to 'indicate certain mysteries through a semblance of history.'[4] In the fifth, Augustine spluttered with prophetic wisdom that if Christians set themselves up as experts on matters of physics and biology when the biblical texts could clearly be interpreted in many different ways, no one would take them seriously when they talked about matters of faith.[5] Throughout the Middle Ages, the Bible was held to be capable of holding any of four different levels of meaning: literal, moral, allegorical or spiritual; only in the sixteenth century, with the new insistence that it could be read as a stand-alone text free of the interpretive framework of the Catholic Church, was the foundation laid for a literalistic interpretation of scripture. The belief that the Earth is less than 10,000 years old is not a traditional Christian one; it became widely accepted only in the early seventeenth century following the calculation by James Ussher and John Lightfoot that God had created the Earth on Sunday 23 October 4004 BC at 9 a.m. London time, or midnight in the Garden of Eden.[6] And what we know now as creationism was first invented in the late nineteenth century by the Seventh Day Adventists Ellen White and George McCready Price; its current popularity dates from 1961, and the publication of a book called *The Genesis*

Flood by an engineer named Henry Morris.[7] Not only does creationism fly in the face of undeniable evidence from geology, palaeontology, genetics, mathematics and physics, it is not, and never has been, a mainstream Christian belief.

As Theodosius Dobzhansky, a prominent scientist and member of the Russian Orthodox church, writes, 'It is a blunder to mistake the Holy Scriptures for elementary textbooks of astronomy, geology, biology and anthropology. Only if symbols are construed to mean what they are not intended to mean can there arise imaginary, insoluble conflicts.'[8] Science and theology are not competitors, and to insist we must choose between them is to offer a false choice. The choice we do have to make is in fact a hidden one: it lies not between evolution and creation (or come to that between M-theory, the latest brainchild of theoretical physicists, and creation) but between materialism and theism – the belief that the physical world is all there is and the opposing belief that there is a God beyond it.[9] Materialism is not a scientific process but a philosophical belief – and therefore in itself a kind of faith. Many materialists acknowledge this. Immunologist George Klein explains: 'I am an atheist. My attitude is not based on science, but rather on faith… The absence of a Creator, the non-existence of God, is my childhood faith, my adult belief, unshakeable and holy.'[10]

In the beginning was the Word…

By faith we understand that the worlds were prepared
by the word of God, so that what is seen was made from
things that are not visible.

Hebrews 11.3

It was our first winter in Somerset, and it snowed. I drove up
into the Mendips to find a silent wonderland of soft drifts,
blue and white landscapes, and buried signposts. Far below, the
Levels glittered green in the sunlight, and millions of starlings
gathered for their pre-roost dance, ready to twist and turn above
the reeds, black against an orange sky. Children laughed on new
sledges, and I was filled with awe, and joy, and delight at being
alive. It was hard, that afternoon, not to think of God. And it is
my experience that life offers such moments regularly; moments
which invite us to look beyond the demands of the everyday
and connect with the bigger picture. The world we can see,
and which increasingly reveals itself to be a place of astonishing
complexity and improbable diversity, leads us by the hand into
the world we cannot see, the world of eternal reality.

The Bible does not attempt to help us to understand the
physical processes by which the universe and everything in
it came into being. But it has plenty to say to us about the
invisible reality on which the visible world depends. It speaks
of these things in precisely the two metaphors which we have
been exploring: Word and Spirit. Word and Spirit, the vehicles
of our relationship with God, are also the vehicles of creation.
In the beginning when God created the heavens and the earth,
we read in the first verse of the book of Genesis, the Spirit of
God was hovering over the waters. In the beginning when all
things came into being, we read in the first verse of the gospel
of John, was the Word. In the beginning, both the Old and
the New Testaments proclaim, there were these two things: the
Spirit and the Word. The biblical language of creation knows
nothing of singularities and strings, nothing of nucleotides and
mitochondria. But if scientists tell us what the words of reality
are, perhaps our faith can tell us who spoke them. Our faith

does not end with science; as the great Christian spiritual writers have always known, it begins there.[11]

Language, as we have already seen, determines how we think. I find it fascinating that scientists often speak about the creation of a living universe in terms of words. 'What lies at the heart of every living thing is ... information, words, instructions,' Richard Dawkins has said, referring to DNA.[12] DNA is commonly referred to as an alphabet, a single 64-word code which has spelt life in all living things since the beginning of time. It is the ultimate way of storing information, information which when decoded spells not just plants, insects and animals but also you and me. Geneticists such as Francis Collins, director of the Human Genome Project, and biochemists such as Denis Alexander, formerly Chair of the Molecular Immunology Programme in Cambridge, see this language both as God-given and as finding continuously developing expression through the mechanism of evolution. Francis Collins has written a book, *The Language of God*, in which he coins the term 'BioLogos' to describe his conviction that God interacts with reality precisely *through* the process of evolution.[13]

The same inclination to talk about creation in terms of speech is found in physicists and mathematicians. Quantum physicist Paul Davies has suggested that the application of information theory to science leads us to believe that 'perhaps the universe is really a frolic of primal information, and material objects a complex secondary manifestation.' Einstein's colleague John Wheeler said that eventually we would learn to understand all of physics in the language of information. John Lennox, professor of mathematics at the university of Oxford and a specialist in the philosophy of science, observes that what needs explaining is not the origin of life but the origin of information, for it is information which is fundamental to the existence of the universe. This, he points out, is no easy task, for information is both invisible and immaterial.[14]

So reality, it seems, is spoken; and this, curiously, is how the people of God have always understood it. In the beginning God spoke, and the world was created. A word, as we have seen, is *dabar*, which means both word and deed. Scripture presents God's words not simply as flat and factual things, but as the active agents of life itself – so that what is seen is indeed, as the writer to the Hebrews knew, made from things that are not visible. Later that word was spoken to us directly by Jesus, its living manifestation; and his words seemed to carry within them the same creative power. Perhaps it is no coincidence that *logos* was the word which John used to describe Jesus; language, we believe, lies at the heart of physical reality. It lies at the heart of our reality too; for it is language which distinguishes us from all other creatures and makes us uniquely human. Perhaps this is what the Bible means when it says we are people made in the image of God, for we have minds which not only have the capacity to communicate directly with God, but which are able to engage in profound and astonishing ways with the universe he spoke. It is language, and not just logic, which makes everything possible. Reality comes in words.

And the Spirit of God was hovering over the waters...

> … *in him all things in heaven and on earth were created, things visible and invisible,… – all things have been created through him and for him. He himself is before all things, and in him all things hold together.*

Colossians 1.16–17

If information is a fundamental property of reality, so too is energy. Energy is fundamental to everything from the initial explosion into being of the universe to the continued existence of every individual atom. Here too we as Christians have inherited a way of thinking about these things; energy, power and life are all properties of the Spirit of God. Throughout the whole of scripture, the Spirit is identified with the power and energy which come from outside the visible world but which govern all that happens within it.[15] This continues in our own experience; we saw in the last chapter that Paul describes the work of the Spirit as 'energising', and that this energy, having been newly released through the death and resurrection of Jesus, is available to work through us in various ways today.[16]

The origin of the energy which created and sustains life remains shrouded in mystery; indeed, it seems that whilst we know that it can be neither created nor destroyed, we do not know what energy actually is. We do, however, know what it does. Physicist John Polkinghorne is content to read the Genesis description of the Spirit hovering over the waters as the universe was created as perfectly consistent with the scientific theory of the Big Bang. He rewrites it like this:

> In the beginning was the big bang. As the world sprang
> forth from the fuzzy singularity of its origin, first the
> spatial order formed, as quantum fluctuations ceased
> seriously to perturb gravity. Then space boiled ...
> blowing the universe apart with incredible rapidity in
> the much less than 10^{-30} seconds that it lasted. ... For a
> while the universe was a hot soup of quarks and gluons
> and leptons, but by the time it was one ten-thousandth
> of a second old, this age of rapid transformation came

to a close and the matter of the world took the familiar
form of protons and neutrons and electrons. The whole
cosmos was still hot enough to be the arena of nuclear
reactions, and these continued until just beyond the
cosmic age of three minutes. The gross nuclear structure
of the universe was then left, as it remains today, at a
quarter helium and three-quarters hydrogen. It was far
too hot for atoms to form around these nuclei, and this
would not occur for another half a million years or so.
By then the universe had become cool enough for matter
and radiation to separate. The world suddenly became
transparent and a universal sea of radiation was left
to continue cooling on its own until, 15 billion years
later, and by then at a temperature of 3°K, it would
be detected by 2 radio astronomers working outside
Princeton.[17]

Terry Pratchett is easier to follow, but says essentially the same thing: 'The current state of knowledge can be summarised thus: In the beginning, there was nothing, which exploded.'[18] What was nothing like, how could it explode, and what came before it (for physicists now suggest there may have been a 'pre-bangian' universe)?[19] We do not know, and we may never know. But what we do know can be talked about in the biblical language of the Spirit as well as in the specialist language of physics; and indeed the Spirit himself can be seen as an adequate theological explanation for a physical conundrum, for the energy which set the whole thing in motion, the source which lies outside the physical reality within which we are confined, cannot by its very nature be explained from within this reality. Astrophysicist Robert Jastrow suggests that 'the essential elements of the astronomical and biblical accounts of Genesis are the same; the chain of events leading to man commenced suddenly and sharply at a definite moment in time, in a flash of light and energy.'[20] The trail of that explosion is still evident all around us: astonishing amounts of energy are locked up not just within the nuclei of uranium atoms but even inside our own bodies: within the frame of a single adult lurks as much energy as would be released in the explosion of thirty large hydrogen bombs.[21]

From this singular beginning, life developed. How, again we do not know. DNA, the vehicle of life, is not itself alive – it's just a natty zip-like structure of amino acids, and the odds against their arrangement into the hundreds of thousands of proteins needed for life is apparently $10^{400,000}$ to 1. Fred Hoyle famously compared this to the likelihood of a tornado sweeping through a junkyard and producing a jumbo jet.[22] As for life itself, Paul Davies describes it as 'the most astonishing phenomenon in nature.'[23] It can be recognised but not defined, and certainly cannot be reduced to a property of an organism's constituent parts; at best, we exist not in our physical components, for those constantly change, but in the patterns between them.[24] There is more to life than can be explained by physics or genetics. 'What *is* it that breathes fire into the equations and makes a universe for them to describe?', Stephen Hawking once asked.[25] It's not a physical question but a metaphysical one. Theologians answer it by talking about the Holy Spirit, the *ruach* or breath of God. What makes you alive? Breath is in fact as good a definition as anyone has yet come up with.

Once we have DNA, evolution can begin. Whilst the evidence for evolution is overwhelming, it too carries its conundrums. In particular, it seems that mathematically there has not been time for it, and it's been suggested that this means it should be seen as a process with an inbuilt 'bias' of some kind.[26] Nonetheless, develop it did, through a gradual evolution of forms, each more complex than the last, in a remarkable unfolding of the diversification of species. Francis Collins, as eloquent and informed an evolutionist as you will find, suggests that that evolution can only be fully understood as a process instigated by God.[27]

If the origin of the universe and the development of life within it remain something of a mystery, so too does the continued existence of the complex system which is life on Earth. James Lovelock was one of the first scientists to think about how the whole thing keeps going. His research led him to conclude that 'the only feasible explanation of the Earth's highly improbable atmosphere was that it was being manipulated on a day-to-day basis from the surface, and that the manipulator was life itself'.[28] Theologians, who over the centuries have wondered whether not just the original creation of the universe but also its continued existence can be thought about in spiritual terms, have with good biblical authority referred to this 'manipulator' as the Spirit of God. Reflecting on passages such as Psalm 104, Ambrose wrote in the fourth century: 'If it were possible to remove the Spirit from creation, all beings would become confused and the life in them would appear to have no law, no structure, no ordered purpose whatsoever. Without the Spirit, the entire creation would be unable to continue in being.'[29] Sir Thomas Browne remarked in the seventeenth century that

> *ther may be (for ought I know) an universall and*
> *common Spirit to the whole world ... I am sure there*
> *is a common Spirit that playes within us, yet makes no*

> part of us, and that is the spirit of God, the fire and
> scintillation of that noble and mighty Essence, which
> is the life and radiall heat of spirits. This is that gentle
> heate that brooded on the waters, and in six days
> hatched the world... whosoever feels not the warme gale
> and gentle ventilation of this Spirit (though I feel his
> pulse) I dare not say he lives.

In the nineteenth century philosopher Georg Hegel suggested that the whole of reality is the continued manifestation of one universal Spirit, and in the twentieth, theologians Teilhard de Chardin and Paul Tillich both wrote of the Spirit as the power directing the processes of life.[30] But the person who has perhaps made the most thorough contribution to our understanding of the role of the Spirit within creation is Wolfhart Pannenberg. For Pannenberg, the divine Spirit is the power of life that both transcends the living organism and yet is intimately present in each individual. The Spirit's presence is what sustains that individual and keeps him alive, so that the act of creation not only occurs in the beginning but is repeated at every moment. Perhaps, Pannenberg says longingly, 'a renewed doctrine of the Trinity would combine the Logos doctrine of the ancient church with contemporary information theory and recognise the activity of the divine spirit in the self-transcendence of life and its evolution.'[31]

What does this mean for us? Vincent Donovan summed the whole thing up in personal terms, offering the Spirit as the explanation for everything from our ability to get up in the morning to the fact that the television continues to work: 'We Christians profess to believe in a continuing creation. We believe that God is continuing to create and to hold in existence the world and everything in it: the atom, and the molecule, the mountain and the chair, the rocket hurtling through space, the television set, my finger and my mind: that if God ceased to create, took away his creative presence, all these things, and we ourselves, would cease to exist on the instant. This creative power is acting now and here.'[32] He is echoed by biochemist Arthur Peacocke: 'the continuing creative power which is manifest ... at all levels of existence ... is, in the Christian tradition, God as "Holy Spirit".'[33]

So for the Christian, it seems that the 'who' behind the universe, the Word and Spirit who spoke and animated it, still speaks and animates today. Metaphysics is not an alternative to physics or biology, but rather their completion; a perspective which helps us to make sense of the information we have discovered and continue to discover. Our faith enables us to put a framework of meaning round the picture of material reality; it both completes the picture and gives us another way of looking at it. It enables us to do something which scientists cannot: to look at things from the outside.

But it does more than that too. In giving us a wider perspective on life than the purely material, faith opens up avenues of thought that lie outside the province of science. Through the language of faith we find that it is possible to think not just about creation and evolution, but about purpose and eternity, about what it means not simply to be alive but to be a human being with all the joys and sorrows, memories and ambitions which materialists wish to limit to the pre-determined behaviour of an assembly of nerve cells and molecules. In insisting that nothing can be known which cannot be known through science, materialists seem to slam shut the door on half of life.[34] As Christians we find that it is indeed possible to think constructively about who we are and where we are going. We find that we can smile at what we know and do not know, and entrust ourselves to a God to whom we can actually speak, and to whom we may clearly listen. This is the living world of faith; this is the framework within which we do our science. It's a bit like being in a room full of immensely complex and interesting things, and then opening the window to find yourself gazing in astonishment at a whole new realm outside it.

Good news for John Ruskin

John Ruskin was the foremost art critic of the nineteenth century. In his book *Modern Painters* he describes his awareness of the spiritual dimension which lies within and beyond the created world:

> *There was a continual perception of Sanctity in the*
> *whole of nature, from the slightest thing to the vastest;*
> *an instinctive awe, mixed with delight; an indefinable*
> *thrill, such as we sometimes imagine to indicate the*
> *presence of a disembodied spirit. I could only feel this*
> *perfectly when I was alone; and then it would often*
> *make me shiver from head to foot with the joy and*
> *fear of it, when after being some time away from hills*
> *I first got to the shore of a mountain river, where the*
> *brown water circled among the pebbles, or when I first*
> *saw the swell of distant land against the sunset, or the*
> *first low broken wall, covered with mountain moss…*
> *If we had to explain even the sense of bodily hunger*
> *to a person who had never felt it, we should be hard*

put to it for words; and the joy in nature seemed to
me to come of a sort of heart-hunger, satisfied with the
presence of a Great and Holy Spirit.[35]

For reflection and discussion

Everywhere, in all the heavens you will find his footprints,
all regions are filled with his mysterious letters,
all heights and depths with his handwriting that only he
    can decipher.
All-powerful one, why do you not teach us to read
    your book?
Why do you not move your finger along the letters
and teach us to piece them together and understand like
    children?
But no, that you do not do. You are no schoolmaster,
You let things be as they are, incomprehensible as they are.
Then, one day in the evening of time, will you delete them
    all again,
let everything become darkness, as it was before you arose
    from your thoughts
and wandered off to set them down while on your way with
the burning coal in your hand?

PÄR LAGERKVIST

**Do you identify with Ruskin and Lagerkvist in their awareness
of the spiritual dimension which lies beyond the world we
can see?**

'Living in an urban area feels to me a bit like being covered
with a paving stone, but I'm always secretly pleased when I
see paving stones being cracked by the roots of trees – I am
all on the side of the tree. Paving stones do crack and life
goes on and I might not get what I wanted, but there are so
many things I never imagined and didn't know how to want

that now I am eternally grateful for' – Anna Farago. Do you find, like Anna, that God can speak to you through even the most ordinary details of the world around you? How can you make the space and time for him to do this more easily?

'Either half my colleagues are enormously stupid, or else the science of Darwinism is fully compatible with conventional religious beliefs – and equally compatible with atheism' – Stephen Jay Gould.[36] Do you find that there is tension between the theory of evolution and faith in God? What about people you know outside the Church? How can we help them to think clearly about the relationship between faith and science – do you see this as a ministry opportunity?

'Ever since the creation of the world, his eternal power and divine nature, invisible though they are, have been understood and seen through the things he has made' (Romans 1.20). Meditate on this verse.

Part III

Doing Things Differently

Chapter 12

Living beautiful lives

What matters is not your outer appearance… but your inner disposition. Cultivate inner beauty, the gentle, gracious kind that God delights in.

1 Peter 3.2–4 (TM)

Last month I spoke at an event in Painswick, Gloucestershire, as part of a 'Think Twice' mission series aimed at drawing people together to discuss topics of common interest. My brief was to talk about the relationship between science and faith, and afterwards a man came up to continue the conversation. "It's all very well," he said, "but everyone has their own idea of God – how can we know who he really is?" The answer, I suggested, is to be found in Jesus. God, uniquely of all gods, took the trouble to show himself to us in the physical person of his Son – and that is our message, the good news with which everything begins. A long silence followed, and then a second question: "How, then, do we know Jesus?" And that, of course, is the issue.

This book has been full of the stories of people who have come to know Jesus. For some of them the encounter has been a direct one, in dreams, in church porches, or through scripture. But for most, Jesus has been encountered through those who already know him: in conversation, in prayer, through simple acts of kindness. We are, as Paul said, ambassadors for Christ, and our lives are a letter that others can read – a letter written not with ink, but by the Holy Spirit who is at work within us, and not on paper but in our hearts. We, who through knowing Jesus are being changed to become more like Jesus, act as models for what is on offer. Others will be won, Peter remarked, primarily by the beauty of our lives. It worked; a couple of hundred years later Minucius Felix was able to affirm: 'Beauty of life causes strangers to join our ranks. We do not talk about great things; we live them.'[1]

We have already seen, to our perhaps faithless surprise, that people are interested in Jesus and are willing to talk about him. We have seen too that there are few other effective answers available to the spiritual questions which burst like green shoots through the concrete of a materialistic society. If we become like Jesus, loving others with the passion and power he makes available to us, people will want to join our ranks. If ever there was a time to rediscover Jesus, we have noted, it is now: not the Jesus of history or the Jesus of ceremony or the Jesus of children's picture books, but the actual living Jesus who heals our wounds, answers our prayers and intrudes upon our lives with his inconvenient demands – the one who comes into the kitchen and bleeds all over the floor, to quote Thelma Laycock. To discover Jesus means not just that we believe in him; it means that we follow him and in the process change to become more like him, both in who we are and in what we do.[2] We are meant to be different from those around us. The biblical word for this process is discipleship, 'the irreplaceable and lifelong task of becoming like Jesus by embodying his message.'[3]

The problem is that surveys tend to show that for most of us this does not in fact happen; on the whole Christians do not change as a result of their faith in God, and it seems that there is in practice no discernible difference between their lives and the lives of those around them; to use Jesus' analogy, we are not salty, and we do not shed light.[4] It's time to do things differently; and we need to start with ourselves.

The Christian disciple

Go therefore and make disciples of all nations, baptizing them in the name of the Father and of the Son and of the Holy Spirit, and teaching them to obey everything that I have commanded you.

Matthew 28.19–20

As Jesus prepared to leave his friends for the last time, he gave them one simple instruction: they were to go and make disciples. Whatever else we do, it is clear that if we aren't making disciples we aren't doing what Jesus meant us to do. It is also clear that becoming a disciple means being baptised into something – it's a distinct moment at which something happens, something which involves not just the individual but also God, Father Son and Spirit. And it seems too that becoming a disciple involves doing things – everything, in fact, which Jesus had told his first followers to do.

So how are we getting on? Are we being baptised into the living reality of God, Father, Son, and Holy Spirit? Are we actively absorbing and obeying the commands of Jesus? Are we fully dependent upon the tools of Word and Spirit which have been made available to us? Or are we, in most cases and most places across this green and pleasant land, falling short of our potential?

When we think about disciples and discipleship, we tend to think in academic terms. The word disciple comes from the Latin, *disco*, to learn. Learning, to us, usually means classrooms and colleges; it's about what we know and understand. And yet this is not what the gospels seem to mean by discipleship at all. The New Testament word is not Latin but Greek, and it's *mathetes*. *Mathetes* is not a classroom kind of word – a disciple is not so much a student as an apprentice.[5] Gospel discipleship is about learning on the hoof, with a clear emphasis on putting what's being learnt into practice. "Watch me," Jesus said as he healed the sick, freed the oppressed and offered good news to the poor. Then, "Off you go in pairs, you have a go, and we'll go through it when you get back." Then finally, "I'm leaving now, but you are to keep on doing it, and teach others to do it too – and you will find that I am still with you." It's clear from exchanges like these that Jesus was not training rabbis. He could engage in theological reflection with the best of them; but we don't once see him teaching his disciples to do that. Christian discipleship is meant to be practical. It's fun to watch Nicodemus, a leading teacher of the law, so struck by Jesus' miracles that he sneaked back under cover of darkness to find out more. "How do you do it?", he asked. "You must be born of the Spirit," said Jesus, "this is not about qualifications." So impressed was Nicodemus by this that he is later said to be 'one of them', and it was he who helped Joseph of Arimathea bury Jesus' body. It's clear from the outset that you can't get to be a disciple by going on a study course; to be a disciple of Jesus is to learn to do the things that Jesus did.[6]

Secondly, discipleship is most commonly understood today in individualistic terms. Again it's not hard to see why – we live in an individualistic society. My daughters have just made their choice of subjects to study for AS level; they chose them according to their own interests and abilities, and now they are meeting their new teachers. This is radically different from the New Testament concept of discipleship – for Jesus, discipleship was not an individual process but a collective one. His disciples didn't choose a syllabus, they chose a person, leaving behind their families and throwing their lot in with one another as they set out to follow him. For them it meant learning in community, learning to abandon their individual agendas and to think about one another as branches on the same vine or members of the same body. The same is true for us: Jesus is no longer here physically, but he explained (and Paul emphasised it again in his letters to the Christians in Rome, Corinth, and Ephesus) that he would be with us in an even more powerful way, for we would find him both within ourselves and also in and through one another.[7] Discipleship is by its very nature relational – which should perhaps come as no surprise, for we have, as Jesus remarked, a relational God: Father, Son, and Spirit.

Discipleship, then, can be defined as a form of apprenticeship undertaken in community. To recognise this radically alters our understanding of it. It means that our focus should be not on what we know, but rather on who we are becoming. To become a disciple of Jesus is to embark, with others, on a journey; it is to decide to submit our whole life, in all its parts, to God. Discipleship cannot be done by turning up once a week for an evening class, or even a sermon; it is a courageous, collective vote for change.

We watch the journeys of some of the first disciple-apprentices in the gospels and Acts of the Apostles – a group of people who, as the title of Acts suggests, became not just people who believed things but people who, in the tradition of *dabar*, actually did them – and furthermore who did them together. We see Simon, an impulsive, irascible fisherman, changing before our very eyes into a man so reliable and steadfast that, now named Peter ('The Rock'), he became the leader of the first Christian church, preaching the gospel fearlessly and performing signs and wonders in the name of Jesus. We see James, who with his family once thought that Jesus was mentally ill, leading the infant church in Jerusalem and writing about the importance of being people who do not just listen to the word but who actually do it. And, perhaps most strikingly of all, we meet Saul, the church's greatest persecutor, struck blind one day on the Damascus Road as Jesus spoke to him, opening his eyes three days later to begin a new life as apostle to the Gentiles. No one believed it had happened, but Saul – renamed Paul – went on to plant churches all over the Roman empire and, eventually, to die for his faith.[8]

Peter, James, and Paul must rank as among the most influential individuals in history. It is clear that their impact was not due to their qualifications – Peter in particular had none, and as far as we can tell none of the other eleven initial disciples of Jesus had any either. Nor was it due simply to their own strength of character or ability to command others. These men were conspicuous for two things: for the thoroughness of their discipleship, manifest in their ability to do the things which Jesus did; and for their unquestioning grasp of the importance of relationships. Having shared the gospel, they drew those who responded into small, radical communities of people who shared their possessions, ate and studied the scriptures and prayed and ministered together. In so doing they laid the foundations for the spread of the gospel all over the known world.[9]

The same process of apprenticeship and community has

been played out throughout history, the greatest growth coming always when both factors are present. The ascetics of the fourth century, alarmed by the increasingly fuzzy discipleship of the church, left their towns and cities for a life of prayer in the desert. Francis of Assisi, heir to a successful textiles business, devoted himself, after a direct encounter with Jesus in an abandoned church, to a Christ-like life of travelling poverty. John Wesley, a young priest released from a deep sense of failure through hearing Luther's commentary on the epistle to the Romans, set off on horseback to preach the gospel all over England. All three submitted themselves completely to Jesus, and all realised that he cannot be followed independently – that Christians, in Rowan Williams's words, are people who not only encounter the risen Jesus but who also commit themselves to sustaining and deepening that encounter in their encounter with each other.[10] The great monasteries of the Middle Ages, the worldwide Franciscan movement, and the Methodist church all drew their strength from the small, mutually accountable communities into which they gathered their members. The same seems to be true of the remarkable church growth in China today – forbidden to meet in groups of more than fifteen, to erect dedicated church buildings or to set up institutions, numbers of Christians meeting in small, mutually accountable communities are rocketing.[11] Lone disciples are not true disciples.

Depending on the Holy Spirit

The key to our discipleship is to be found, as Jesus explained to Nicodemus, in our interaction with the Holy Spirit. We cannot travel physically with Jesus, but the Holy Spirit enables us to travel with him spiritually, to embark on a journey which is played out in three dimensions.

First of all, it's a journey inwards. In Exodus 15.26 God tells us for the first time what kind of a God he is – "I am the Lord who heals you." In Luke 4 Jesus too speaks of his ministry in terms of healing, understood in the broadest sense. It seems that a Christian is someone who is being healed and made whole – salvation, healing and wholeness all come from the same root word.[12] Healed first of all of our sin, gradually made whole in our hearts and minds, and ultimately healed from the death which afflicts our bodies, Christian discipleship is a process of gradual change. If we are prepared to take Jesus seriously, we will find that we are indeed, as Paul says, transformed day by day into his likeness – transformed in our minds and hearts, our habits and our relationships.[13] We will find that we grow, as we see those first disciples grow, into the potential we have in Christ. I am, it's been said, a shadow of my future self.

All this is brought about by the Holy Spirit who teaches, encourages, and ministers to us. Paul gives us a first-hand description of his work in us. To the Romans he talks about the power of the Spirit to help us overcome sin and to become the people we yearn to be. To the Galatians he talks about the fruit of the Spirit which grows in us, so that we become full not of fear, envy or anger, but rather of love, joy, peace, patience, kindness, generosity, faithfulness, gentleness, and self-control. To the Ephesians and Colossians he says it's like putting off an old identity and putting on a new one, a process once acted out in baptism by walking into the river wearing one set of clothes and coming out of it to change into another. Or, he says, mixing his metaphors rather, it's like walking in light rather than in darkness. But whether you go for fruit, clothing, or light, it's clear that our commitment to Jesus is meant to change us, and furthermore that this happens not as we acquire information but as we become willing, as Jesus and Paul put it, to be born again, washed through the water of rebirth and renewed by the Holy Spirit.[14]

In Chapter 1 we met Lisa, who at the time of her first encounter with Jesus was a single parent with a history of abuse, violence and drugs. Lisa joined an Alpha group, then a cell group. Pastored by the cell leader, she asked if she could spend an evening with two of us, offering her past, present, and future life to God in prayer. Listening as she poured out her story, then waiting on God in silence, we sat and watched as Lisa was overwhelmed with an almost physical sense of his love for her. Within two years she was sufficiently healed and changed to travel as part of a ReSource mission team to Milford. Such was the impact she had there that within a week they had offered her a job on the staff of the church. Lisa's story is an example of what can happen when a damaged individual begins to grow, through her relationship with other Christians, into the space made available to her by Jesus.[15]

Secondly, our journey is a journey upwards. It begins in the ripping of the temple curtain as Jesus, dying, opens up the way back to God. It takes us through the heavens in the company of Jesus, our high priest, into a place where we stand before the throne of grace and discover what it means to enter into the presence of God. It takes us back to the beginning of time in the presence of the one who spoke the world, and forward into eternity and the place he has prepared for us in a new heaven and a new earth.[16]

The journey upward begins here. For Amy, aged twenty-two and working with orphans in Uganda, surrounded by nightly gunfire, by deaths and funerals and rabid dogs, it meant throwing herself on the Lord to whom she'd given her life, alone, in a little Methodist chapel ten years earlier. She wrote home: 'The Lord flows in my veins – I can feel his love spreading into my very fingertips, into the core of my soul, and into my sight, so that I may see as he sees. Awesome feelings; the power within, the power upholding you and surrounding you is so real, so true – it is a living part of you, and yet it is so much greater than you. God is with me so massively, it's scary.' She finished the letter with a question: 'Why didn't you tell me he was like this?' Amy went on to work with World Vision, managing their relief operation in Banda Aceh; she is I think one of the most fearless people I have ever met – for Amy knows what it is to stand before God in a place of utter vulnerability.

Finally, our journey is directed outwards; it's a journey towards other people. "Go, and make disciples of all nations," Jesus said, adding, according to John: "As the Father has sent me, so I send you." We may be sent to the people next door or we may be sent to the other side of the world, but what is sure and certain is that we are sent, equipped by the Holy Spirit whom Jesus breathed on those first disciples as he commissioned them for ministry, and which they in turn passed on to others.[17] There would be no more puzzling conversations about fasting or sabbaths, no masterclasses in casting out particularly resistant evil spirits, no incomprehensible trips up mountains or nights spent in gardens, no surreal stories, no disappearing and reappearing tricks. From now on they would find their resources within themselves, in the person of the Holy Spirit, who would continue to apprentice them as Jesus had apprenticed them. And if the fruit of the Spirit characterises our journey inwards, so we find that the gifts of the Spirit characterise our journey outwards. For us, this is the primary way in which our discipleship impacts the lives of others; to return to John Wimber's analogy, it's how we move from being people who read the menu to people who enjoy eating the meal. It's been said that instead of asking ourselves whether we believe or not, we should ask each day whether we have done just one thing because Jesus told us to do it – for it is absurd to say we believe, or even want to believe, if we do not do anything he tells us to do.[18] Authentic discipleship is not just about what goes on in our heads; it's about what goes on in our lives; and that means, as it meant for Jesus, engaging with people.

The journey outwards can be every bit as dramatic today as it was for Paul. In 2003 Carl Medearis found himself with a group of six Lebanese Christian friends in Basra, in Iraq. "What are you doing here?" they were asked. "Well," they said, "we are followers of Jesus, and we are looking for him. He always seemed to be in places the religious leaders didn't expect to find him in, and ours don't expect to find him here – so we are looking for him; have you seen him?" This led to a surprise ninety-minute brainstorming session with a group of Muslim clerics on what Jesus would be doing if he were in Basra, and then to an offer of protection. In the months that followed, 25,000 copies of the New Testament were sold in the city, and many people gave their lives to Jesus in a remarkable process, which, somehow, never made it onto our television screens.[19]

Closer to home, a vicar in Dorset was pleasantly surprised to find his church growing, but unsure why. So he took a map of the village, and put a red pin in it for every established member of the church and a green pin for every new one. Finding that almost all the green pins were clustered around one particular red pin, he went to ask why. One by one they told their stories: "The car wouldn't start, and John came out to help me"; "the children were ill, and Sue offered to look after them while I was at work." The conversation always ended the same way: "and we knew they went to church."[20]

Lisa, Amy, Carl, John, and Sue are all on a journey, changing inwardly, connecting with God, moving in service outwards towards others. Ivan Illich, who said that we can change society only by telling an alternative story, points out that we have to *live* the changes we want to see – we cannot simply think them.[21] For us, this means doing what the first disciples did, and signing up as apprentices of Jesus, depending together on the Holy Spirit, and using the gifts which he makes available to us. This may mean Basra and it may mean Dorset; it may mean miracles and it may mean simple acts of kindness. We don't know and we won't know – until we start to follow Jesus and find out.

It seems then that the kind of learning we do as disciples is a travelling kind of learning. Being a disciple is about going somewhere. It's not really an alternative to not going anywhere, because life sweeps us up in its own agendas anyway. It's about intentionally going somewhere, choosing the narrow path rather than the broad one, following Jesus, finding our part in his story and inviting others to find theirs. And this, presumably, is why the first Christian disciples were known as followers of 'The Way'.[22]

The great spiritual writer William Law summed all these things up in the eighteenth century: 'Christianity is not a school for the teaching of moral virtue, the polishing of our manners, or forming us to live a life of this world with decency and gentility. It is deeper and more divine in its designs, and much nobler ends. It implies an entire change of life, a dedication of ourselves, our souls, our bodies unto God in the strictest and highest sense of the words.'[23]

Becoming part of God's story

One of the defining characteristics of our contemporary society is, as we saw in Part I, a loss of meaning. The solution, we suggested, lies in recovering a faith-based world view. We do not have to create our own story; it is open to us simply to find our part in God's story. And this is another way of thinking about what it means to be a follower of Jesus; we are words woven into the narrative of God's story. We begin to speak with power, the power of *dabar*. We become brothers and sisters of Jesus, the *logos* who created and sustains the world, joined to him on one vine and in one body. And together we are woven into sentences, sentences which carry the message, *rhema*, of the gospel itself. None of this is easy; as theologian Stanley Hauerwas remarked recently, "to be a Christian is to learn to live in a story you haven't chosen," and there's a clear cost to that.[24] But it's the only way to join in with reality, not reality as we might like it to be but reality as it actually is.

Sarah was a young fashion designer in Leicester, and she had been praying for the people of Greece since a childhood holiday there. One summer she joined a mission team to Brazil, where a woman she had never met prophesied that God was calling her to work in a big city in a country which she thought was called 'Greece'. Other prophecies followed, and eventually Sarah found herself in Athens, where she now works with Hellenic Ministries distributing Bibles and planning evangelistic outreaches all over the country. Sarah's life today is not the one she planned; but she is convinced it is the one God intended.[25]

Martin was a partner in a firm of solicitors. He writes: 'About 16 years ago I was completing my daily reading when a verse, Genesis 26.18, leapt off the page at me in a way I had never experienced before: "Isaac reopened the wells that had been dug in the time of his father Abraham, which the Philistines had stopped up." All I could see in that moment was the churches across Britain, including 16,000 Anglican ones; and all I could feel was the intense conviction that God wanted to remake them all as the provision of living water for his people. I understood in that second what it was I was called to in my work then with Springboard and since with ReSource. Confirming words and pictures followed – but the foundation was that vision from God's written Word, living and active.'[26]

If we are not willing to listen to God in this way, we may miss out on our own future, and God will have to write his story in other ways. But if we do learn to listen to him, we will find that our lives will become unique words spoken by him. Mary Jo Leddy puts it well: 'I believe that each one of us has at least one significant word to say with our lives. This word is who we really are, who we are meant to become, our calling in this world. Within this word lies the secret of our happiness, the source of our power, and the mysterious point of our being. Through this particular word of our lives we bring the one thing still wanted and awaited in the world, the one thing necessary that no other can give.'[27] When we hear and become this word, we find our part in God's story, however large or small, spectacular or ordinary it may be. In hearing his voice, we find ours.

Depending on each other

Becoming a disciple of Jesus is about going on a journey, or finding our part in a sentence. How does it come about, and how do we get started? Often I think we assume either that it happens by some kind of spiritual magic, or that it's a nice idea but in practice unrealistic. In fact true discipleship becomes possible only as leaders make space for people to grow in – and not any kind of space, but relational space, for we have a relational faith. It happens as individuals become part of a community of people willing to travel together to places defined by Jesus. And this means that we must recreate, in our church fellowships, places where people can together become apprentices of Jesus, study his word, rely on his Spirit, listen to his voice, and learn to do the things that he did – things which will actually make a difference not just to the lives of those concerned but also to the lives of others. No one can do this stuff alone. If we are serious about our responsibility to present the gospel to the people of this country we must realise, as Bishop Graham Cray has said, that the very core of our calling is to be a disciple-making community; we must begin to cultivate 'open, authentic, learning and praying communities focussed on making whole-life disciples who live and share the gospel wherever they relate to people in their daily lives.'[28] It is difficult to see how that can be done other than through relationships, through helping people to make the transition from being passive consumers of Sunday services to becoming active members of a community committed to travelling inwards, upwards and outwards. It's long been recognised that we need process evangelism; I suggest that we also need process discipleship. We know it works in Africa; it is time to do it here, to unshrink our classroom conception of discipleship and realise that it is not an attendance record or a syllabus but a whole new approach to life. Anything less and we sell the whole gospel short.[29]

Good news for Martin

Martin Mlaka is the eighth of eleven children, born in Malawi into a family of refugees from Mozambique. Money was short, and Martin was taken out of school to look after the family's goats and sheep so that his siblings could continue their education. Martin had no shoes and only one set of clothes, and he lived on what he could find in the bush; if he lost an animal he was beaten and sent out to find it, even if that meant searching overnight while lions and hyenas prowled. Martin was a diligent shepherd, and gradually he built up the flock from twenty-two animals to 400. But, to his dismay and despair, when his brothers and sisters completed their education they sold the flock, scorning their peasant brother and leaving him to fend for himself. Martin took a job as a messenger boy at a computer company in Blantyre. There he gave his life to Christ, discovered with joy that his name 'Mlaka' means 'victory', and set himself a course of home study. Martin began to grow into the space opened up to him by Jesus. Others noticed his faith, confidence, and ability, and in 2002, by now a successful computer engineer, Martin was invited to become head of evangelism in the diocese of Southern Malawi. I first met him when he invited us to introduce the *Rooted in Jesus* discipleship programme to the diocese. 'It is my desire to make the diocese of Southern Malawi a model of Christ's ministry,' he wrote.

Martin knows what it is to travel with Jesus, to leave behind what is past and to strain for what is ahead. He has learned what it is to serve, to suffer, and to forgive. He has discovered the need to depend on God and the pain that comes from not being able to depend on others. And all these things fuel his determination to help people become disciples of Jesus. Martin is now studying for ordination in Nairobi.[30]

For reflection and discussion

JOURNEY

In a village by the sea, with painted beach huts
I stood and waited, not knowing who would come, or why.
The village was my childhood, and the sun rose high
over the marshes. Harriers hunted, a bittern boomed,
fishing nets and glass floats decked the church
where the future unfurled its misty wings.
I left the sea behind and travelled overland;
libraries bestowed degrees, and marriage children
the passing of the years, maturity
but as I return to walk along the pebbled shore
a carnelian glows amongst the other stones
never previously noticed, but gathered now as mine.
The sea ebbs and flows, unfolds my life's design.

ALISON MORGAN

What is your life's design?

'We must become holy not because we want to feel holy but because Christ must be able to live his life fully in us' – Mother Teresa.[31] How do you respond to that thought?

'For the follower of Jesus, discipleship is not the first step toward a promising career. It is in itself the fulfilment of his or her destiny' – Alan Hirsch.[32] Do our church programmes help people to fulfil their destiny, or do we sometimes settle for just helping them to live comfortably within the parameters set for them by a secular society?

'Following Jesus is a unique way of life. It is like nothing else.

There is nothing and no one comparable. Following Jesus gets us little or nothing of what we commonly think we need or want or hope for. Following Jesus accomplishes nothing on the world's agenda. Following Jesus takes us right out of this world's assumptions and goes to a place where a lever can be inserted that turns the world upside down and inside out. Following Jesus has everything to do with this world, but almost nothing in common with the world' – Eugene Peterson.[33] What is your own experience of following Jesus? Do you think we can do it alone?

Read Matthew 28.18–20 again, and then 2 Timothy 2.2, and reflect on their implications for the church today.

Chapter 13

Reimagining Church

Do not remember the former things, or consider the things of old. I am about to do a new thing; now it springs forth, do you not perceive it?

Isaiah 43.18–19

We are coming to the end of our journey. We have a confident gospel. We have the spiritual resources we need to help us share it. And we have the capacity to become people who individually and together are learning to live beautiful lives. And so we come now to the final question: what does all of that mean in practice when we think about church?

Examining assumptions

I often reflect on how easily things can get lost in translation. We have looked at our tendency to shrink words and concepts, and we have seen how this affects the way we think about everything from scripture to discipleship. Now it is time to come full circle and to end where we began: with the Church. How can we welcome more people into it, is the usual question. But there's a prior question: what is it? What do we actually mean by this word 'church'? If we can't answer that question convincingly and attractively we will by default continue to muddle onwards into yesterday. It is time, in other words, to re-examine our ecclesiology.[1]

It is my privilege to meet each year with groups of African church leaders, and to look together at our assumptions about the nature of church. For many of us, church is a building. First modelled centuries ago on Roman temples and basilicas, and built all over the world since then in wood, brick, and stone, a church is a large indoor space where we can meet together to worship God. But this cannot be right, for whereas we do find the word 'church' in the New Testament, we also know that the first dedicated church buildings were not put up until the third century, after (and not before) two centuries of spectacular numerical growth. Before that Christians met in people's homes. So it's not the building.[2]

For others, church is an institution; we talk in this country about the established Church, about the Methodist Church, the Roman Catholic Church. Institutions have leaders and representatives, boards and committees, financial and administrative structures, and so inevitably do our major denominations. And yet it cannot be quite right to think of the Church as an institution either, and certainly not right to model it on the secular institutions which dominate our lives, for both the Old Testament word *qahal* and its New Testament translation *ecclesia* refer not to an organisation but to people – in particular, to a group of people who have been 'summoned' or 'called out'. A church, it seems, is a gathering or assembly of people who move from where they are in order to meet together with God. The English word 'church' carries this meaning even more clearly: nothing to do with the beautiful medieval buildings which still dominate our villages, it derives from the

Greek *kurios*, or 'Lord'. Verbal archaeology can lead to some surprising discoveries: church is not about our structures but about our focus.[3]

These are the most common misunderstandings of the word church. But there are others too which we play with as we toss things about in Africa, and they are usually less conscious. For many, church is a classroom; a place where the faithful gather to be led and taught by an appointed and authorised minister. Sometimes this classroom view of the church extends beyond Sundays, as we have seen, and affects our whole understanding of Christian discipleship. For the appointed and authorised minister – and here usually comes a laugh of recognition – a church is often more like a bus full of people, and the task of the minister is the rather lonely and tiring one of driving them safely to their eternal destination: lonely because somehow the driver gets left out of the jokes, and tiring because he's doing nearly all the work.

At this point I usually offer a simple suggestion. We each live in a house. If there are two or three together, we just call them houses. But if there are many houses, we call them a village – village is the plural of house. Similarly, each one of us is a disciple or apprentice of Jesus. If there are two or three of us together, we are disciples. But if there are many, we call ourselves a church – church is the plural of disciple. Like God himself, a church is an association of relationships between people who are united under the headship of Christ, filled and supported by the Holy Spirit, and held in the love of the Father. One person stepping out to follow Jesus becomes a disciple; a lot of people stepping out to follow Jesus become a church. Church, said Paul Tillich, is simply and primarily a group of people who express a new reality by which they have been grasped. It is not an institution or a building; it's people – people who are growing and changing into the likeness of Christ.[4]

Now of course we know these things; but we don't always live as if we do. The English character and way of doing things has been formed cautiously, conservatively; it has been said that we have a natural preference for slow evolutionary change, measured, discussed, and weighted with checks and balances.[5] This approach has stood us in good stead: the medieval monarchy, the Elizabethan Navy, the Victorian empire brought us in a slow and steady crescendo through the centuries to our present niche as a nation that has, in shaping a place for itself, left its mark upon the world. The difficulty is that the world is an increasingly complex and interactive place, and change is now being poured into the global melting pot at a speed we aren't always equipped to deal with. We live in a time of unprecedented cultural change; and unless we consciously examine what we are doing we are likely to find ourselves stranded in something of a historical backwater.[6] People are still interested in God – think of Sharon and Matthew in Nottingham – but Sally Gaze sums up their predicament: 'For many people the idea of going to a medieval building to sing to an organ, read some prayers and listen to a talk based on the text of an ancient book does not appear as if it would help them discover the meaning of the universe, never mind have any bearing on everyday struggles with work, debts, addictions or relationships.'[7]

If we think of church as a building it is a short step to thinking about faith as participation in a church service. Again, the outlook is not good. If Christian faith is measured by passive attendance at a carefully crafted religious performance, it is no different from attendance at any other kind of performance, and it certainly bears little relationship to the kind of active apprenticeship-in-community offered by Jesus to his followers.[8] What worked beautifully as the collective yearning for God expressed by a tight-knit rural community as they gathered together each week for worship makes an inadequate vehicle for faith in a scattered suburb of people who do not know one another – it certainly passes the time, but it actually *prevents* relationships, and it keeps Sunday not so much special as separate from the reality of Monday to Friday. Dallas Willard comments: 'we must flatly say that one of the greatest contemporary barriers to meaningful spiritual formation into Christlikeness is overconfidence in the spiritual efficacy of "regular church services". They are vital, they are not enough, it is that simple.'[9]

The solution, of course, is not to knock down our beautiful buildings or to cancel our services. It is simply to do what we are already in many places doing, and think more deeply about who we are, why we meet, and where we are going. We need to recognise that the buildings and the services are not the destination, not what church is all about, but simply a part of the journey – which is why relocating the service to the pub, or reviving the liturgy with the kaleidoscopic magic of modern technology, is not in itself the answer. John Drane puts it like this: 'To continue as we are may be comfortable, but could also be institutionally suicidal. Our options are simple. We either do nothing, and the decline continues, or we ask fundamental questions about how faithful discipleship might be incarnationally embedded in the culture, and take whatever steps may be necessary to re-imagine church life.'[10] It's all a perfect illustration of the paradox that we must change in order to stay the same.

Examining expectations

I have just returned from a family holiday in Southwold, a place I have known and loved since childhood. When I was little we would stay in an old semi owned by a friend of my grandmother, and from this little black and white house we would sally forth to explore the Suffolk coast. Beaten day and night by the roaring sea, it was, and still is, the fastest eroding coastline in the world, and I would marvel as I watched the fragile landscape change with the passing years. Over the centuries whole towns have come and gone here; but even within my lifetime I've seen the road drip gently off the edge of the cliff, the wartime pill box recede into the sea, new salt lagoons form behind the shifting shingle and inland pines march onto the beach. As the cliffs crumble, the teeth of sabre-toothed tigers emerge onto the sand, and rare birds colonise a habitat which is endlessly dying and being reborn.

Just up the coast, above the crumbling cliffs, stands the village of Covehithe. Once a thriving town, it is now a hamlet with fewer than twenty inhabitants. It has an unusual church. Built in the heyday of the medieval wool trade to cathedral proportions, it became, as the sea encroached and the community shrank, too large and costly to maintain. So the local people decided to downsize. In the year 1672 they took off the roof and built a smaller structure within its walls. The trim little thatched church still nestles beside its monumental tower, the original walls rising jagged in the mist around it like a vast stone shell. Creeping ever closer to the cliff edge, it has about fifty years to go before it too merges with the sea.

Covehithe is unusual in that the decline of the church is measured in stone; but perhaps it offers a salutary warning.

It is tempting to respond to decline by downsizing – not just our buildings but our expectations, our hopes and dreams. As we saw at the beginning of this book, decline is real, and it is discouraging. But the good news is that it is not inevitable. During the 1980s and 90s, generally recognised as a time of considerable reduction in church attendance, it turns out that 1.6 million people actually joined a church. In the 1990s, 22% of all UK churches grew by 10% or more, and 7% of Anglican churches grew by over 60%. This growth has continued: over the two-year period 2004–2006, fourteen out of the Church of England's forty-four dioceses registered an increase in all-age weekly attendance – a trend which has marked every year of the first decade of the new century. Midweek, cathedral, Christmas, and Easter attendance is rising steadily, as are the numbers of children under the age of sixteen.[11] And the official figures do not take account of the many 'fresh expressions' or experimental forms of church established primarily for the benefit of those who are not connected with any existing church, or come to that of the million Christians who have left the institutional church but continue actively to express their faith. Nor do the statistics measure the level of interest in the gospel among those who do not regularly attend church: 2.5 million people across the country have completed Alpha courses over the last seventeen years, many finding faith for the first time, and each Christmas 35% of the population choose to come to a church service of some kind.[12] So while it is clear that the overall decline continues, it is equally clear that there is no universal factor preventing growth; indeed, it seems that there are signs of growth wherever we look. All the evidence suggests that decline is optional.

Doing things differently

We saw in Chapter 7 that our first response in a changing cultural context must be to train ourselves to think in new ways. Common sense would suggest that if we do that we should naturally also find ourselves acting in new ways. What might they be? It is worth reminding ourselves of Ken Blanchard's story about the response of children making sandcastles on the beach and faced with a rising tide: one group built a new and improved sandcastle higher up the beach, and the other came up with a whole new way of playing the game. Which is better, Blanchard asks, to improve what is, or to create what isn't? The answer, he says, is 'Yes!'[13] We would do well to heed his advice as we think about the church. The task is not to preserve our buildings, keep our service patterns going and downsize our expectations, however tempting it may be to embrace such modest goals. The task is much bigger than that. If we are prepared to think creatively about what a church is and what it's for, we will find that God is indeed, as Isaiah foresaw, able to do new things. Some of those new things will be radically new expressions of faith among currently unreached groups of people – in Blanchard's terms, creating what isn't. Others will involve the renewal and revitalisation of what is already there – improving what is.[14] It's happening already – a cursory glance at our churches today shows that there are innovative projects going on all over the country which aim to meet the spiritual needs of people who would not dream of walking through a lychgate; but that there are also uncomplicated local initiatives which welcome back those who have simply got out of the habit.[15] There are creative new resource materials which help explain the Christian faith in culturally relevant ways to those who have never heard it; there are also many straightforward acts of community service performed by local churches.[16] Let's look at some stories from around the UK, and then consider what they tell us about what the church is and what it's for.

Creating what isn't

A few years ago, a hotel developer offered a little Methodist congregation of seven elderly people £3.5m for its chapel by the sea. They prayed, and turned the offer down; "God's got bigger ideas than that," they said. Reflecting on the church's history of beach missions, they raised some money and appointed a couple of young leaders, Henry Cavender and Kris Lannen. Henry and Kris refitted the building and opened it not just as a church but also as a surf centre, with the aim of reaching out to the local community. As the website says, 'Tubestation is about serving the community and presenting the Gospel in unforced, creative, culturally relevant, down-to-earth practical ways. The project has created an environment where faith can be caught as well as taught.' It's going well. They have Café nights with Bible study, Christian surfers' Saturday mornings, and an annual Jesus Longboard Classic open competition which attracts people from far and wide. From the original seven members, all still there, they have built up to a regular congregation of sixty, and in the summer it's standing room only. They do some unusual things – they baptise those who come to faith in the Atlantic Ocean, and they hold night prayer meetings standing chest deep in the sea, wearing wetsuits and carrying flaming torches – a nice reminder of the seventh-century saint Cuthbert's habit of praying at night immersed in the ocean. Encouraged by the

Methodist Church, Tubestation is now planning to plant new churches all round Cornwall.[17]

In 2003, a Church Army evangelist named Andy Milne picked up his skateboard in Bradford and began to talk to kids in the local park. As he began to build relationships with young people in an area of social deprivation, Andy found himself creating a Christian youth community centred on a Portakabin in the grounds of the local secondary school. Working now with some fifty-five young people aged eleven to seventeen in a ministry they call 'Sorted', Andy's aim is to help them find faith, gain self-respect, and become leaders for their peer group. 'Sorted' runs evenings of prayer, discussion, Bible study, and practical activities, and Andy has formed partnerships with local schools and with the city council. "I was a mess on the streets," says one teenager; "I've now realised what I want to do in life." "People seem to think religion is just about going to church, but it's a lot more than that – it's about having fun," says another. Andy himself remarks that he is "often the only Bible that some of these young people will ever read."[18]

The need to create what isn't is perhaps most acute amongst young people, who are particularly unlikely to feel at home in a traditional Sunday service. But the same need is there among other groups too. Happy participation in mother and toddler activities run by the local church led seven young mums from four Norfolk villages to join a Christian basics course. Five of them made a commitment to follow Jesus. Only one, however, felt she could join a local Sunday congregation. They gave different reasons – the pressure to keep the children quiet during the service, the embarrassment of not knowing the hymns or 'what to do when you do that thing up at the altar,' the clash with the needs of the family on a Sunday. The vicar,

Sally, formed them into a daytime cell group. They began to reach out to their own network of young parents, and started an informal afternoon service they called '4All.' Soon they were welcoming thirty to fifty participants, many of whom had not previously attended any church. With other youth and post-Alpha adult cells, they now form a new cell church within a traditional rural benefice.[19]

Improving what is

Sometimes the very creativity of these initiatives can discourage members of small, ordinary churches who feel they could never do anything like that. One of the most helpful writers on this topic is Bob Jackson, a down-to-earth Yorkshireman who has conducted years of painstaking statistical research into church growth. Bob's catchphrase is 'It's not rocket science.' He concludes that it doesn't seem to matter what you do to make your church grow, as long as you do *something*. Churches which change their service styles and patterns grow. Churches which employ a youth worker grow. Churches which cater for different people groups grow. Churches which run nurture courses grow. Churches whose leaders get together to talk about growth grow. Churches which have small groups grow; churches which evaluate what they are doing grow; churches which develop lay leaders grow. My favourite story comes from a church anxious to spare no expense in its desire to reach out more effectively to the community. They invited Bob to come as a consultant. Bob came, and carefully reviewed everything they were doing. "What do we need to do in order to grow?" they asked nervously as he prepared his conclusion. "Just one thing, really," said Bob. "You need to put in a toilet."[20]

The age profile of this country is rising, and yet many older people have never had any meaningful contact with Jesus. One church in Lincolnshire had been declining for many years, and the diocese appointed a new part-time vicar, telling her they had no expectation of change; her brief was simply to care for the remaining members until the time came for the church to close. She found that although the church was open for only four services a year (Mothering Sunday, Easter, Harvest, and Christmas – Pentecost was thought 'too obscure' to have any appeal), there were three home communions. Disabled herself, she suggested to each of these people that they might like to invite their friends. Within a few months she had a congregation of forty-five people meeting regularly in these three homes, growing in their relationship with one another and with God.

How about run-down town churches, is there any future for those? St Michael and all Angels is located on a roundabout in Middlewich. With no facilities and no families, it was living on its investments. Ian, its new vicar, found that there were people within the congregation longing to see growth. They began a new family service and started to run Alpha courses and then build cell groups where people could together deepen the faith they had found. Then they held a parish renewal weekend to which over 100 people came, and which proved to be a turning point. 'The Holy Spirit is loitering with intent,' the weekend facilitator wrote afterwards. Attendance and income began to grow. St Michael's appointed a youth worker, bought the shop over the road and converted it into a venue for children's work and community activities. A few years on, the heating pipes still leak, but the congregation has doubled, and Ian is left musing on Ezekiel's description of the river in the desert, bringing life where none seemed possible.[21]

Why do all these things work? Because people are not looking for something super duper from us. The adventure is not one we ourselves have to create, it's one which has been going for centuries; our role is simply to invite people to join in. People are looking for God, and God is looking for them, and our part is to welcome them into the community of those who are already following him. In so far as there is a human factor, Bob Jackson observes, it's not the sophistication of our resources but the quality of our relationships which counts. It turns out in fact that there is only one constant feature of every growing church, and it's not expertise but joy and laughter.[22]

Those are just a few stories, but there are many, many others, stories both of innovation and of renewal. Reordering the church building in Marks Tey, Colchester, made it possible for children to join holiday clubs, for hospitality to be offered through shared meals, for concerts and exhibitions to be held and Alpha courses to be hosted; 'a building which used to look backwards has become a mission statement,' Richard, its rector, wrote. In Newcastle, going out of the church altogether to take part with Christians from other denominations in a Healing on the Streets programme has enabled many who would never think of venturing inside a church building not just to receive healing but to make a commitment to Jesus; fascinated teenagers, many unexpectedly healed of skateboard injuries, stand around and photograph the proceedings on their mobile phones. Sending a team into a local school in Leicester to pick up litter, run revision courses and support children close to exclusion led to a growing afterschool club in which one afternoon half the kids present said they'd like to follow Jesus; the sending church now has 200 members under the age of eighteen and is having to rent additional premises to cater for them – and the headteacher was so bemused by the litter-picking that she joined an Alpha course in order to find out what made these Christians tick.[23] There are many ways forward: there are community centre churches, post office churches, virtual churches, soup kitchen churches, student churches, café churches, school churches, surf churches, network churches – the list is as varied as the types of people involved and the places in which they meet.

So, what *is* a church?

The problem with stories such as the ones above is that although they are encouraging, they are not necessarily transferable. We like blueprints, and the history of the church in recent times is littered with them, often uncritically embraced in the hope that what worked there will work here. Alas, usually it is not so. Perhaps growing a church is more like making a cake than following a blueprint: there are some shared and essential elements – the baking agent which makes the cake rise, the heat which binds the ingredients together – but once we've got those right we can use all sorts of different ingredients and produce cakes which are uniquely shaped for particular occasions.

What then are the essential characteristics of an authentic church? I suggest there are four, all of which we have already touched on.

First of all, a church is a group of people who have responded to the call to follow Jesus: people who are learning to do the things which he did, using the tools which he makes available, and in the process becoming more like him. Secondly, a church is a group of people who have committed themselves to doing that together; church is not just about individual apprenticeship to Jesus but about apprenticeship in community. Thirdly, a church is a group of people who are outwardly focussed, who have a purpose bigger than themselves – for Jesus does not just call disciples, he also sends them. And fourthly, a church is a community living in daily dependence upon the Holy Spirit, discerning the needs of its context and allowing its mission and ministry to be shaped accordingly.

1. A community centred on Jesus

> *"For where two or three are gathered in my name, I am there among them."*

Matthew 18.20

Usually, Bob Jackson remarks, it is Jesus who attracts people and the church that puts them off.[24] Our primary preoccupation should not be the Church, which is after all a transitional body, an outpost of the kingdom for travellers on the way, but Jesus. And yet so often we focus our attention not on Jesus but on ourselves; 'we have reduced the gospel message so that it is inseparable from the institution of church,' Neil Cole laments.[25] This is a shame – because we live in an increasingly anti-institutional age. To put it another way, it's the product, not the packaging, which should command our attention.[26]

Twenty years ago Martin Down, vicar of two Norfolk villages, was touched by the Holy Spirit. He formed no plans, developed no strategies, but simply began to try and do each day what he thought Jesus was telling him to do. A church member was healed in her electrical shop as he prayed with her; people began to come forward to repent of their sins and to receive the Holy Spirit during services; small changes began to be made in the way they did things. Slowly, unspectacularly, Martin noticed a gradual shift in people's focus: they began to talk about Jesus instead of about the church. He comments: 'the problem ... arises when the attention of people and their worship is focused on the church and its services and not on God himself. It is always discernible in people's conversation... Do they talk about the services or about the Lord?'[27] If we are not focusing primarily on Jesus as a living, present reality, then we are not a church; if we are, then we are learning to play our part in the most exciting story on earth.

Christian discipleship begins with a simple decision to follow Jesus. Our primary task is to become effective disciples of Jesus, apprentices who grow and change so that, in becoming more like him, we find ourselves living confident and beautiful lives. A church is first and foremost a group of people who are doing this together.

2. A united community

> As in one body we have many members, and not all
> the members have the same function, so we, who are
> many, are one body in Christ, and individually we are
> members one of another.

Romans 12.4–6

We saw in Chapter 4 that one of the greatest problems in contemporary Western society is a loss of community, leading to increasing personal isolation and an endemic sense of loneliness. 'No man is an island,' wrote poet John Donne in the seventeenth century; for us, who live in a society which all too often assumes just the opposite, this is a hard thing to take on board – and yet it is at the heart of the Christian message. As fellow apprentices of Jesus we are, as Paul stressed repeatedly to the jostling personalities of the first Christian churches, joined together as surely and irrevocably as the parts of our own bodies: Christian discipleship is not a career choice but a decision to become part of the body of Christ. A Christian is a member of a community centred on Jesus, living in mutual dependence and love and making an individual contribution to the life of the whole. To see ourselves otherwise is to become a disconnected limb, a lone organ, handicapped and disabled in our Christian lives – or, to revert to an earlier metaphor, to find that we are not so much sentences woven into God's story as isolated words written in the middle of a blank page.[28] When, on the other hand, we succeed in sharing our lives as Jesus intended us to, we offer a unique model: one which guarantees personal fulfilment and yet also provides the security that comes from knowing that we belong. It's one of the most remarkable gifts we have to offer to our broken world – our world where, as Nigerian journalist Suni Umar noticed, people no longer greet each other. It is indeed good news.

And yet it is not simply about belonging. The biblical image of the Church as a body is particularly instructive when it comes to the question of our calling, for bodies not only exist, they do things; and if the existing offers an answer to our need for belonging, it is the doing which offers an answer to our need for fulfilment. The body of Christ does all the things that Christ himself did; it is not passive but active. This is a lesson that was learned by a church in Little Rock, Arkansas which, although taking its internal life seriously, was in fact not doing many of the things which Jesus did. From the outside it appeared that all was well. Teaching and worship were of the highest standard, and every church member was offered the chance to be part of a small group, in the conviction that spiritual growth takes place in the context of honest, loving relationships. But something wasn't quite right, and in 1989 the church reached a crisis point. The church leaders decided to survey the membership through a questionnaire. Its pastor, Robert Lewis, tells the story: 'The results were stunning. We discovered that after four to five years of involvement in the small group ministry that is central to our church, people began to feel unchallenged and stifled. Their excitement about church dramatically declined. They had always been told that they were to be "equipped," but the data raised a greater question: "Equipped *for what*?"'[29] The church discovered that it is not enough to build community; it is necessary for that community to be *about* something – it has to have a purpose bigger than itself.

The discovery that community is not an end in itself but rather the means to an end is a key one. Jesus did not invite his disciples to form a comfortable group of friends who could go fishing or watch television together, or even who could invite others to join them as they did these things. He invited them to follow him, to move out of their comfort zones and learn how to proclaim the good news of the kingdom of God. He said that on the one hand this would mean caring for the hungry, the thirsty, the stranger, and the destitute, and that on the other it would involve learning to heal the sick, raise the dead, cleanse lepers, and cast out demons. And it wouldn't end there; their task would then be to find others and teach them to do the same.[30]

The church in Little Rock set about the first of these imperatives, finding ways to serve needy groups within their city. Many churches here now do the same: one of the best known initiatives was 'HOPE 08', which saw 1,500 churches reaching out in practical ways to their communities, often working in partnership with local government, police, and media organisations, under the strapline 'Do more, do it together, do it in word and action.' An independent report by Theos found that over 80% of those involved felt the initiative had inspired their congregations, nearly 60% said that overt evangelism in words had increased as a result of the practical engagement with the community, and nearly 50% said their churches now pray more. The report concludes: 'A new model of mission seems to have emerged across the UK in recent years combining words and actions, being good news as well as proclaiming good news. HOPE 08 has been an important champion of this change.'[31]

Paul wrote to the Christians in Rome, Corinth and Ephesus about the spiritual gifts which would empower them to proclaim good news, heal the sick and cast out demons. In 1990, after seven years of prayer and seeking the will of God, Damian Stayne founded a small Roman Catholic community in Chertsey, Surrey, of people who would live together with the twin aim of building up a common life of prayer and worship, and reaching out in mission to others using the charismatic gifts which characterise the body of Christ. Known as the Cor et Lumen Christi, members of the community live according to a Rule and share a common life of prayer centred around the Blessed Sacrament and the daily Divine Office of the church. Uniquely, they combine this with leading Catholic Miracle Rallies and Signs and Wonders conferences both in this country and abroad; in the last three years over 20,000 people have given public witness to having received physical healing through the ministry of the community. Cor et Lumen Christi is a united community; but it is also a community with a purpose.[32]

Jesus was a man with a purpose too, and we, called together to be part of his body, are intended to be the people through whom he continues to pursue that purpose. Michael Frost suggests that the difference between the kind of dynamic, purposeful community which Jesus had in mind and the comfortable, static group we often settle for is so great that we really need different words to describe them. Drawing on the work of anthropologist Victor Turner, he proposes that we distinguish between 'community' and 'communitas', or community-with-a-purpose. It is good to build community; but it is only in discovering a shared purpose that a community comes to life. To attend regular church services, to belong to a supportive home group or good youth group – or indeed to any Christian group which has no aim beyond itself – is belonging for the sake of belonging.[33] It's essentially static. It may help us to stay sane, but it won't play any great part in shaping the future, and it's not likely to inspire others to follow Jesus. 'A church,' writes Robert Lewis, is 'a community of people who present living proof of a loving God to a watching world.'[34]

3. A missional community

"As the Father has sent me, so I send you."

John 20.21

Mark Russell, of the Church Army, is passionate about evangelism. Speaking at the Rochester Diocesan Conference in 2009, Mark told how as a new youth worker he suggested to his vicar that he show him around the town. As they walked together up the high street they passed the betting shop. "Let's go in," suggested Mark. "I couldn't do that!", gasped the vicar. "Someone might see us go in! Someone might see us come out! And I haven't the faintest idea what goes on in there!" That,

Mark pointed out, is exactly how most people feel about the local church. Welcoming though we may be, we cannot welcome those who are afraid to step through the door; something more is required of us.

Over the last hundred years or so, many parts of the Western church have been touched by a spiritual renewal which has brought fresh dependence on the presence and gifts of the Spirit. It has been exciting to rediscover the healing ministry, to learn to minister to one another prophetically, to pray and praise God in the tongues of angels. But as time has gone on, many have begun to wonder what this renewal was actually for – what *is* renewal, one theological college lecturer mused, when renewal isn't new? Like a top spinning faster and faster and then slowly running down, many 'charismatic' churches have lost their momentum – "we've discovered our gifts, yes, but that was a while ago now, surely it's time to move on?" The key to the dilemma is found in John's account of the evening of Jesus' resurrection. Appearing before the disciples, Jesus first invited them to receive the Holy Spirit, and then told them why: "As the Father has sent me, so I send you." The Holy Spirit is given to us so that we may continue the work of Jesus; renewal is for mission. Mission is not an add-on, it is part of our identity. Mission is not something which we do – it is who we are. First equipped, we are then sent.

To whom then are we sent? When Jesus told the disciples that their task was to go and make disciples of all nations, he actually used the word *ethne*, or 'people groups'. Our word 'nation' tends to have political overtones; a nation for us is a people living within a defined geographical unit, and so we have often assumed that to take the gospel to 'all nations' means that we must travel overseas and offer the good news about Jesus to those who live under other governments and within other geographical units. In fact the word nation simply comes from the Latin verb 'to be born'. The gospel must be offered to all those who have been born, to every people group within every country and every society – not just the 120 tribes of Tanzania but also the unemployed youth, wealthy bankers and senior citizens of England.[35]

As living parts of the body of Christ, our mission is his mission, defined as "to proclaim the good news of the kingdom of God."[36] Jesus demonstrated by his own ministry that this may be done through both word and deed. In recent years, as we saw in Chapter 6, different parts of the Church have learned to proclaim the good news in different ways – through acts of loving service, through verbal explanation, through exercising the gifts of the Spirit and through the celebration of the sacraments. Taking an overview, the Anglican Consultative Council has suggested that we engage effectively in mission not just when we share the good news of the kingdom in words, but also when we make disciples, serve others, work for justice, or strive to safeguard creation. These are the 'five marks' of mission, and examples of all of them are to be found in this book.[37]

For most of us, mission starts as we learn to live as disciples of Jesus in the home, in the workplace and in the streets. For Stephen Oake, it meant expressing open allegiance to Jesus in his daily life as a Manchester police officer, in the face of frequent taunting by his colleagues who regarded his faith as a sign of weakness: "Why do you need a crutch?" they would ask. "Can't you just be a man, like us?" It soon became apparent that it wasn't quite as simple as that. On 14 January 2003 Stephen was called to a flat in Crumpsall to arrest a man suspected of involvement in an illegal chemical weapons laboratory. The man had a knife; unarmed himself, Stephen deliberately placed his own body between the man and his colleagues and attempted to restrain him. Stabbed eight times through heart and lungs, he died at the scene. His colleagues not only nominated Stephen for a bravery award, they also asked the church to run Alpha courses in five local police stations.[38]

For John, working in the missile industry in the Midlands, his new faith meant not leaving his job (as he had at first thought) but remaining as the sole representative of Jesus within the company. By the time he left seven years later there were several Christians among the workforce, a daily shop floor prayer meeting and a weekly workers and management prayer meeting; and the management were planning to bring the company out of missile production altogether, which they subsequently did.[39]

Stephen and John were sent into difficult situations. Most of us are not; most of us are sent to share our faith in simple ways amongst our family, friends and neighbours. We do that not as isolated individuals but as part of the body of Christ; and it is in that, and not in our own talents, that our effectiveness lies. I think of a dustman in Manchester, ordained as a local minister. People on his round heard about it, and began, spontaneously, to leave prayer requests written on post-it notes attached to their dustbins. Or of a story told by John Drane, whose hairdresser, traumatised by her brother's suicide but who knew John belonged to the local church, asked him to teach her to pray – then and there, in the salon, while the staff gathered round to listen; and then went home to teach her children. Or of Warren, who went to church to make his peace with God before committing suicide; taken aback to find he'd known the minister, Matt, twenty years before when they were teenagers, he recommitted himself to Jesus instead. A few months later

Warren was in the post office when armed robbers burst in; he comforted a terrified fellow customer, Tracy, and a few weeks later Tracy also gave her life to Christ. She told her hairdresser all about it, and the hairdresser in turn came to faith.[40] The gospel can be most infectious when we least expect it.

What about children and teenagers? I think of Ed, aged seven, who lacked the words to share his faith with his friend David but invited him to the church holiday club, where David leapt at the chance to connect with Jesus, followed in the next few months by his mother, brother, and sister. I think too of Lisa, who once wondered how she could get an invitation to church, working now with young people in Syston, where a combination of litter-picking and street parties has encouraged some of those involved to try out the church youth activities; liking what they found, two teenagers recently gave their lives to Christ.[41] Or of our own experiment in Wells, where a small group of Christians has begun a monthly café evening for young people, based around muffins, games, video clips and discussion of common life issues; average attendance so far is about fifty, of whom four, plus fifteen of their friends, have already asked if we can help them find out about the Christian faith.[42]

It seems that Christian mission is just ordinary people, banded together in their determination to follow an extraordinary God, opening doors for their friends and neighbours. If we live as disciples of Jesus in our everyday circumstances, sharing our lives with one another and serving those around us, we are doing what Jesus asked us to do. We do not need to be highly trained or unusually articulate; we simply need the confidence to welcome others to join in with what we ourselves have discovered.

4. A community shaped and formed by the Holy Spirit

Come to him, a living stone, though rejected by mortals
yet chosen and precious in God's sight, and like living
stones, let yourselves be built into a spiritual house, to be
a holy priesthood, to offer spiritual sacrifices acceptable
to God through Jesus Christ.

1 Peter 2.4–5

Peter offers a beautiful, practical, and innovatory way of thinking about what it means to be a Christian. Individually, we are like living stones – stones which are of little use on their own, but which together can be built into a spiritual house where people can relate in new and immediate ways to God. For Peter's hearers, used to the stones of the temple and the ceremonies conducted by specialist priests, this was a radical redefinition of what it meant to have faith. Don't think building and services, Peter seemed to be saying – think people, and allow yourselves to be shaped by your identity in Christ and your calling in ministry.

If we are to minister effectively today, it seems that we must allow our mission and ministry to be shaped by our context and calling rather than by our traditions. This is harder than it seems – Steven Croft has written perceptively of the way in which as we move away from a simple understanding of church as building or institution we sometimes end up just substituting modern secular models for old religious ones. It is all too easy to fall into the trap of seeing the church as a chain of cinemas all showing the latest film, or a network of local franchises buying into the same centralised model of ministry, or a production unit narrowly focussed on a particular output, rather than as something formed and breathed by the Holy Spirit.[43] Perhaps it is not surprising that Peter should place so much emphasis on the Spirit: the church is and always has been a charismatic community, William Abraham has written.[44] The same must be true today; if we are going to count for anything in the world in which we now live, we must allow the presence of the Spirit within the gathered community of Christ to shape the way we do things.

When Paul first stepped outside the familiar religious environment of Jerusalem, he said that he would allow his ministry to be shaped by the nature of the community into which he was sent – he would be a Jew to Jews, a Greek to Greeks – he would in fact be whatever was needed in order to present the gospel accessibly to the people he was with. Throughout the Book of Acts we find ourselves watching the apostles debating which of their traditions were essential and which were merely reflections of their own cultural background, with God demanding repeatedly, often through the direct intervention of the Holy Spirit, that they step outside their religious comfort zones. It's an essential process of challenge and discernment which is familiar to every overseas missionary. It is also a process which we ourselves must increasingly embrace as we reach out to the different communities in our country today.[45]

We live in a diverse society in which there are many different people groups. Some of the differences are regional: people in Stoke do not see things the same way as people in Salisbury. Some are to do with the physical environment: people in high-rise estates do not experience life in the same way as people in rural communities. Some are to do with age profile: teenagers rarely have the same values or lifestyle as the retired. Some are to do with occupation: probation officers tend to have a different outlook from accountants. But increasingly the differences are to do with choice: bikers, city professionals, reiki specialists, clubbers, full-time mums, artisans, farmers – we live in a world where people define and express themselves in many different ways. In the Middle Ages, when our church buildings were put up and our service patterns created, it was not so; the world then was a much simpler one in which one community was much like another, and everybody knew their place within it. Today things are very different; and it seems obvious that different people groups will need and want to express their faith in different ways. It is no more appropriate to lure teenagers to sing hymns in pews than it is to persuade grannies to pray in wetsuits.

It seems, then, that we should be open to changing the way we do things as we shape ourselves to the contexts in which we are placed. It goes against the grain, when we have done things so consistently and for so long. But we should not be surprised. Not only do we live in a diverse society, we worship a God whose own self-expression is characterised by diversity. In the beginning when God created the heavens and the earth, the Spirit of God swept over the waters and the world came into being: mountains and seas, plants and birds and fish and animals and insects, and finally human beings. Filled with the breath of God, the earth became a living tapestry of astonishing variety: rugged mountain ranges, coastal marshes, sweeping estuaries and ancient forests. In each place different life forms arose, remarkable for their diversity: the huge number of different shades and shapes of leaves, the ten thousand different species of bird, the half million types of flower.

Jesus often taught by inviting us to look at the world around us – not just because it was what was there, but more profoundly because it tells us something about the nature of the God who made it. And observation of the world he made suggests that God does not delight in uniformity. How can we presume that the Spirit who created and presides over such variety would have us express ourselves in any other way? How would the Spirit have us worship, where would he have us meet, how would he encourage us to reach out to others? The answer, surely, is that it must depend on the context. Just as parrots won't roost in reedbeds and poppies won't grow in forests, so we must find different ways to help people follow Jesus. More than that, we must help them find their own ways to follow Jesus. We are called to live beautiful lives focussed on Jesus, to find our place as part of the body of Christ, and to be outward looking in all that we do and are. Other than that, there are no blueprints: our task is to follow Jesus through constant and active dependence on the Holy Spirit. This is what it means to find our place in his story – and so to find our true meaning.

Good news for the world...

'There is nothing like the local church when it's working right. Its beauty is indescribable. Its power is breathtaking. Its potential is unlimited. It comforts the grieving and heals the broken in the context of community. It builds bridges to seekers and offers truth to the confused. It provides resources for those in need and opens its arms to the forgotten, the downtrodden, the disillusioned. It breaks the chains of addictions, frees the oppressed, and offers belonging to the marginalized of this world. Whatever the capacity for human suffering, the church has a greater capacity for healing and wholeness. Still to this day, the potential of the local church is almost more than I can grasp. No other organization on earth is like the church. Nothing even comes close' – Bill Hybels.[46]

For reflection and discussion

ODE

We are the music makers,
And we are the dreamers of dreams,
Wandering by lone sea breakers,
And sitting by desolate streams:
World losers and world forsakers
On whom the pale moon gleams;
Yet we are the movers and shakers
Of the world forever it seems.

ARTHUR O'SHAUGHNESSY

What is your dream for your local church? Can you think of anything that has greater potential to change society?

If we see the Church as a community of people focussed on Jesus, sharing a common purpose and sent to proclaim the good news of the kingdom to others, we are in effect saying that it is not so much an institution as a movement. It follows that a sense of movement should be apparent not just to our members, but also to the outsider. Would it seem to a visitor that your church life is characterised by movement, or simply by repetition?

'The Church or something like it must be cherished, criticized, nourished and reformed. The Church of Jesus Christ, with all its blemishes, its divisions and its failures, remains our best hope of spiritual vitality. However poor it is, life without it is worse' – Elton Trueblood. Do you agree?

'Do not remember the former things, or consider the things of old. I am about to do a new thing; now it springs forth, do you not perceive it?' (Isaiah 43.19). Do you think that this is a word for our time, or just a voice from the past?

Appendix

Further resources

We have good news to share; it's still good, it's still new, and it seems people are still interested in it. We have the spiritual resources we need to offer it powerfully and effectively. We know we need to live and work together, and we have plenty of evidence that both traditional churches and fresh expressions of church can grow, irrespective of their size and setting. How, then, do we get going?

Books

Details of the many books cited are given in the bibliography, but here are some for starters:

- For challenge and inspiration, try Michael Frost and Alan Hirsch, *The Shaping of Things to Come*.

- For a no-nonsense analysis of the issues and opportunities facing the Church, try Bob Jackson, *Hope for the Church* and *The Road to Growth*.

- For ideas and good practice, try the *Mission-shaped* series published by CHP.

- For fresh vision of the task to which we are called, try Alison Morgan, *The Wild Gospel*.

Supported resource material

There are many resources and agencies which support churches and Christian groups who wish to grow. I work for ReSource, an independent charity with an Anglican distinctive, which works with local churches of all types and traditions, offering a unique combination of specific resource material and on the ground training and support. These are some of the materials we have developed in response to the needs which have been expressed to us. They are all available through our website, and we can provide support and training for those who wish to use them, through our dispersed team of practitioners.

Churches grow when people are passionate about their faith and committed to the task of sharing it. It doesn't really matter where you start, as long as you start somewhere. Here are some suggestions:

1. Becoming disciples of Jesus

Beyond Ourselves is the first book in a series which takes its inspiration from *Rooted in Jesus*, our practical discipleship course for Africa. It is a response to the increasingly voiced need for similar practical and relational discipleship material for this country – discipleship focussed not on what we know but on who we are becoming. This first book is designed for use with people who are exploring faith for the first time, or with those who wish to take a fresh look at what they believe. Written by a team of contributors, *Beyond Ourselves* is edited by Roger Morgan and Anita Benson. Books 2 and 3 will cover what it means to be part of a Christian community, and how to live as an infectious Christian from Monday to Friday.

- a ten-session course

- interactive and based on discussion (no talks)

- not dependent on the personal charisma of a leader

- based on key verses of scripture

- includes a course member's booklet with session summaries and creative practical exercises for use during the week

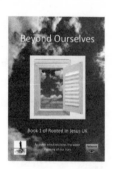

Decision: An explanation of what is involved in becoming a Christian, by Roger Morgan.

Decision is a short booklet designed for those who are thinking of making a step of commitment, and is ideal for use with Alpha or in the context of parish missions and outreach events. It includes illustrations and testimonies, and is being welcomed as the best resource for new Christians.

2. Living beautiful lives

Beautiful Lives is a group course by Roger Morgan, which helps church members develop the confidence to share their faith naturally and effectively with friends, family, colleagues and neighbours. 1 Peter 3.2–4 speaks of the beauty and reverence which should characterise our lives as Christians,

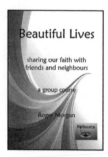

and Roger suggests that it is beautiful lives, lived in the power of the Holy Spirit, which lead others to faith. An eight-session course, offered in a user-friendly format with plenty of interaction and discussion, leading up to an accessible, locally planned invitation event.

> *'It changed the way I looked at people and engaged me differently with the world around me. I have become so much more aware of the possibilities of allowing God to be more clearly present in our interactions.'*

A group member in Pontesbury

3. Ministering to others

In His Name is a practical training course for healing prayer teams by Alison Morgan and John Woolmer. John and Alison combine a characteristically no-nonsense approach with a firm expectation, based on experience, that physical, emotional and spiritual healing is meant to be part of the living reality of every Christian life. A 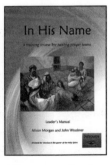 deliberately hands-on course with an emphasis on equipping participants to engage in an active ministry of healing.

> *'Far and away the most balanced, informed, practical guide for church healing teams. The authors have seen much healing – physical, psychological and spiritual, and have the theological and biblical underpinning to ground it. The course is interactive, beautifully written and has been tested over ten years.'*

Michael Green

Doing what Jesus Did: a fresh look at the gifts of the Spirit by Alison Morgan.

A fresh look at the gifts of the Spirit, suggesting they are best regarded as a description of the ministry of Jesus, to be welcomed not as feathers in the caps of individuals but as shared resources given to enable the mission and ministry of the church. With lots of illustrations and plenty of real life stories and testimonies, this is a welcome and readable short introduction to a topic about which little has been written in recent years. It includes a Bible study for use in small groups.

> *'The best theologically rigorous study of the gifts of the Spirit that I have read. Especially because in this new book Alison Morgan, from long experience, includes sensible, practical advice on how to get going.'*
>
> Preb John Collins

4. Renewing the traditional church

Season of Renewal is a Lent course by Alison Morgan and Bill Goodman. Combining traditional elements with a fresh approach, it is ideal for groups and churches who want something a little different which will provide a gentle introduction to the work of the Holy Spirit and act as a stimulus for future growth. It includes spiritual exercises to follow during the week between meetings. The course itself is divided into six sessions – five for the five weeks between Ash Wednesday and Maundy Thursday, and one final session for the week after Easter, structured round a shared meal. Each session includes creative and practical elements as well as a focus on scripture and some times of prayer.

> *'Our five Lent Fellowship Groups have all responded enthusiastically to "Season of Renewal". The music and "arty bit" were movingly effective. It is wonderful to have a course which is "Into God" rather than "About God".'*
>
> Revd Matthew Grayshon, Hanwell

ReSource also publishes a full colour magazine three times a year. Each issue treats a different topic, and contains articles, testimonies, book reviews, poetry and images.

Other networks and agencies

Further resources can be found by visiting any of the following websites:

www.celluk.org.uk – Cell UK supports dynamic small group ministry

www.crosswinds.org.uk – Crosswinds: mobilising, equipping and teaching people on Christian prayer

www.encountersontheedge.org.uk – The Sheffield Centre's series of profiles of fresh expressions of church

www.freshexpressions.org.uk – Fresh Expressions encourages new forms of church for a fast changing world, working with Christians from a variety of denominations and traditions

www.gospel-culture.org.uk – The Gospel and our Culture: networking, stimulating and resourcing the mission of Jesus Christ to Western Culture

www.licc.org.uk – The London Institute for Contemporary Christianity – equipping Christians and churches for whole life discipleship in the world

www.new-wine.org – the New Wine network of local churches working together with a vision to see the nation changed

www.out-there.org – Healing on the Streets

www.rejesus.co.uk – a key evangelistic resource for information and discussion about Jesus

www.renovare.info – Renovaré: discipleship and spiritual formation

www.resource-arm.net – ReSource: helping to build a church which is diverse, local, renewed in the Spirit and effective in mission, through a combination of specific resource material and on the ground training and support

www.resourcechurchplanting.com – ReSource Church Planting: creating church in the emerging culture

www.rootedinjesus.net – Rooted in Jesus: a discipleship programme for Africa

www.somauk.org – SOMA: short-term mission teams to support renewal within the Anglican Communion

www.theosthinktank.co.uk – Theos, the public theology think tank

Notes

Full publication details for the works cited here are given in the bibliography.

Introduction

1. 'Who's shaping you?' by Bishop Graham Cray, p.44 (Cell UK, 2010)

2. Eugene Peterson

3. The late Brother Roger of Taize

4. 'The Church of Irresistible Influence', Robert Lewis

Chapter 1

1. The speed of the Earth's spin varies from 1,675 km an hour at the equator to zero at the poles. In London the speed is 998 km an hour – Bill Bryson, *A Short History of Nearly Everything*, p.45. The Earth itself moves at no less than 64,000 miles an hour in orbit round the sun, and the solar system moves at the speed of 43,200 miles an hour – see Annie Dillard, *Pilgrim at Tinker Creek*, p.32.

2. Figures taken from Bob Jackson, *Hope for the Church*, and Peter Brierley, *Religious Trends* No.5, both using statistics from the 1989 and 2005 English Church Censuses and the 1998 English Church Attendance Survey. For the 2005 English Church Census see www.eauk.org/resources/info/statistics/2005englishchurchcen sus.cfm. Statistics for the Church of England from the Research & Statistics Dept, Archbishops' Council, are available on www.cofe.anglican.org/info/statistics. See also Steve Bruce, who concludes from the 1851 Census of Religious Worship that between 40 and 60% of UK adults were then regular church attenders; *God is Dead – Secularization in the West*, p.63. For an overview see Lynda Barley, *Christian Roots, Contemporary Spirituality*, ch 3.

3. Eleanor Hancock is vicar of Holy Trinity, Carlisle. Stuart Murray tells a similar story, of a teenager who was fascinated by the 'magic square' on Gaudi's Sagrada Familia Cathedral in Barcelona, in which many numerical combinations add up to thirty-three. "Why thirty-three?" she asked. "Because Jesus died at that age."

"That was young – what did he die of?" Walking into the cathedral she continued, "Who's that woman and why does she always have a baby?" Stuart Murray, *Church after Christendom*, p.159.

4. Nick Spencer, *Beyond Belief?: Barriers and bridges to faith today*, p.7; David Hay, *Something There: The Biology of the Human Spirit*, p.8. For more statistics see the summary by Vexen Crabtree on www.vexen.co.uk/UK/religion.html 'Religion in the United Kingdom: Diversity, Trends and Decline.'

5. Lesslie Newbigin, *The Gospel in a Pluralist Society*, p.243; Tom Wright, *Simply Christian*, p.17; Russ Hughes, *Church Times* 12 September 2005.

6. Lisa Warland wrote her testimony for ReSource, issue 11, www.resource-arm.net/articles/godslove.html. A Tearfund telephone survey suggested that 3 million people in the UK would go to church if someone invited them. See Bob Jackson and George Fisher, *Everybody Welcome Leaders' Manual*, p.7.

7. Tony Shelley wrote his story for ReSource, issue 10; online at www.resource-arm.net/articles/alcoholismtochrist.html.

8. For a discussion of the way our cultural climate impacts negatively on faith see David Hay, *Why Spirituality is Difficult for Westerners*.

9. Brian Appleyard, looking back in *The Sunday Times* over 'a decade of shock and awe', 27 December 2009.

10. *The Times* leader, 27 October 2006; article by Rowan Williams on the same day.

11. The individuals concerned were Nadia Ewida, Duke Amachree, Caroline Petrie, Olive Jones. The Christian Legal Centre run by Andrea Minichiello Williams acted for fifty cases of religious discrimination in 2009; www.christianlegalcentre.com. A classroom assistant in Dewsbury, Aishah Azmi, was also suspended for wearing a niqab. In many places the niqab is seen at best as oppressive, at worst as a political statement; France banned Muslim headscarves from schools in March 2004, and is now exploring legislation which would make it illegal to wear a full veil in any public place.

12. BBC One, 4 April 2010, presented by Nicky Campbell. See www.bbc.co.uk/programmes/b00rx7tj. See also the series of reports on the role of faith in society published online by the public theology thinktank Theos, including *Free to Believe? Religious freedom in a liberal society* by Roger Trigg, *Neither Private nor Privileged – the role of Christianity in Britain Today*, by Nick Spencer, and *Doing God – a Future for Faith in the Public Square*, also by Nick Spencer. www.theosthinktank.co.uk

13. Nick Spencer, *Beyond Belief?*, p.20.

14. *Resourcing Mission for a 21ˢᵗ Century Church*, p.21

15. See for example José Comblin, a Roman Catholic theologian working in Latin America: 'There has never, since the origins of Christianity, been such a radical change in the world as the one that is now taking place. For the church, this transformation is more radical than the transition from Israel to the Gentiles, more important than the establishment of the institutional church under Constantine or the Protestant Reformation: the present transformation forces it to a more radical reappraisal of itself and challenges many more aspects of it than have been challenged hitherto'. José Comblin, *The Holy Spirit and Liberation*, p.10. For a full treatment of the gospel in contemporary society see my book *The Wild Gospel*.

16. See Luke 11.33.

17. Mark 2.17; see also 1 Thessalonians 5.23, where Paul prays the Thessalonians may be kept whole in spirit, soul, and body.

18. e.g. Psalm 1, Jeremiah 17.7–8, Colossians 2.6–7, Ephesians 3.17. See also Galatians 5.22–23.

19. Nicky's story appears in ReSource, issue 14, and online at www.resource-arm.net/pdf/nickycox.pdf.

Chapter 2

1. See Annie Dillard, *Pilgrim at Tinker Creek*, ch 2, 'Seeing'. Also Donald E. Carr, *The Forgotten Senses* – a book about the sensory puzzles of life, and Marius Von Senden, *Space and Sight: The perception of space and shape in the congenitally blind before and after operation*.

2. Research into the development of language shows that the abstract terms we use to discuss concepts all derive from simple, concretely based forebears. Concepts have no independent existence – we create them from the physical building blocks of the interpreted sense world in which we live. So for example when we de*clare* or clarify something, we are making it physically clear – as when mud sinks to the bottom of water. When we say we are inde*pendent*, we meant, originally, that we are not hanging from anything. When we ex*press* something, we press it out, like butter. Every abstract concept has its roots in a physical experience. See Steven Pinker, *The Stuff of Thought: Language as a Window into Human Nature*, ch 5 'The metaphor metaphor'.

3. Definitive proof that the earth goes round the sun was provided in 1632 by Galileo. For a discussion of the implications of this event see *The Wild Gospel*, pp.141–42.

4. A worldview can be defined as 'a framework or set of fundamental beliefs through which we view the world and our calling and future in it… the integrative and interpretative framework by which order and disorder are judged, the standard by which reality is managed and pursued. It is the set of hinges on which all our everyday thinking and doing turns' – James H. Olthuis 'On Worldviews', online at www.gospel-culture.co.uk.

5. John Finney, *Emerging Evangelism,* cites Smart's definition of a religion as a six-dimensional organism containing doctrine, myths, ethical teachings, rituals, and social institutions, and animated by religious experiences of various kinds.

6. The Hebrew world view is described in more detail by Lesslie Newbigin, *Proper Confidence: Faith, Doubt & Certainty in Christian Discipleship,* especially ch 1, 'Faith as the way to knowledge'.

7. See my book *The Wild Gospel,* ch 2, for a more detailed treatment of this theme.

8. Brian O'Brien, *She Had a Magic: The Story of Mary Slessor;* see also www.maryslessor. com. An excellent short biography of William Wilberforce can be found on www. bbc.co.uk. His mentor told him 'If you carry this point in your whole life, that life will be far better spent than in being Prime Minister many years.'

9. 'Does God impose a meaning on my life from the *outside,* through event, custom, routine, law, system, impact with others in society? Or am I called to *create from within,* with him, with his grace, a meaning which reflects his truth and makes me his "word"' spoken freely in my personal situation?', Thomas Merton, *Contemplative Prayer,* p.84.

10. In his essay 'Advent – hope or delusion?' 1964.

11. See C. H. Haskins, *The Renaissance of the Twelfth Century,* ch 9.

12. For a virtual visit to the museum go to www.brunelleschi.imss.fi.it/museum.

13. The change from a Hebrew to a Greek world view is explored by Michael Frost and Alan Hirsch, *The Shaping of Things to Come: Innovation and Mission for the 21st-century Church,* ch 7. For an overview of the changing intellectual foundations of Western society see Alison Morgan, *The Wild Gospel,* chapters 4–5. For a discussion of the new scientific approach see Alister McGrath, *Science and Religion,* ch 1.

14. Whewell was Master of Trinity College, Cambridge (and a clergyman). The word did not come into general use until much later in the century. See Denis Alexander, *Creation or Evolution: Do We Have to Choose?,* p.39. Alexander defines science as 'an organised endeavour to explain the properties of the physical world by means of empirically testable theories constructed by a research community trained in specialised techniques.'

15. Charles Darwin, in a letter to Henry Ridley. To John Fordyce he wrote 'It seems to me absurd to doubt that a man may be an ardent Theist & an evolutionist. In my most extreme fluctuations I have never been an atheist in the sense of denying the existence of God' – Denis Alexander, *God, Darwin and Evolution* p.9. For a full discussion see Nick Spencer, *Darwin and God*, ch 3. Atheist scientist Stephen Jay Gould offers: 'Either half my colleagues are enormously stupid, or else the science of Darwinism is fully compatible with conventional religious beliefs – and equally compatible with atheism' – writing in *Scientific American*, and quoted by John Lennox, *God's Undertaker: Has Science Buried God?*, p.90.

16. *The God Delusion*, p.2. Dawkins also describes himself, with curious lack of scientific objectivity, as 'militantly anti-religion', interview with Jheni Osman, *Focus Magazine*, July 2007. Peter Atkins, Professor of Chemistry at Oxford University, supports this view when he says 'there is no reason to suppose that science cannot deal with every aspect of existence'; see John Lennox, *God's Undertaker*, p.39.

17. Terry Eagleton, reviewing *The God Delusion*.

18. P. B. Medawar, *Advice to a Young Scientist*, ch 8 'The scientific process'. Another Nobel laureate, quantum physicist Erwin Schrödinger, puts it even more starkly: 'I am astonished that the scientific picture of the real world around me is very deficient. It gives us a lot of factual information, puts all of our experience in a magnificently consistent order, but is ghastly silent about all that is really near to our heart, that really matters to us. It cannot tell us a word about red and blue, bitter and sweet, physical pain and physical delight; it knows nothing of beautiful and ugly, good or bad, God and eternity. Science sometimes pretends to answer questions in these domains but the answers are very often so silly that we are not inclined to take them seriously.' Quoted by Henry Schaefer in a lecture given at the University of Georgia, 'Stephen Hawking, the Big Bang and God', from Schrödinger's 1954 book *Nature and the Greeks*.

19. Ecclesiastes 3.11.

20. John Drane, *The McDonaldization of the Church*, p.20.

21. Jean Houston, quoted in Michael Frost and Alan Hirsch, *The Shaping of Things to Come*, p.182.

22. Chinese academic Carver T. Yu, quoted by Lesslie Newbigin, *Proper Confidence*, p.46.

23. All recent Turner Prize entries – Damien Hirst (winner 1995), Tracey Emin (shortlisted 1999), Martin Creed (winner 2001). Carrie O'Grady comments in *The Guardian* that the 1990s Britart movement explores 'everyday alienation', 1 November 2003.

24. One of the gospel's clearest promises is that persecution awaits Christians (e.g. John 15.20; 2 Timothy 3.12). Some have lost their jobs – but most of us have little more to worry about than the momentary possibility of unpopularity.

25. Susan Hope, *Mission-shaped Spirituality*, p.50.

26. Paul Taylor was at the time managing the Cheddar branch of NatWest. Shortly after his conversion, Paul was diagnosed with stomach cancer. He died, strong in faith and full of peace, just over two and a half years later.

Chapter 3

1. 'Stone walls do not a prison make/ Nor iron bars a cage;/ Minds innocent and quiet take/ That for an hermitage;/ If I have freedom in my love,/ And in my soul am free;/ Angels alone, that soar above,/ Enjoy such liberty' – from his poem *To Althea, from Prison*.

2. For a more detailed discussion see David W. Smith, *Crying in the Wilderness: Evangelism and Mission in Today's Culture*, p.43, and Andrew Walker, *Telling the Story: Gospel, Mission and Culture*, p.115.

3. A 2006 survey for National KidsDay found that children under ten identified celebrity as their top priority (Andrew Johnson and Andy McSmith, *The Independent*, 18 December 2006); a NUT survey of teachers in 2008 found that two thirds said their pupils aspire to be sports stars or pop singers; many seek to be famous with no discernible talent. As the NUT remarks, 'this compounds the subsequent sense of failure, alienation and low self-esteem when celebrity status is not achieved' (Nicola Woolcock, *The Times*, 14 March 2008). See also the article by Jane Thynne based on interviews with parents, *The Sunday Times*, 2 January 2005, 'Parenting: I want A-levels in fame, celebrity and being a star.'

4. 'Traditional A-levels "disappearing" according to new statistics', article on www. education.icnetwork.co.uk, 20 August 2009. See also the BBC news article, 18 August 2005, 'Media studies overtakes physics', www.bbc.co.uk.

5. Statistics for the last five years are given on www.ucas.ac.uk

6. Bayes's theorem, developed in the eighteenth century, shows that an experiment cannot prove or disprove a scientific theory, but only change the evidence for that theory relative to others. While this seems like common sense, it contradicts the notion that science is an objective process in which theories are on an even footing until disproved by experiment – an idea popularised only in the twentieth century by philosopher Karl Popper; see Andrew Pontzen and Hiranya Peiris, 'Cosmology's

not broken so why try to fix it?'. Physicist John Polkinghorne explains 'The simple account of science sees its activity as the operation of a methodological threshing machine in which the flail of experiment separates the grain of truth from the chaff of error. You turn the theoretico-experimental handle and out comes certain knowledge. The consideration of actual scientific practice reveals a more subtle activity in which the judgements of the participants are critically involved,' *One World: The Interaction of Science and Theology*, p.12.

7. J. B. S. Haldane, quoted by Bill Bryson, *A Short History of Nearly Everything*, p.16. For a non-technical discussion of the implications of science after Einstein see Albert Nolan, *Jesus Today: A Spirituality of Radical Freedom*, ch 4.

8. About 20,000. Worms, flies, and simple plants have a similar number. See Francis Collins, *The Language of God: A Scientist Presents Evidence for Belief*, p.125.

9. Thorpe, quoted by Lesslie Newbigin, *Foolishness to the Greeks*, p.69.

10. British astronomer and physicist Sir James Jeans, quoted by Annie Dillard, *Pilgrim at Tinker Creek*, p.132. For a discussion of the way in which the whole is more than the sum of the parts see Albert Nolan, *Jesus Today*, ch 4 'Science after Einstein', p.44. This understanding goes back to James Lovelock's *Gaia*.

11. See for example Colin Gunton: 'It is now widely accepted that almost all intellectual advance takes place by means of metaphor.... Metaphor is not mere ornament, but an indispensable means of articulating the shape of reality. Metaphors are the means of interpreting one part of the world by another, by imaginatively transcending the power of language' (in Hugh Montefiore, *The Gospel and Contemporary Culture*, p.91). Polkinghorne remarks that 'The recognition of a role for judgement in the scientific enterprise... gives it a kindred character to aesthetic, ethical and religious thinking,' *One World*, p.16.

12. Writing on the eve of his 2010 Reith Lectures, *The Times*, 31 May 2010. See also Jeremiah 51.15–17!

13. Bryan Appleyard, *The Sunday Times*, 3 June 1990.

14. *God and the New Physics*, quoted by Bryan Appleyard, *The Sunday Times*, 3 June 1990, 'God and the scientists join hands in a quantum leap.'

15. In his *A Brief History of Time*, Hawking wrote about 'knowing the mind of God'. He is also on record as follows: 'My work on the origin of the universe is on the borderline between science and religion, but I try to stay on the scientific side of the border. It is quite possible that God acts in ways that cannot be described by laws' – quoted in a lecture by H. F. Schaefer III, 'Stephen Hawking, the Big Bang, and God' at the University of Georgia in 2001 (www.leaderu.com/offices/

schaefer/docs/bigbang.html). Hawking's most recent statements are made in *The Grand Design*, Stephen Hawking and Leonard Mlodinow.

16. *The Times*, 25 April 1992, in an article launching Bryan Appleyard's book *Understanding the Present: Science and the Soul of Modern Man*.

17. See Brian Appleyard, speaking of both Hawking and Dawkins, *The Sunday Times* 3 December 2006. Dawkins writes 'the God hypothesis is a scientific hypothesis about the universe, which should be analysed as sceptically as any other' – *The God Delusion*, p.2.

18. Mary Midgley, *New Scientist*, 7 October 2006: 'It seems not to have struck Dawkins that academic science is only a small, specialised, dependent part of what anybody knows. Most human knowledge is tacit knowledge – habitual assumptions, constantly updated and checked by experience, but far too general and informal ever to be fully tested… With the largest, most puzzling questions, we have no choice but to proceed in mythical language which cannot be explained in detail at all, but which serves (as Einstein's did) to indicate what sort of spiritual universe we perceive ourselves to be living in. This is the province of religion. Adding God is not, as Dawkins thinks, adding an illicit extra item to the cosmos, it is perceiving the whole thing differently.'

19. Julian Baggini, himself an atheist, in 'The rise, fall and rise again of secularism', p.207. Francis Collins, Director of the Human Genome project, remarks in his Amazon review of Alister McGrath's 2007 book, *The Dawkins Delusion*, that 'Dawkins has abandoned his much-cherished rationality to embrace an embittered manifesto of dogmatic atheist fundamentalism.'

20. 'Science is the only reliable way to understand the natural world, and its tools when properly utilized can generate profound insights into material existence. But science is powerless to answer questions such as 'Why did the universe come into being?', 'What is the meaning of human existence?', 'What happens after we die?'. One of the strongest motivations of humankind is to seek answers to profound questions, and we need to bring all the power of both the scientific and spiritual perspectives to bear on understanding what is both seen and unseen.' *The Language of God*, p.6.

21. Statistic given by J. M. Houston, 'Modernity and spirituality', in *Faith and Modernity*, p.183.

22. 'The leaders of the western world have adopted an incredibly naive and shallow analysis of the problem of evil itself. They act as if they'd assumed that the world's problems were basically solved, that all we needed was a bit more free trade and parliamentary-style democracy, and then any remaining pockets of evil would wither away. So the reaction to 9/11 was astonishingly immature: "Goodness,

there seems to be some serious evil out there after all! What on earth shall we do? I know – let's go and drop some bombs on it, that'll sort it out!"', from 'Where is God in "The War on Terror"?' – a public lecture given in Durham Cathedral, 9 November 2006. For a more detailed treatment of the subject see also his William Temple Lecture, Blackburn Cathedral, 22 June 2006 'Believing in the Real World: The Challenge of Faith to Secularism and Fundamentalism'.

23. Even more than that said they believe in the devil (32%) and in hell (28%). David Hay, *The Spirituality of the Unchurched*, BIAMS Day Conference 2000; *Something There*, pp.8–11, 21–22.

24. *The Sunday Times*, 24 May 2009.

25. Alain De Botton, *The Pleasures and Sorrows of Work*, pp.45–46.

26. Richard Dawkins deals with science's inability to answer questions about purpose by dismissing them as illegitimate: 'Why on Earth should anyone assume that there IS a purpose? You are assuming that the "why" question is a sensible or legitimate question. Not all questions are. You have no right to expect an answer to a silly question' – from a webchat with Ruth Gledhill, published in *The Times*, 3 September 2010 (and see chapter 2 note 18).

27. See Lesslie Newbigin, *Foolishness to the Greeks*, ch 2 'Profile of a culture'.

28. e.g. N. L. Etcoff, *Liking, Wanting, Having, Being: The Science of Happiness*.

29. Matt Munday, 'How to con friends and influence people', *The Sunday Times*, 4 April 2010.

30. 'Postmodernism is consumption', in Craig Bartholomew and Thorsten Moritz (eds), *Christ and Consumerism: Critical reflections on the spirit of our age*, p.114. See also Michael Moynagh, *Emergingchurch.intro*, ch 3, 'New world, new church'. One study of life in the Scottish islands comments: 'It may be that, in the long term, the growth, vigour and beauty of Western materialism will prove to have been not the life-giving dynamism of youth but a malignant cancer in the throat of the world.' Timothy Neat, *When I was Young: Voices from Lost Communities in Scotland – The Islands*, p xi. There are signs of rebellion, with young professionals beginning to declutter their lives in favour of a mobile, online existence – see 'The Cult of Less', *The Times Magazine*, 30 October 2010.

31. *British Medical Journal*, March 2008. On 27 November 2010 *The Times* ran an article by Chris Smyth entitled 'My name is Manchester, I have a drink problem', showing that nationally we drink three times more than we did after the Second World War, with a quarter of deaths among men under twenty-five now caused by alcohol. Five of the worst affected areas are in Manchester.

32. Brian Draper writes sensitively and accessibly about our collective spiritual stuntedness: 'Our ultimate source of identity does not spring from our dominant capitalist world view, which tells us that we need to purchase and consume in order to become who we truly are. Somewhere deep down, something whispers the real alternative: that it is in our nakedness, our stripped-bare self, that we are most fully open to the possibilities of becoming the person we were born to be', in his *Spiritual Intelligence: A New Way of Being*, p.58.

Chapter 4

1. *Jesus Today*, p.7.

2. See 'The Lonely Society' – a report by Jo Griffin for the Mental Health Foundation. Broadband users spend the equivalent of a day a week online – 2¾ hours a day, plus 2½ hours watching television. In the UK as a whole the average person spends half their leisure time watching television. See also Lynda Barley, *Community Value*, pp.5–6. In the UK in 2009, the NHS issued 39 million prescriptions for depression (up from 22 million in 2002, which in turn was up from 9 million in 1991) – *The Sunday Times*, 19 January 2003, and *The Times*, 21 July 2010. A report 'Co-operative Streets: Neighbours in the UK' based on a YouGov poll commissioned by the Co-op found that in 1982 76% of people said they never felt lonely, but by 2010 this had fallen to 32%; it seems people have more acquaintances, particularly online, but fewer close friends – www.uk.coop/node/7687. Mother Teresa is quoted by John Ortberg, *Everybody's Normal Till You Get To Know Them*, p.29.

3. The journalist's name was Suni Umar. Richard Dowden, *Africa: Altered States, Ordinary Miracles*, p.2.

4. The word *ubuntu* stems from the Zulu folk saying 'Umuntu ngumuntu nagabantu', which means 'A person is a person because of other people'; *The Fifth Discipline Fieldbook*, by Peter Senge et al., p.3. See also Albert Nolan, *Jesus Today*, ch 2 'Signs of our times – the crisis of individualism.'

5. A good analysis of Western individualism and its consequences is given by Albert Nolan, *Jesus Today*, ch 2. Clinical psychologist Steve Ilardi suggests that the explanation for the high prevalence of depression lies in our lifestyle: 'Our standard of living is better now than ever before, but technological progress comes with a dark underbelly. Human beings were not designed for this poorly nourished, sedentary, indoor, sleep-deprived, socially isolated, frenzied pace of life. So depression continues its relentless march.' *The Depression Cure*.

6. Similar headlines: 'The good life fails to make Britain happy'; 'Happy daze – we are richer than ever, but no happier than in the 1950s, says the government'; 'What money can't buy – we are more prosperous than ever, but our melancholy has been rising in eerie synchronisation with our riches' (*The Sunday Times*, 8 January 2006; 19 January 2003; 28 December 2003). See the excellent summary of this trend in Lynda Barley's booklet *Community Value*, and the Downing Street Strategy Unit's report on the state of the nation's happiness, January 2003. Nick Spencer notes that between 1971 and 2004 per capita GDP almost doubled, with disposable income reaching nearly 2½ times its 1971 level by 2003, but that surveys report unchanged rates of life satisfaction over the same period – a third of people in UK said 'very satisfied' both in the early 1970s and in the late 90s (*Doing God*, p.51).

7. Sarah-Kate Templeton, *The Sunday Times*, 5 December 2004, reporting on a team of economists who had suggested that we should measure a country's gross national happiness. In 2009 a 'Science of Happiness' research project looked at the factors which lead to happiness (*The Times*, 12 August 2009), and in 2010 Richard Layard, professor at the London School of Economics, launched a 'Movement for Happiness' (*The Sunday Times*, 28 March 2010). The BBC series was screened in 2006.

8. Oliver James, *Affluenza: How to Be Successful and Stay Sane*, Vermilion 2007. A new charity, Action for Happiness, founded by Lord Layard of the LSE and Anthony Seldon, master of Wellington College, began work in 2011, researching what makes people happy and how they can improve their lot – see *The Times* article by Margarette Driscoll 'If you're happy they want to know it', 21 November 2010, written in response to David Cameron's instruction that the Office for National Statistics gauge the population's happiness and create a happiness index.

9. Kathleen Wallace, *This is Your Home: A Portrait of Mary Kingsley*, p.85.

10. Graph based on the research findings reported by David Hay in *Something There*. The research was conducted by the Opinion Research Business (ORB) for the BBC series *Soul of Britain*, written and presented by Michael Buerk and broadcast in nine episodes in June and July 2000.

11. Lynda Barley, *Christian Roots, Contemporary Spirituality*, p.4. Lynda provides an excellent summary of the various spirituality statistics to date.

12. Nick Spencer, *Beyond the Fringe: Researching a Spiritual Age*, p.12.

13. ORB 2000; 72% defined themselves as Christian believers in the 2001 census, and an additional 3.5% Muslim or Jewish believers. See www.statistics.gov.uk/focuson/religion/default.asp

14. Lynda Barley, *Christian Roots, Contemporary Spirituality*, pp.23, 25; *Community*

Value, p.25 (figures from the year 2005). The poll in December 2010 was conducted by ComRes on behalf of Theos – see www.theosthinktank.co.uk

15. Alister McGrath, *The Twilight of Atheism*.

16. www.nhsdirectory.org

17. Paul Heelas and Linda Woodhead, *The Spiritual Revolution*. See also www.lindawoodhead.org.uk and 'The Kendal Project' on www.lancs.ac.uk

18. *Glastonbury Oracle*, February 2009.

19. William Temple Lecture, Blackburn Cathedral, 22 June 2006: 'Believing in the Real World: The Challenge of Faith to Secularism and Fundamentalism'. I note with interest that it now seems that China, where for many years any form of religion was banned, is heading rapidly towards becoming a Christian country, with an estimated 100m believers; in 2007, 50m copies of the Bible were printed there – more than in any other nation. See www.timesonline.co.uk and www.christiansinchina.com

20. Extracts from 'Beyond belief' by Rachel Dobson and Jonathan Ungoed-Thomas, 2 November 2003.

21. Fleur Britten, 'Office Om', *The Sunday Times* 1 May 2005.

22. See Lynda Barley, *Christian Roots, Contemporary Spirituality*, p.8.

23. www.cofe.anglican.org/info/statistics/cathedralattendances1995to2007.pdf

24. Quoted by Roy McCloughry, *Living in the Presence of the Future*, p.32.

25. Questions is still running at Holy Trinity; see www.holytrinityleics.force9.co.uk/questionsmp3.htm.

26. Ann Murphy's account is printed in ReSource magazine, issue 13.

27. Gerard Kelly, *Get a Grip on the Future*, p.79.

Chapter 5

1. *Daily Mail*, 11 April 2009 (extracts). The full article is on www.dailymail.co.uk/news/article-1169145/Religion-hatred-Why-longer-cowed-secular-zealots.html

2. *New Statesman*, 2 April 2009. Full article www.newstatesman.com/religion/2009/04/conversion-experience-atheism

3.   David Hay, *Something There*, p.63.

4.   David Hay, *Something There*, p.226.

5.   *Mission-shaped Church: Church Planting and Fresh Expressions of Church in a Changing Context*, p.40.

6.   Copeland was interviewed in *The Church Times*, 14 November 2008. See also Brian Draper, *Spiritual Intelligence*, p.97.

7.   The old global frameworks of capitalism or communism have long since lost their lustre. In the run up to the 2010 UK general election, Anatole Kaletsky commented in *The Times* that 'the problem for all parties, as many commentators have noted, is the absence of any overarching narratives, ideological worldview or even tribal and class loyalties'. We have lost the big picture; all that is left is a mass of details – *The Times*, 14 April 2010.

8.   Illich is quoted by Neil Cole, *Organic Church*, p.123

9.   I have written about the way this happens in *The Wild Gospel*, ch 2.

10. *The Gospel in a Pluralist Society*, p.125.

11. David Lochhead, quoted by Gerard Kelly, *Get a Grip on the Future*, p.116. For more on the spirituality of print see chapter 8.

12. See *The Wild Gospel*, chapter 8, 'Living in the truth of Christ'; and John 1.1–14; John 5.39–40.

13. Nick Spencer: *Beyond the Fringe*, pp.160, 19. See also his *Beyond Belief?*, a study among non-churchgoers in London and Nottingham which concludes that church culture is one of four major barriers to belief for people today.

14. Luke 19.10 (TM).

15. Michael Polanyi, *Personal Knowledge: Towards a Post-critical Philosophy*, p.266. It was Einstein who first remarked that knowledge comes not in a vacuum but as a hypothesis. Polanyi is hard to read, but Lesslie Newbigin summarises his thought in *Proper Confidence*, chapters 3–4. Newbigin also cites Roy Clouser, *The Myth of Religious Neutrality*, who shows how major theories in maths, physics, and psychology involve a prior decision as to what is fundamental in the area studied. Newbigin concludes that we have to believe in order to know, and that the certainty which Descartes claimed is available only within a mental world that is not in contact with a reality beyond itself.

16. See note 6 of Chapter 3.

17. 2 September 2010, responding to the publication of Stephen Hawking's *The Grand Design*.

18. Carver T. Yu comments, 'While philosophers are busy ascertaining the verification of truth, we have to ask, is it not possible that truth may have to be verified in a different way? Is it not true that in our Christian experience, truth has to be verified with our life, precisely in this age when man has gained everything except life?' – from his paper 'Truth and authentic humanity'.

19. The Portuguese word *feiticeirios* was adopted from the Latin *factitius*, or magically artful – see Mary Kingsley, *West African Studies*, p.115. For more details see Nick Middleton, *Kalashnikovs and Zombie Cucumbers: Travels in Mozambique*, ch 8.

20. *The Gospel in a Pluralist Society*, p.61. See also his remark 'If the ultimate reality... is the being of the triune God, then the response of personal faith to a personal calling is the only way of knowing that reality. To rule this out... is to make an a priori decision against the possibility that ultimate reality is personal.'

21. Christopher Hart, *The Sunday Times*, 23 March 2008; he concludes, 'Just because Church of England attendance figures are dropping through the floor does not necessarily mean the end of religion.'

22. Michael Frost and Alan Hirsch, *The Shaping of Things to Come*, p.113; Michael Riddell, *Threshold of the Future*, p.115.

23. For a full discussion of the ways in which the gospel has been articulated effectively into the culture at different times see *The Wild Gospel*, pp.125–29.

24. Oliver Wendell Holmes, quoted by Steven Croft, *Mission-Shaped Questions*, p.186. The concept is further developed by De Bono in his book *Simplicity*.

25. 1 Corinthians 2.2–6; see also 1 Corinthians 1.22–23: 'the Jews demand signs, Greeks demand wisdom, but we preach Christ crucified'.

26. *The Jesus Way: A Conversation in Following Jesus*, p.270.

27. Richard Taylor tells his story in his autobiography *To Catch a Thief*. His website is www.richardtaylor.org.uk

Chapter 6

1. See Stuart Murray, *Church After Christendom*, ch 2. The figure of 1 million does not include those who die or move away.

2. An excellent way of learning how to do things better is to use *Everybody Welcome: The Course where Everybody Helps Grow their Church*, by Bob Jackson and George Fisher.

3. Dallas Willard remarks that changing the way we do our services may be good but it is not enough – 'reacting against the modern church is not a gospel' – 'The Apprentices', p.25.

4. A 'mystery worshipper' visiting a church to see what it feels like to an outsider – see www.ship-of-fools.com. See also Nick Spencer's *Beyond Belief?*

5. Revelation 3.20.

6. James M Washington (ed), *A Testament of Hope: the essential writings and speeches of Martin Luther King, Jr*, pp.37–38. Another advocate was Archbishop Oscar Romero, who highlighted Jesus' preference for the poor and whose insistence that the Church should do the same led to the development of the base communities in El Salvador, small groups in which people could together consider the application of the gospel to every dimension of their lives. The price they paid for this radical insistence on following the example of Jesus was the same price paid by Jesus himself – King was assassinated in 1968 and Romero in 1980. Both men are discussed in William J Abraham: *The Logic of Renewal*, ch 5.

7. William Booth's last public address, in the Royal Albert Hall, London, on 9 May 1912, included the following: "While women weep as they do now, I'll fight; while little children go hungry as they do now, I'll fight; while men go to prison, in and out, in and out, as they do now, I'll fight; while there is a drunkard left, while there is a poor lost girl on the streets, while there remains one dark soul without the light of God, I'll fight – I'll fight to the very end." See www.cyberhymnal.org/bio/b/o/o/booth_w.htm. Mother Teresa said: "Without our suffering, our work would just be social work, very good and helpful, but it would not be the work of Jesus Christ, not part of the Redemption. All the desolation of the poor people, not only their material poverty, but their spiritual destitution, must be redeemed. And we must share it, for only by being one with them can we redeem them by bringing God into their lives and bringing them to God" – www.quotationsbook.com

8. Romans 10.17.

9. I was particularly helped by F. F. Bruce, *The New Testament Documents: Are They Reliable?*, Frank Morison, *Who Moved the Stone?*, and Norman Anderson, *The Evidence for the Resurrection*.

10. Mark 12.24.

11. Gordon D. Fee, *Paul, the Spirit and the People of God*, p.xiii.

12. 2 Corinthians 3.2–4.

13. Tom Smail, *Charismatic Renewal*, p.49.

14. José Comblin, *The Holy Spirit and Liberation*, p.41. 1 Corinthians 12 is often treated out of context and given a distorted and over-individualistic interpretation; its importance lies not in the listing of spiritual gifts available to us as individuals but in the fact that it describes the ministry of Jesus – see Alison Morgan, *Doing what Jesus Did: A Fresh Look at the Gifts of the Spirit.*

15. Susan Hope argues: 'In talking about the fullness of the Spirit, I am not arguing that all should become "charismatics" in the sense of embracing the particular tradition that has become known as the charismatic movement. But I am convinced that we should all become charismatics in the sense of having a healthy, robust and living experience of the power and presence of the Spirit of God in our ordinary everyday lives and in the ordinary, everyday lives of our churches.' *Mission-shaped Spirituality*, pp.70–71.

16. *Contesting the Rise of the Nazis* will be published by Blackwells in 2012 – see www.lboro.ac.uk/research/theview/archive/aw09/articles/rise-of-nazis.html

17. Mark and Helen Van Koevering went to Niassa in 2003, and we visited to train leaders to use the *Rooted in Jesus* discipleship course in 2006 and again in 2007. For more information see www.rootedinjesus.net or read Helen's article in ReSource magazine, issue 15, summer 2009, 'God is doing things differently in Mozambique'.

18. Rosemary Ruether, 'The Free Church Movement in Contemporary Catholicism', p.47. See William Abraham, *The Logic of Renewal*, ch 4.

19. St Bene't, Cambridge. She goes on, 'We were greeted by someone whose eyebrows were raised in wonder over whether we had actually come for the service' – www.ship-of-fools.com

20. Brian McLaren, *A Generous Orthodoxy*, offers an inspiring advocacy of an integrated approach to faith which goes beyond the insights of any one grouping to create something strong and exciting.

Chapter 7

1. *Faith in a Changing Culture*, p.176.

2. Hebrews 11.1–3.

3. The combination of prayer and pastoral care offered by Christians stood in marked contrast to the nail-them-up-and-run reaction of the average Roman – see Alison Morgan, *The Wild Gospel*, ch 4, 'The gospel in history'.

4. Quoted by Michael Frost and Alan Hirsch, *The Shaping of Things to Come*, p.185.

5. See www.freshexpressions.org.uk. See also the LICC's project 'Imagine', which invites us to begin by 'starting to recover a way of seeing'; www.licc.org.uk/imagine

6. We need, Michael Frost and Alan Hirsch suggest, to reawaken the latent apostolic imagination at the heart of the biblical faith, *The Shaping of Things to Come*, p.xi; see in particular chapter 11, 'Imagination and the leadership task'. See also Walter Brueggemann, *Texts under Negotiation: Bible and Postmodern Imagination*, with its insistence that the Bible itself is the paradigm through which we practise imagination; and Michael Riddell, *Threshold of the Future*, especially ch 6, 'Dreaming the forbidden dream.' For the visionary nature of Jesus' teaching see Alison Morgan, *The Wild Gospel*, ch 3.

7. Speech at Harvard University, 6 May 1943.

8. Ken Blanchard and Terry Waghorn, *Mission Possible: Becoming a World-Class Organization While There's Still Time*, p.xviii.

9. See *The Shaping of Things to Come*, ch 11, from which many of the ideas in this section are drawn.

10. Conrad Gempf points out that in the sixty-seven episodes with conversation in the gospel of Mark, we find no fewer than fifty questions asked by Jesus – *Jesus Asked What He Wanted To Know*, p.19.

11. William P. Young, *The Shack*; Nick Page, *The Church Invisible*; Rob Bell, *Velvet Elvis: Repainting the Christian Faith*; Alison Morgan, *The Wild Gospel*; Stuart Murray, *Church after Christendom*; Michael Frost, *Exiles: Living Missionally in a Post-Christian Culture*; Michael Riddell, *Threshold of the Future*; Alan Hirsch, *The Forgotten Ways*. For summaries of these and other challenging books see www.alisonmorgan.co.uk

12. 'Retreat on the Street' is a powerful activity that enables you to spend a day on the streets with just 50 pence in your pocket and freedom from your usual preoccupations and busyness – see www.cuf.org.uk/pray/retreat-street

13. For ideaviruses see Alan Hirsch, *The Forgotten Ways*, pp.210–12; for memes see Richard Dawkins, *The Selfish Gene*, p.193. Dawkins understands the meme as a unit of self-replicating information, the psychological equivalent of the gene. As a piece of science it is unsupported by any evidence; but as a metaphor it is useful.

A good discussion of the meme is given by Mario Beauregard, *The Spiritual Brain: A Neuroscientist's Case for the Existence of the Soul*, pp.217–223.

14. Acts 7.29 (echoing Exodus 2.22); 1 Peter 2.11. The words 'parish' and 'parishioner' actually come from this term 'resident alien' or 'temporary sojourner' – *paroikos* in the Greek. We are resident aliens, foreigners in our own land. Funny how now the word 'parish' carries exactly the opposite connotations…

15. For more details see www.biblesociety.org, 'campaigns'. Similar events were run in Bristol in 2005 and Manchester in 2007.

16. Charles Colson and Nancy Pearcey: How Now Shall We Live? Colson's story is told in *The Washington Post*, www.washingtonpost.com

17. www.rejesus.co.uk

18. Exodus 31.2–6. Tim Keller spoke at the Lausanne III Congress in Cape Town, October 2010, about the need for city churches to empower artists through concerts, drama workshops, exhibitions, poetry performances, music and so on. See the helpful chapter by John Holbrook, 'Mission-shaped civic church', in *Mission-shaped Parish: Traditional Church in a Changing World*, Paul Bayes and Tim Sledge (eds), especially p.97.

19. Nick Spencer, *Doing God*; John Micklethwait, *God is Back: How the Global Rise of Faith is Changing the World*.

20. Identified by the Northwest Regional Development Agency in their 2003 report 'Faith in England's North West'.

21. See Nick Spencer, *Doing God*, p.54.

22. *Julius Caesar*, IV.iii.218–25.

23. 1 Corinthians 2.2–6.

24. John Samways, *More to Life: A Model for Mission for the Local Church in the 21*[st] *Century*. See also www.moretolife08.org.uk

25. *The Irresistible Revolution: Living as an Ordinary Radical*, p.225.

Chapter 8

1. *The Stuff of Thought*, p.24.

2. The story is told in *The Wild Gospel*, pp.16–21.

3. Statement made in a lawsuit, Commissioner v National Carbide Corporation, 1948, quoted in *The Oxford Dictionary of Literary Quotations*, Peter Kemp (ed), p.43.

4. Steven Pinker, *Words and Rules*, p.3.

5. Lewis Carroll, *The Annotated Alice*, p.269.

6. For the Piraha see Steven Pinker, *The Stuff of Thought*, pp.138–40 (NB Pinker notes that the Yanomano tribe, also from Amazon, have been shown not to need precise number words because they remember things individually – e.g. they notice a particular arrow is missing, rather than that they have one too few.) For the Eveny of Siberia see Piers Vitebsky, *CAM Magazine*, Lent 2006 issue; Vitebsky is the Head of Anthropology at the Scott Polar Research Institute. For a discussion of the way literacy changes the nature of our thinking see the research conducted by Russian Alexander Luria, reported in David Hay, *Why Spirituality is Difficult for Westerners*, ch 3. It seems that the thinking of illiterate peoples is structured through memory rather than through concept, and that this in turn produces a society which is more conservative and communally minded than that of literate peoples, whose strengths lie instead in innovation.

7. For a readable account of string theory see Bill Bryson, *A Short History of Nearly Everything*, p.148. For the limitations of human thought see Jeremiah 51.15–17.

8. Matthew Fox is extremely forthright about our failure to understand this: 'a theology of the word of God has practically killed the word of God. This very paradoxical statement is true to the extent that theologians have been translating the Hebrew word "Dhabar" as "word" practically without regard to what the words "word" and "words" have come to mean in our culture. The word "Dabhar" simply does not mean what we now mean by "word" or "words"', *Original Blessing*, p.36.

9. 'The Word of God in the Old Testament', p.205.

10. Genesis 1.1–27; Psalm 33.6–9; Hebrews 11.3.

11. 2 Peter 3.5–7; Isaiah 50.2–3.

12. Psalm 102.25–26; Revelation 21–22.

13. Psalm 147.15–18; Psalm 104.2–30.

14. *Pilgrim at Tinker Creek*, p.132.

15. 'Prayer is not only worship; it is also an invisible emanation of man's worshipping spirit – the most powerful form of energy that we can generate.' He goes on, 'The influence of prayer on the human mind and body is as demonstrable as that of secreting glands. Its results can be measured in terms of physical buoyancy, greater

intellectual vigour, moral stamina, and a deeper understanding of the realities underlying human relationships.' Quoted by Morris Maddocks, *The Christian Healing Ministry*, p.236.

16. Most Christians are happy to identify the Big Bang as a different way of talking about the events of Genesis chapter 1. For the energy of the sun as words of information see James Lovelock, *Gaia*, ch 8.

17. Colossians 1.17. The theological way of describing this is to say that God is 'immanent' in his creation. See especially Psalm 104, but there are many other passages in the Psalms, Isaiah, and Job, which make it clear that God is intimately involved in continued creative activity in relation to his universe. For a good discussion see Denis Alexander, 'The Biblical doctrine of creation', in *Creation or Evolution: Do We Have to Choose?*

18. Exodus 20.1; Exodus 24.3–4; Matthew 5.17–19.

19. All this is laid out in Deuteronomy chapters 28–30. It is interesting to compare Nehemiah 9–10, where Ezra reacquaints the returning Israelites with the books of the law, recognises that their misfortunes are due to their failure to live by the word of God, and leads them in prayers of repentance and recommitment.

20. David Lochhead, quoted by Gerard Kelly, *Get a Grip on the Future*, p.116.

21. From Contemplations (1856), quoted in *The Oxford Dictionary of Literary Quotations*, p.203.

22. 'Jesus speaks and enacts the holy word of God in ways that "pluck up and tear down," that "plant and build."... Jesus is not only an utterer of the word, but is himself the uttered word. That is, Jesus' own person is God's word of life, which shatters all idolatrous forms of life and makes new community possible' – Walter Brueggemann, *Texts that Linger, Words that Explode*, p.38.

23. 'Jesus is thus the final event of the Word of God in history; he is that word "issuing forth from the mouth of God" that, like the rain, has come down upon the earth and watered it so it can bear seed to sow and bread to eat, and, once everything has been completed that God sent him to do, returns to him, saying to the Father, "I have accomplished the work you gave me to do",' – Raniero Cantalamessa, *The Mystery of God's Word*, p.12.

24. These incidents are recorded in Matthew 8, Mark 2, John 11, Matthew 8, and Mark 1.

25. John 5.39–40. For a more detailed discussion of people's responses to Jesus see *Who Do You Say That I Am?: The Unexpected Jesus*, and *The Wild Gospel*, chapters 2–3. See in particular John chapters 3, 4 and 8.

26. Acts 1.4, 8. See also John 14.12, where Jesus promises his disciples that they will do the works that he does.

27. For testimonies of healing at New Wine events see www.new-wine.org/your-stories. For Healing on the Streets, pioneered by Mark Marx in Coleraine, Northern Ireland and now functioning in many places, see www.out-there.org, or just google 'healing on the streets'. Many testimonies of healing and deliverance can be found in the ReSource healing course 'In His Name', by Alison Morgan and John Woolmer – details on www.resource-arm.net, where you will also find first-hand individual stories. See also *The Wild Gospel*, particularly ch 8, 'Changing Individuals.'

28. This story was told to me by Helen Bence, associate minister at St Luke's, Thurnby.

29. 1 Peter 1.25.

30. Tom Wright puts it well: 'When you announce the good news that the risen Jesus is Lord, that very word is the Word of God, a carrier or agent of God's Spirit, a means by which, as Isaiah had predicted, new life from God's dimension comes to bring new creation within ours' – *Simply Christian*, p.114.

31. See for example Acts 6.7; 12.24; 19.20; 1 Thessalonians 1.8; 1 Peter 1.23; James 1.18.

32. See www.free2live.org.uk, where you can also read the online edition of Liesl's book, *Free to Live and God Heals Today*. The visit to the church is on p.86.

33. Deuteronomy 30.12–14.

34. Romans 10.8.

35. Mark 4; see also Colossians 1.5–6, 'you have heard of this hope before in the word of the truth, the gospel that has come to you. Just as it is bearing fruit and growing in the world, so it has been bearing fruit among yourselves from the day you heard it and truly comprehended the grace of God'.

36. Robert's story is told in *A Boy and his Bible*, by Robert Hicks and Jill Gupta. For an interview with Robert by Dan Wooding see www.assistnews.net/Stories/2010/s10030176.htm. Now sixty-nine, Robert lives in Bath.

37. Richard Foster, *Life with God: A life-transforming new approach to Bible reading*, p.134.

38. Richard Foster, *Life with God*, p.3.

39. Gary Ralls is a member of Oakhill Methodist Chapel in Somerset. He

wrote his testimony for ReSource magazine, issue 19, Winter 2010. See
www.resource-arm.net

40. From 'Le porche du mystère de la deuxième vertu', quoted by Raniero Cantalamessa,
The Mystery of God's Word, pp.20–21.

41. A. W. Tozer, *The Pursuit of God*, p.75.

Chapter 9

1. Thessalonians 1.8. For full information on *Rooted in Jesus* see
www.rootedinjesus.net

2. A similar story was told at New Wine 2010 by Jackson ole Sapit, now bishop of
the new Anglican diocese of Kericho in Kenya, who was sent to school (to the
initial dismay of his mother, who was relying on him, her only son, to provide the
family with cattle) through sponsorship from World Vision.

3. A stunning visual portrait of all these factors is given by Brazilian photographer
Sebastiao Salgado in his book *Africa*.

4. Deuteronomy 8.3; Matthew 15.17–20. DR Congo is one of the poorest countries
in the world, and yet it possesses 70% of the world's coltan, more than 30% of
its diamonds, and vast quantities of copper and cobalt. It also has a river system
extensive enough to provide hydro-electric power to the whole continent of Africa.
See the Foreign Office (www.fco.gov.uk) and BBC websites for more information.
For a recent description of the country see Tim Butcher, *Blood River: A Journey
to Africa's Broken Heart*; one cobalt trader sums up the situation in the simple
statement: "If you think you can solve Africa's problems with money, you are a
bloody fool. There has always been plenty of money, and there is more money
around today for African raw materials than ever before. The point is the money
goes only to a few people, not to the country in general." A report in *The Lancet*,
January 2006, estimates that 1,200 people a day still lose their lives in Congo as a
direct result of the endemic violence and insurgency there.

5. www.timesonline.co.uk/tol/comment/columnists/matthew_parris/article5400568.ece

6. Acts 9.2; 19.9; 19.23, 22.4; 24.14; 24.22.

7. For example Jeremiah 17.7–8; Psalm 1; Ephesians 3.17; Colossians 3.6–7.

8. You can read their testimonies on www.rootedinjesus.net

9. A survey in Uganda found that 41% of men admitted to beating their wives;

Robert Guest, *The Shackled Continent*, p.110. Amorim's sister was beaten to death by her husband while we were with him.

10. 'Spirit and Word belong together like breath and voice', Jean-Jacques Suurmond: *Word and Spirit at Play: Towards a Charismatic Theology*, II.1.

11. For the link between Spirit and Word see Psalm 33.6, Isaiah 59.21, Ezekiel 2.2; John 3.34, 6.63; Acts 1.8, 2.41 Corinthians 2.4; 1 Thessalonians 1.5. All these texts indicate that the word on its own is not enough; what gives it its power is the Spirit. See José Comblin, *The Spirit and Liberation*, ch 5 'The two hands of God'.

12. Simon Ponsonby, *God Inside Out*, p.15.

13. Translating into Rukiga, in SW Uganda.

14. Matthew 4.4. See Walter Brueggemann, *Texts that Linger, Words that Explode*, p.8.

15. John Wimber and Kevin Springer, *Power Evangelism*. Something similar was said by A. W. Tozer: 'I believe that much of our religious unbelief is due to a wrong conception of and a wrong feeling for the Scriptures of Truth. A silent God suddenly began to speak in a book and when the book was finished lapsed into silence again forever. Now we read the book as the record of what God said when He was for a brief time in a speaking mood. With notions like that in our heads how can we believe? The facts are that God is not silent, has never been silent... He is by nature continuously articulate.' *The Pursuit of God*, p.75.

16. *Texts Under Negotiation*, pp.24–25. See also *The Word That Redescribes the World: The Bible and Discipleship*.

17. Quoted by Ray Simpson, *Church of the Isles*, p.41. Similar prophecies have been given by Jean Darnell and by David du Plessis.

18. Jeremiah 21.28–29, Luke 4.18, John 20.21–22, John 14.12.

19. Hebrews 4.12. Eugene Peterson remarks: 'we do not progress in the Christian life by becoming more competent, more knowledgeable, more virtuous, or more energetic. We do not advance in the Christian life by acquiring expertise. Each day... we return to Square One: God Said' – *Subversive Spirituality*, p.30.

20. Jeremiah 1.12.

21. *Eat this Book*, quoted by Richard Foster, *Life with God*, p.1.

Chapter 10

1. 1 Corinthians 2.1–4; Romans 15.18; 1 Thessalonians 1.5.

2. Luke 4.18–19; Acts 1.8 "you will receive power when the Holy Spirit has come upon you, and you will be my witnesses in all Judea and Samaria, and to the ends of the earth."

3. See Luke 7.22; the story is told in the Acts of the Apostles.

4. e.g. Acts 1.8; 2.4; 2.14; 4.31; 7.55; 8.29; 9.17–20. This of course is also a pattern familiar from the Old Testament, in particular to the prophets who spoke as the Spirit came to them.

5. Dutch theologian Hendrikus Berkhof once wrote that 'to a great extent, official church history is the story of the *defeats* of the Spirit' – D. J. Hall, *The End of Christendom and the Future of Christianity*, p.18. Simon Ponsonby gives a good description of the process, *God Inside Out*, ch 4 'The Holy Spirit in historical development'. For a summary see Alison Morgan, *Doing What Jesus Did*, pp.1–10.

6. Lenin said 'Electricity will replace God. The peasants should pray to it; in any case they will feel its effects long before they feel any effect from on high' – quoted by Philip Yancey, *Prayer*, p.105.

7. Raniero Cantalamessa, *The Mystery of God's Word*, p.61. Simon Ponsonby gives a good description of this process of marginalisation of the Spirit, *God Inside Out*, ch 4 'The Holy Spirit in historical development'.

8. All Christians are of course 'charismatic' in the sense that all have received the Holy Spirit (see 1 Corinthians 12.3), but not all are taking full advantage of what is available to them through him. For the figures see the *The New International Dictionary of Pentecostal and Charismatic Movements*, Stanley Burgess (ed), p.284.

9. See especially John 14–16. I use 'him' merely as a convenience, for the Spirit is in fact feminine in Hebrew (*ruach*), neuter in Greek (*pneuma*), and masculine only in Latin (*spiritus*). Through the gender of nouns is a theology formed; we do well to remind ourselves again of the way in which language both enables and limits our thinking.

10. John Owen, *The Spiritual Gifts (Pneumatologia* Book IX). See Simon Ponsonby, *God Inside Out,* p.15; Simon remarks that the Spirit has been called 'the orphan doctrine of theology' and 'the Cinderella of theology' – and yet also 'the stealth weapon of the Church'.

11. The 'gifts' are described in 1 Corinthians 12–14; the fruit in Galatians 5.

12. For a detailed discussion of the work and person of the Holy Spirit see Alison Morgan, *Doing What Jesus Did*. The fruit of the Spirit is grown as we become mature in Christ. Entering prayerfully into life's experiences accomplishes this; the ministry of inner healing can also help.

13. 1 Corinthians 12.12–2; John 14.12–14; Ephesians 2.10.

14. For more detail See *Doing what Jesus Did*, pp.23–24.

15. Tom Wright was speaking at the first Fulcrum conference at St Mary's Islington, April 2005 – see www.fulcrum-anglican.org.uk. For John Owen see *The Spiritual Gifts*, p.82.

16. Steven Croft, in *Mission-shaped Questions*, p.21.

17. Alison Morgan, *Doing What Jesus Did*, p.24.

18. Mark 2, 3, 7 and 12; John 8; Matthew 13.54.

19. Luke 21.15; Acts 4 (Peter and John); Acts 6 (Stephen).

20. Acts 6.1–6; Acts 15.7–21; 2 Peter 3.15. He adds that they are sometimes hard to understand!

21. See Ephesians 1.17–19 – 'I pray that the God of our Lord Jesus Christ may give you a spirit of wisdom and revelation so that, with the eyes of your heart enlightened, you may know what is the hope to which he has called you, what are the riches of his glorious inheritance, and what is the immeasurable greatness of his power for us who believe.' See also James 1.5–6.

22. John 4.16–18; 13.11; see also 18.4; 21.4–6.

23. Acts 5.3; Acts 27.21–26.

24. Luke 5.20; 7.9; 8.48.

25. Matthew 14.28–31; Acts 15.8–9.

26. See the great chapter on faith, Hebrews chapter 11; 'faith is the assurance of things hoped for, the conviction of things not seen.'

27. Many books have been written about George Muller. For Andy and Claudia Fanstone see www.holytrinityleics.force9.co.uk/fanstones.htm

28. Jesus announces his ministry of healing and deliverance in Luke 4, referring to Isaiah 35.5–6 and 61. He sends out the disciples to heal, Matthew 10.8. He challenges them to believe in him because of his works, John 10.38.

29. For Martin of Tours see *Doing What Jesus Did*, pp.12–13; for an overview of the gifts of the Spirit in history see p.16. More information about healing (and other spiritual gifts) in history is given by: John Wimber, *Power Evangelism*; Mark Stibbe, *Know Your Spiritual Gift*; John Woolmer, *Healing and Deliverance*; Simon Ponsonby, *God Inside Out*; Mark Cartledge, *Encountering the Spirit*; Jack Deere, *Surprised by the Voice of God*; Guy Chevreau, *Turnings*.

30. For the ministry of John Lake see Guy Chevreau, *Turnings* p.205. For the Bakers see Rolland and Heidi Baker, *Always Enough: Miraculous Ministry in Mozambique*. See also Bill Johnson, *When Heaven Invades Earth*; Johnson comments 'Any revelation from God's Word that does not lead us to an encounter with God only serves to make us more religious. The Church cannot afford "form without power", for it creates Christians without purpose,' p.87. Recent testimonies to healing can be found in the ReSource healing course *In His Name*, in ReSource magazine and on www.resource-arm.net/onlinearticles.html. See also Alpha News at www.uk.alpha.org, or google 'Healing on the Streets'.

31. For more examples see my other writings: *The Wild Gospel,* the ReSource healing course *In His Name*, and *Doing What Jesus Did*.

32. This was the experience that led ultimately to the writing of *In His Name*. It is interesting that Bob Johnson, brother to Bill and pastor of a church in San Francisco, estimates that they see a 65% success rate of answered prayer for healing in church, but an 85% rate on the streets. See Guy Chevreau, *Turnings*, p.210.

33. Some commentators distinguish between miracles and healings by saying miracles are instantaneous whereas healings are gradual – but as there is only one recorded instance of Jesus performing a healing gradually (Mark 8, the blind man who saw 'trees walking'), and as the word 'power' is used repeatedly for healing, it seems to make more sense to distinguish between healing miracles and other miracles.

34. Exodus 7ff (plagues), Exodus 14 (Red Sea), Exodus 16 (manna), 1 Kings 17–18 (Elijah), 2 Kings 2–4 (Elisha), John 2 (water into wine), Matthew 14 (feeding of the 5,000), Luke 8 (storm), Luke 7 (raising of the widow's son), John 11 (of Lazarus), Luke 8 (of Jairus's daughter).

35. Acts 9 (Tabitha), Acts 20 (Eutychus), Acts 8 (Philip), Acts 6 (Stephen), Acts 16 (earthquake).

36. Both were writing within living memory of the saints' deaths. Gregory's *Dialogues* include the stories of an immovable stone carried away easily after prayer, a violent rainstorm brought on by the prayers of Benedict's sister Scholastica, the rescue of a drowning boy by a monk named Marcus who found himself running over the water to reach him, and the often illustrated restoration to life by Benedict of a boy crushed by a falling wall. Bonaventure claimed to have been healed from a

dangerous illness as a child by the prayers of Francis, and miracles recorded in his life of Francis were illustrated by Giotto in the Upper Church at Assisi – water springing from a rock, the restoration of a woman from death who needed to confess a sin committed in her lifetime, and various posthumous miracles.

37. For John Welsh see Jack Deere, *Surprised by the Voice of God*, pp.82–83; the original account is found in a work by John Howie published in 1775. Paul Thigpen has demonstrated that miracles have occurred consistently in every century up to our own. His doctoral thesis is summarised in the article 'Come, Holy Spirit! – 2,000 years of miracles'; a summary is given by Mark Stibbe, *Know Your Spiritual Gifts*, p.97. John Wesley remarked, 'I do not recollect any Scripture wherein we are taught that miracles were to be confined within the limits either of the apostolic age or the Cyprian age, or any period of time, longer or shorter, even till the restitution of all things' – *The Works of John Wesley*, vol 8, quoted by Guy Chevreau, *Turnings*, p.205. One way of affirming the medieval belief in miracles is to browse the pages of the book *Marvellous to Behold: Miracles in Medieval Manuscripts*, by Deirdre Jackson, which shows not only biblical scenes but also images of medieval saints performing miracles.

38. The prison riot took place in the high security prison at Narok, Kenya, and was quelled as I prayed with the chaplain on the phone. The dry rot disappeared from Holy Trinity Leicester between a Sunday and a Thursday in October 2004. The light story was told at the Baptist Mainstream Leaders' Conference at Swanwick in January 2008 by a representative of Open Doors, which works with persecuted Christians; it had been told to her first hand by a minister in Cairo. The ball bearings story was told by Baroness Cox at New Wine in 2007. For all these, see *Doing What Jesus Did*, pp.41–45. The Haiti story was told at a healing day in Chichester Diocese by a man who had received it from his son, at that time working in Haiti as part of the relief effort following the earthquake in January 2010.

39. A boy named Katshinyi Manikai returned to life having been certified dead from malaria in a clinic in DR Congo, when Mahesh Chavda prayed for him in a meeting attended by his father – see Mark Stibbe, *Know Your Spiritual Gifts*, pp.98–101 (which includes a copy of the boy's death certificate). Eleven people have been healed from death through the prayers of Iris Ministries in Mozambique – see Guy Chevreau, *Turning: The Kingdom of God and the Western World*, pp. 53–56. Another well-known modern-day 'resurrection' story is that of Nigerian pastor Daniel Ekechukwu, taken to Emezurike Hospital in Owerri on Friday 30 November 2001 following a car crash. Pronounced dead on arrival, he was transferred to St Eunice's Clinic where a death certificate was issued. His body was sent to the mortuary and partially embalmed. On Sunday morning the body was taken at his wife's insistence to the Grace of God Mission church in Onitsa, where that afternoon as people prayed it seems that Daniel was raised from the

dead; the event was partially captured on video. See *Doing What Jesus Did*, p.43, and www.heavensfamily.org/ss/daniel_main. A similar story is told by Australian Ian McCormack, laid out as dead in a hospital in Mauritius after being stung by a notoriously lethal box jellyfish, and restored to life fifteen minutes later to the terror of the medics attending him. Ian's story is told by John Woolmer, *Encounters: Authentic Experiences of God*, pp.105–110. Both Daniel and Ian's stories have been the subject of endless scrutiny – google either name and you can read the details and watch video testimonies by the protagonists. Both men are undoubtedly alive today. Such stories are unusual but not unprecedented; for historical examples see Alison Morgan, *What Happens When We Die*, pp.75–76, or *Dante and the Medieval Other World*, pp.1–4.

40. There is a clear scriptural distinction between the office of prophet (in the Old Testament but also in the New, see, for example, Ephesians 4.11) and the gift of prophecy, which Paul urges all believers to seek – see 1 Corinthians 14.1). F.L. Godet says a prophecy is a 'miracle in the form of speech,' and produces an effect in the spiritual domain similar to that produced on the sick man by the 'rise and walk' command pronounced by a person exercising the gift of healing. Ellicott summarises the purpose of prophetic words as building up, stirring up, cheering up. See J Rodman Williams, *Renewal Theology* vol. 2 p.383.

41. Joel 2.28–30 and Acts 2.17–18; 1 Corinthians 14.3.

42. John 1; John 11.51–52; Luke 1.67, 2.34, 2.38.

43. Mark 7.24–30.

44. Acts 11 and 21 (Agabus), 15 (Judas and Silas), 19 and 21 (the Ephesians and the daughters of Philip).

45. John 14.26; 15.15–20; 21.18.

46. Acts 13, 20 and 27.

47. See C. M. Robeck, 'Prophecy', in *The New International Dictionary of Pentecostal and Charismatic Movements*, Stanley Burgess (ed), pp. 1008–09.

48. Given through Michael Hogg, it went like this: 'I have called you with a fresh calling, anointed you with a fresh anointing, that you may be my apostle to the lost churches, to those who are broken, downtrodden, lost their faith, those whose faith is dying, in whom the embers of the gospel are dying; I am causing you to go to them and to blow on them to rekindle the flame in their hearts, that my name may rest upon them, that those on the margins may be raised up; through you I will minister a ministry of lost hope, that many will turn their hearts towards me, be healed from the wounds and arrows, so that you can pour oil into their wounds

and they will see clearly, and speak out of their hurt, and that they will trust in me and know that I am the one who rebuilds, restores, refreshes, and I will pour my Holy Spirit into them by the bucketload, not by drips, and heal fully those determined to serve me, who have been turned out of the way, and I will be to them a guard, a shield, a protection, so that they may be no longer wounded and set aside. I will put a fresh hope in their hearts and cause them to walk before me in purity before this generation, so that my church will be one of purity, holiness and righteousness, looking towards the eternal city. My reward is great for those who serve me; know my restoration and my peace.'

49. Luke 8.43, 13.11; John 9.6–7, Luke 11.14.

50. Acts 13.6–12, 16.16–18, Mark 1.21–27.

51. For Olive's story and others see Alison Morgan, *Doing What Jesus Did*, pp.50–54. See also *The Wild Gospel*, p.275.

52. Ephesians 6.12. Many people are uncomfortable with the idea that Freemasonry is spiritually dangerous, pointing out that the majority of Freemasons are well motivated, caring people, and often also Christian. However, at its heart and at its highest levels Freemasonry does not honour Jesus but rather a composite deity, and its initiation ceremonies are not compatible with a full commitment to Christ. I have prayed with many people damaged by their family's involvement in Freemasonry. Others have written in more detail about this, but see the article by Trevor Lake on www.resource-arm.net/articles/freemasonry.html

53. Mark 16.17 – part of the 'longer ending' of Mark held by many scholars to have been added to the gospel at a later date.

54. *The Book of Margery Kempe*, chapters 33 and 40 – for an extract see *Doing What Jesus Did*, pp.14–15. Francis of Assisi and Ignatius of Loyola are also said to have spoken in tongues – see Simon Ponsonby, *God Inside Out*, 'Historical evidence for the continuity of the remarkable charisms', p.272.

55. This story was confirmed to Bishop Martin Breytenbach by John Lowes himself. John later became a community priest in South Africa.

56. This took place in 1995. For more on the gift of tongues see *Doing What Jesus Did*, pp.56–59.

57. Matthew 10.8. 1 Corinthians 12 is one of several biblical passages which talk about the ways in which the Spirit works through us for the benefit of others – see for example Exodus 31.2–6 (the first place where the Spirit is given for ministry, in this case one of craftsmanship); Daniel 5.11–12; 1 Corinthians 7.1, 6–9; Romans 12.4–8; Ephesians 4.8–12; 1 Peter 4.8–11.

58. See chapter 1, note 14.

59. *Surprised by the Voice of God*, p.413.

Chapter 11

1. Owen Gingerich, *God's Universe*, p.6. Wolfhart Pannenberg, *Toward a Theology of Nature*, p.48. See also Francis Collins, head of the Human Genome Project: 'There is no conflict in being a rigorous scientist and a person who believes in a God who takes a personal interest in each one of us. Science's domain is to explore nature. God's domain is in the spiritual world, a realm not possible to explore with the tools and language of science. It must be examined with the heart, the mind, and the soul – and the mind must find a way to embrace both realms.' *The Language of God*, p.6.

2. Viewing Genesis as a scientific text leads to some remarkable results. In 2007 a 27 million dollar Creation Museum opened in Kentucky. It sets out to demonstrate that the universe was created in six consecutive twenty-four hour periods, that the earth is 6,000 years old, and that all human beings are descended from two individuals named Adam and Eve. It has a special effects theatre, complete with vibrating seats, where you can watch a video of the Great Flood and learn how dinosaurs survived on board the Ark. See www.creationmuseum.org and the related www.answersingenesis.org, which asserts that 'The Bible – the history book of the universe – provides a reliable, eye-witness account of the beginning of all things' – though they don't explain exactly *whose* eyes witnessed these things (certainly not those of Moses, supposed author of the book, or those of the person or persons who centuries later wrote it down).

3. A category mistake is one which uses the information at hand (scriptural, scientific) to answer the wrong question. In this instance, scriptural information cannot be used to tell us how, and scientific information cannot tell us why. (Mary Midgley comments: 'with the largest, most puzzling questions, we have no choice but to proceed in mythical language which cannot be explained in detail at all, but which serves… to indicate what sort of spiritual universe we perceive ourselves to be living in. This is the province of religion. Adding God is not, as Dawkins thinks, adding an illicit extra item to the cosmos, it is perceiving the whole thing differently'– *New Scientist*, 7 October 2006.) Creationism is at least in part a reaction against the so-called 'social Darwinism' of the early twentieth century, which coined the term 'survival of the fittest' and taught that it can be applied not just to biological species but to whole people groups – thus paving the way for racist philosophies such as Nazism. Many Christians felt that if this was what evolution taught, they wanted nothing to do with it; but it does illustrate the dangers of building a philosophy out of a scientific theory.

4. See Nick Spencer and Denis Alexander, *Rescuing Darwin: God and Evolution in Britain Today*, pp.46–48 'Genesis in history'.

5. 'Usually, even a non-Christian knows something about the earth, the heavens, and the other elements of this world, about the motion and orbit of the stars and even their size and relative positions, about the predictable eclipses of the sun and moon, the cycles of the years and the seasons, about the kinds of animals, shrubs, stones, and so forth, and this knowledge he holds to as being certain from reason and experience. Now, it is a disgraceful and dangerous thing for an infidel to hear a Christian, presumably giving the meaning of Holy Scripture, talking nonsense on these topics; and we should take all means to prevent such an embarrassing situation, in which people show a vast ignorance in a Christian and laugh it to scorn. The shame is not so much that an ignorant individual is derided, but the people outside the household of the faith think our sacred writers held such opinions, and, to the great loss of those for whose salvation we toil, the writers of our Scripture are criticized and rejected as unlearned men. If they find a Christian mistaken in a field which they themselves know well and hear him maintaining his foolish opinions about our books, how are they going to believe those books and matters concerning the resurrection of the dead, the hope of eternal life, and the kingdom of heaven, when they think their pages are full of falsehoods on facts which they themselves have learned from experience in the light of reason?' From *On the Literal Meaning of Genesis*, quoted by Francis Collins, *The Language of God*, p.156.

6. See Adam Nicholson, *Power and Glory: Jacobean England and the Making of the King James Bible*, p.149. Nick Spencer points out that even Darwin only realised in 1861 that the marginal notation in standard Bible editions claiming the world began in 4004 BC was derived from James Ussher, and not from the Bible itself – Nick Spencer, *Darwin and God*, p.42.

7. For the rise in creationism in the twentieth century see Nick Spencer and Denis Alexander, *Rescuing Darwin*, pp.26–27. Collins, *The Language of God*, p.206.

8. Stephen Hawking, having previously thrown statements about 'knowing the mind of God' into his work, suggests in his recent book on M-theory that the law of gravity is sufficient explanation for the existence of the universe; 'it is not necessary to invoke God'. Professor Hawking does not attempt to explain how or why the law of gravity should itself exist, and early responses suggest that most scientists (including many atheists) and theologians see no incompatibility between the potential implications of the (as yet unproven) M-theory and the Christian faith. See Stephen Hawking and Leonard Mlodinow, *The Grand Design*. Hawking, like Nietzsche before him, may be premature in his declaration that God is unnecessary. Frank Close, theoretical physicist at the University of Oxford, comments: 'I don't see that M-theory adds one iota to the God debate, either pro or con' – see Hannah Devlin, *The Times*, 2 September 2010.

9. Geneticist Richard Lewontin agrees: 'our willingness to accept scientific claims that are against common sense is the key to an understanding of the real struggle between science and the supernatural. We take the side of science... because we have a prior commitment... to materialism.' See John Lennox, *God's Undertaker*, p.34–35. Science itself, on the other hand, is simply a method; it can be defined as 'an organized endeavour to explain the properties of the physical world by means of empirically testable theories constructed by a research community trained in specialised techniques' – Denis Alexander, *Science, Friend or Foe?*, quoted Nick Spencer and Denis Alexander, *Rescuing Darwin*, p.52.

10. Romans 1.20. Bonaventure's thirteenth-century *Ascent of the Mind to God* describes the ways in which contemplation of the physical world can lead us, as if by the rungs of a ladder, into the presence of God; see the article by Alison Morgan in ReSource magazine issue 2, Spring 2005, online at www.resource-arm.net. Or try eighteenth-century Jonathan Edwards, *Images or Shadows of Divine Things*. Many examples of such writings are given by Matthew Fox, *Original Blessing*, particularly in Appendices A and C.

11. *The Blind Watchmaker*, p.112.

12. Francis Collins, *The Language of God*. Denis Alexander, *Creation or Evolution*.

13. Paul Davies, *New Scientist*, 30 January 1999 (Davies has written many books, including *God and the New Physics* and *The Goldilocks Enigma: Why is the Universe Just Right for Life?* John Lennox, *God's Undertaker*, quotes Bernd-Olaf Kuppers, *Information and the Origin of Life*: 'the problem of the origin of life is clearly basically equivalent to the problem of the origin of biological information', p.139. For Wheeler see p.167; see also Lennox's full discussion in chapter 9, 'Matters of information'.

14. Examples of biblical passages referring to the role of God in creation can be found in Alison Morgan, *Praying with Creation*; in addition to those cited in this chapter see especially Psalm 104. Other examples are Job 12.10; Job 33.4; Job 37–39; Psalm 33.6–9; Psalm 65.5–13; Psalm 102.25–26; Psalm 135.6–7; Psalm 148; Proverbs 8.22–31; Jeremiah 10.12–13; Wisdom of Solomon 11.17–12.1; Wisdom 13.1–9; Jeremiah 10.12–13; Matthew 6.25–30.

15. It is notable that both the coming of the Spirit upon Jesus at his baptism and the release of the Spirit to all believers after his crucifixion are represented as irruptions of energy which tear open the heavens (see Mark 1.10 and Mark 15.38). The resurrection itself is an event which depends upon divine energy.

16. *Science and Christian Belief: Theological Reflections of a Bottom-up Thinker*, p.71. See also quantum chemist Henry Schaeffer, who remarks: 'A Creator must exist. The Big Bang ripples and subsequent scientific findings are clearly pointing to an ex

nihilo creation consistent with the first few verses of the book of Genesis', quoted by John Lennox, *God's Undertaker*, p.29.

17. Terry Pratchett, *Lords and Ladies*, p.7.

18. See for example the article 'The Myth of the Beginning of Time', by Gabriele Veneziano, founder of string theory, *Scientific American*, May 2004.

19. Quoted by Francis Collins, *The Language of God*, p.67. Collins also notes that the laws of physics work perfectly from the first 10^{-43} seconds after the Big Bang onwards, but break down if we attempt to reach backwards beyond that point.

20. 'You may not feel outstandingly robust, but if you are an average-sized adult you will contain within your modest frame no less than 7×10^{18} joules of potential energy – enough to explode with the force of thirty very large hydrogen bombs, assuming you knew how to liberate it and really wished to make a point. Everything has this kind of energy trapped within it. We're just not very good at getting it out. Even a uranium bomb – the most energetic thing we have produced yet – releases less than 1 per cent of the energy it could release if only we were more cunning' – Bill Bryson, *A Short History of Nearly Everything*, p.109.

21. For the statistical odds see John Lennox, *God's Undertaker*, ch 7, 'The Origin of Life.' For a layman's summary see Bill Bryson: 'By all the laws of probability proteins shouldn't exist. To make a protein you need to assemble amino acids (which I am obliged by long tradition to refer to here as 'the building blocks of life') in a particular order, in much the same way that you assemble letters in a particular order to spell a word. The problem is that words in the amino-acid alphabet are often exceedingly long. To spell 'collagen', the name of a common type of protein, you need to arrange eight letters in the right order. To make collagen, you need to arrange 1,055 amino acids in precisely the right sequence. But – and here's an obvious but crucial point – you don't make it. It makes itself, spontaneously, without direction, and this is where the unlikelihoods come in. The chances of a 1,055-sequence molecule like collagen spontaneously self-assembling are, frankly, nil. It just isn't going to happen.' Bill Bryson, *A Short History of Nearly Everything*, p.254.

22. Paul Davies, *God and the New Physics*, p.58.

23. Consciousness cannot be accounted for in physical terms; research in the new discipline of neuroscience suggests that logical, emotional and spiritual processes occur as mutually distinct patterns of activity in the brain – see Danah Zohar and Ian Marshall, *SQ – Spiritual Intelligence*, ch 3 'Three kinds of thinking'.

24. *A Brief History of Time*, p.209. See also John Lennox: 'All theories on the origin of life run aground on the question "how did the genetic code, along with the

mechanisms for its translation, originate?" – for it seems not that DNA created life but rather that life created DNA', p.134–36.

25. For the maths see John Lennox, *God's Undertaker*, pp.109–10, 'What say the mathematicians?'. For the bias see Hugh Montefiore, *The Probability of God*, p.161: 'although there is no external force imposed on species, and in particular on their genetic systems, mutations occur which would not be expected by random mutation. This is not because of external pressure, but because of the bias implanted in matter. Such bias is not, of course, to be detected by scientific measurement (and so the hypothesis is not testable) since there is no possibility of setting alongside it matter which is not implanted by the bias towards complexity and integration. Another way of describing this bias would be to call it the Holy Spirit working with the matter of the universe, unfolding the purposes of the Creator by immanent operation.'

26. *The Language of God*, ch 10, 'BioLogos'.

27. 'The entire range of living matter on Earth, from whales to viruses, and from oaks to algae, could be regarded as constituting a single living entity, capable of manipulating the Earth's atmosphere to suit its overall needs and endowed with faculties and powers far beyond those of its constituent parts.' Lovelock called this mechanism 'Gaia'. James Lovelock, *Gaia*, pp.6-9.

28. *On the Holy Spirit*, 2 May 1933, quoted by Simon Ponsonby, *God Inside Out*, p.94. Simon has a whole chapter on the Spirit and creation.

30. Thomas Browne, *Religio medici*, *Major Works* p.99. For Hegel see Simon Ponsonby, *God Inside Out*, p.76. Pierre Teilhard de Chardin's *The Divine Milieu* is an extended essay on the role of the Spirit in the created world. Paul Tillich deals with the Spirit and creation in vol 3 of his Systematic Theology, *Life and the Spirit*.

31. Wolfhart Pannenberg, *Toward a Theology of Nature*; see especially pp.65–66. The theological perspective which holds that creation is a continuous process in which the universe is actively sustained in being by its creator is often called process theology or panentheism. A good summary is given in the Church of England's report *Man and Nature*, edited by Hugh Montefiore.

32. Vincent Donovan, *Christianity Rediscovered: An Epistle from the Masai*, pp.133–34.

33. Arthur Peacocke, *Creation and the World of Science*, p.151.

34. Francis Crick, one of the discoverers of the structure of DNA, had this to say about human identity: 'You, your joys and your sorrows, your memories and ambitions, your sense of personal identity and free will, are in fact no more than

the behaviour of a vast assembly of nerve cells and their associated molecules' – *Astonishing Hypothesis – the scientific search for the soul*, p.3. Peter Atkins, Professor of Chemistry at Oxford, offers these contributions to the human search for meaning: 'There is no reason to suppose that science cannot deal with every aspect of existence. Science has no need of purpose. All the extraordinary, wonderful richness of the world can be expressed as growth from the dunghill of purposeless interconnected corruption', *Creation Revisited – the origin of space, time and the universe*, pp.127–28. Richard Dawkins asks 'Why on Earth should anyone assume that there IS a purpose? You are assuming that the "why" question is a sensible or legitimate question. Not all questions are. You have no right to expect an answer to a silly question'– in a webchat with Ruth Gledhill, *The Times*, 9 September 2010. They would do well to heed the advice given by Nobel Laureate Sir Peter Medawar: 'There is no quicker way for a scientist to bring discredit upon himself and upon his profession than roundly to declare – particularly when no declaration of any kind is called for – that science knows, or soon will know, the answers to all questions worth asking, and that questions which do not admit a scientific answer are in some way non-questions.. that only simpletons ask and only the gullible profess to be able to answer.' *Advice to a Young Scientist*, Harper and Row 1979, p.31.

35. John Ruskin, *Modern Painters* (1843) – quoted in *The Creation Spirit: An Anthology*, p.19.

36. 'Impeaching a self-appointed judge', *Scientific American*.

Chapter 12

1. 1 Corinthians 3.1–3, 1 Peter 3.2–4. Minucius Felix, *Octavius* 31.7, 38.5; Minucius lived in Rome, 160–240 AD. Quoted by Alan Kreider, *Worship and Evangelism in pre-Christendom*, p.19. *Beautiful Lives* is the title of ReSource's evangelism course – it is not by the coherency of our words but by the beauty of our lives that people will be initially drawn to Jesus. See the Appendix for more details.

2. For the way in which we are transformed to become like Jesus see Romans 8.29; 2 Corinthians 3.18; 5.20; Galatians 4.19; Philippians 3.7–11; Colossians 1.28–29; 1 Peter 2.21.

3. Alan Hirsch, *The Forgotten Ways*, p.24. See also Matthew 5.13–16 – we are meant to be salt and light, different from those around us.

4. See for example the September 2010 survey by the Barna Group in the US: 'survey finds lots of spiritual dialogue but not much change,' www.barna.org/

transfomation-articles/433, or the 1990 'Study of Protestant Congregations: A Summary Report on Faith, Loyalty, and Congregational Life' conducted by the Minneapolis-based Search Institute, www.religion-online.org. Compare Matthew 5.13–16, where Jesus says we are to be like salt and light to our communities.

5. Our understanding of the word 'disciple' shows how the words we use influence the way we think! The word 'disciple' or *mathetes* is particularly associated with Jesus – its equivalent appears only once in the Old Testament, and not at all in the New Testament outside the gospels and the Acts of the Apostles. It indicates a person who follows a particular master, who himself determines what form the learning should take. For *mathetes* and apprenticeship see Michael Wilkins, *The Concept of Disciple in Matthew's Gospel As Reflected in the Use of the Term Mathetes*; or his more readable *Following the Master: Discipleship in the Steps of Jesus*. See also the helpful overview by Bill Hull, *The Complete Book of Discipleship: On Being and Making Followers of Christ*, especially ch 1, 'Biblical Foundations of Discipleship'.

6. For Nicodemus see John 3.1–10, 7.50, 19.39. Jesus announced that his ministry would be one of healing, deliverance and the proclamation of good news (Luke 4.18–19). As he began to do these things, he said others would need to do them too (Matthew 9.35–38). He sent first twelve disciples (Matthew 10.1, 8) and then seventy (Luke 10.1) to have a go; evaluated their work with them (Luke 10.17–20, Mark 9.28–29) and parted from them with a lasting commission to continue this process (Matthew 28.18–20). For more, see Alison Morgan, *Doing What Jesus Did*, and ch 10 of this book.

7. For the vine see John 15; for the body see Romans 12; Ephesians 4; 1 Corinthians 12. Some things can be learned only in community – for example, not to compete or judge: Mark 10.35–40, Matthew 7.1–5.

8. Peter the rock: Matthew 16.18. Peter's impetuosity is shown all through the gospels, from his walking on water and refusal to allow Jesus to wash his feet to his cutting off the ear of a Roman soldier in the Garden of Gethsemane. James: Mark 3.21, James 1.22–25. Paul: Acts 7.54 – 8.3; 9.1–30; 11.25–26 and onwards. Paul speaks of the way we are transformed into the likeness of Christ in Romans chapters 7–8 and Ephesians chapters 4–5.

9. This process begins in Acts 2.41–47 and continues throughout Acts with the planting of the first churches; see too Paul's letters to those early Christian communities in Rome, Ephesus, Corinth and elsewhere.

10. Rowan Williams describes the church in terms of encounter in *Mission-shaped Church*, p.vii. See also his lecture 'Being Disciples' given on 27 April 2007 to the Fulcrum Conference (www.fulcrum-anglican.org.uk), reprinted in ReSource magazine issue 12, *Being Disciples*, Summer 2008.

11. For the ascetics, Francis and Wesley see Alison Morgan, *The Wild Gospel*, ch 4. The decline of the Methodist Church began once it abandoned its system of group discipleship in 'classes' – see Alan Hirsch, *The Forgotten Ways*, ch 4, 'Disciple making', citing research done by Steve Addison. The standard study of Methodism is HD Rack, *Reasonable Enthusiast: John Wesley and Rise of Methodism*; Methodists became the agents of social transformation, campaigning for the abolition of slavery, and for the reform of education, prisons and working conditions. For the Methodist 'classes' and 'bands' see Paul Bayes and Tim Sledge: *Mission-shaped Parish*, ch 2. For China see Alan Hirsch, *The Forgotten Ways*, pp.188–89. There are estimated to be upwards of 80 million Christians in China, with 35,000 a day coming to faith.

12. The biblical words for healing, wholeness and salvation are all derived from the single Greek verb *sozo*.

13. John 3.3–7; Luke 4.18–21. Peter talks about salvation and our healing from sin in 1 Peter 2.8–9 and 2.24–25. Paul talks about our transformation in 2 Corinthians 3.18, 5.17; in the great prayers of Ephesians 1.17–22 and 3.14–21; in Romans 12.1–2.

14. See Romans chapters 7–8; Ephesians 4.17–5.20 and Galatians 5.16–26; Colossians 3.1–17; Titus 3.5.

15. Rowan Williams talked about discipleship as moving into the space opened up for us by Jesus in his address to a Fresh Expressions day conference in Lincoln, 5 March 2010.

16. Mark 15.38; Hebrews 4.16; Ephesians 3.18; John 1.1–3; Revelation 21.1–2.

17. Matthew 28.19–20; John 20.21–22. See also Acts 19.2–7, where Paul asks the Ephesian believers if they received the Holy Spirit, and prays for them to do so.

18. George MacDonald, quoted by Bill Hull, *The Complete Book of Discipleship*, p.117.

19. Carl told his story at New Wine at Shepton Mallet in August 2006; see also Ted Dekker and Carl Medearis, *Tea with Hezbollah*.

20. John Richardson, the incumbent in Radipole, Dorset.

21. Quoted by Alan Hirsch, *The Forgotten Ways*, p.101. See 1 Peter 3.2.

22. The narrow path – see Matthew 7.13–14. The Way – see Acts 9.2; 19.9; 19.23; 22.4; 24.14; 24.22.

23. William Law lived in the eighteenth century and is best known for his classic

A Serious Call to a Devout and Holy Life. For this quote see Bill Hull, *The Complete Book of Discipleship*, p.26.

24. In an interview with Christopher Landau in the Grand Committee Room of the Houses of Parliament, 21 October 2010. See also Alan Hirsch: 'For the follower of Jesus, discipleship is not the first step toward a promising career. It is in itself the fulfilment of his or her destiny' – *The Forgotten Ways,* p.103.

25. Sarah Wheway wrote her story for ReSource magazine, issue 5, Spring 2006. See also Alison Morgan, *Doing What Jesus Did*, p.48.

26. Martin Cavender became the Director of Springboard, the Archbishops' Initiative for Evangelism, which ran from 1992 to 2004; he is now Director of ReSource.

27. *Radical Gratitude*, p.1.

28. See www.licc.org.uk/imagine. Imagine is a project whose vision is to 'recover the central vocation of whole-life missionary disciplemaking in our church communities.'

29. Following the success of *Rooted in Jesus* in Africa, ReSource is developing a new process discipleship course for use in the West – see the Appendix for more details.

30. Martin wrote his testimony for ReSource magazine, issue 12, *Being Disciples*, Summer 2008. It included these words: 'My experience as a shepherd helps me to understand both Christ and his ministry. The painful experiences have also made me realize the importance of team work. It is my broken hearted prayer that the Lord will help me to safeguard my lifetime calling to serve others, from serving the flock to serving the people of God as a minister of the Word.'

31. Quoted by Alan Hirsch, *The Forgotten Ways,* p.113.

32. *The Forgotten Ways*, p.103.

33. *The Jesus Way*, p.270.

Chapter 13

1. A task given a recent boost by the *Mission-Shaped Questions* collection of essays edited by Steven Croft, which includes a contribution from me, 'What does the gift of the Spirit mean for the shape of the Church?'.

2. For the word 'Church' in the New Testament see Matthew 16.18; 18.17; and many refs in Acts and the Epistles – especially in the opening salutations, 'to the

church in…'. For the church meeting in homes see Romans 16.5 (the house of Priscilla and Aquila), Colossians 3.15 (the house of Nympha), Acts 16.40 (the house of Lydia). For the history of the early church and its buildings see Owen Chadwick, *A History of Christianity*, ch 1.

3. For the Hebrew and Greek words and their meanings see William Barclay, *New Testament Words*, pp.68–72. Both *qahal* and *ecclesia* are in origin secular words referring to assemblies of citizens. It's particularly helpful for us to realise that Church is not by its nature an institution, because although people may be more inclined to explore the spiritual aspect of life, they are far less inclined to join institutions and organisations (of any kind) than in previous generations.

4. Paul Tillich, *Theology of Culture*, pp.40–41. See Romans 7–8, 2 Corinthians 3.18, 5.7. Other biblical metaphors for church are organic – it is compared to a body (Romans 12, Ephesians 4, 1 Corinthians 12) or vine (John 15). For a helpful discussion see Frank Viola, *Finding Organic Church*.

5. *Mission-shaped Church*, p.132.

6. Thomas Merton remarks: 'we are living in the greatest revolution in history, a huge, spontaneous upheaval of the entire human race. Not a revolution planned and carried out by any particular party, race or nation, but a deep elemental boiling over of all the inner contradictions that have ever been in people, a revolution of the chaotic forces inside everybody. This is not something we have chosen nor is it anything we are free to avoid,' quoted by Robert Warren, *Being Human, Being Church*, p.42.

7. Sally Gaze, *Mission-shaped and Rural: Growing Churches in the Countryside*, p.10.

8. See the comments by Elton Trueblood in Bill Hull, *The Complete Book of Discipleship*, p.264. He concludes, 'The fact that this is not generally understood is one of the chief evidences of the spiritual erosion which distresses us.'

9. *Renovation of the Heart: Putting on the Character of Christ*, p.250. See also Robert Warren, who suggests that our current model of church is essentially feudal; *Being Human, Being Church*, ch 1.

10. John Drane, *After McDonaldization – Mission, Ministry and Christian Discipleship in an Age of Uncertainty*, p.vii.

11. For church growth statistics see Bob Jackson, *Hope for the Church*, ch 1. Church of England statistics are collected and analysed by Lynda Barley, and her reports can be found on www.cofe.anglican.org/info/statistics. See also her article 'Can fresh expressions of church make a difference?', in *Mission-shaped Questions*, CHP 2008.

12. For Alpha see www.alphafriends.org/facts-figures; to these numbers may be added those who follow one of the many other introductory courses available. Alan Jamieson tells the story of those who feel they have no alternative but to leave the church in *A Churchless Faith – faith journeys beyond the churches*. Stuart Murray estimates that 1,500 people leave the UK church each week (not including those who die or move away); in the 1980s and 90s 1.6 million people joined churches – but 2.8 million left them: *Church After Christendom*, ch.2. For Christmas attendance see www.churchofengland.org 'Facts and stats'; a Christmas poll conducted by Demos and reported in *The Week*, 11 December 2010 found similar results. Actual attendance figures from recent years suggest the figure who actually do make it is more like one in five, or 20% – but that is still a marked increase on the 6% who attend regularly during the year.

13. Ken Blanchard and Terry Waghorn, *Mission Possible*, p.xviii.

14. There is room, as the Church of England's *Mission-Shaped Church* report affirms, both for fresh expressions of church and for inherited models of church. Jesus talked about a master who brings out of his storehouse what is new and what is old – Matthew 13.52.

15. Many tell their story on www.freshexpressions.org.uk, which also produces a series of DVDs featuring individual projects. 'Back to Church Sunday' is a good example of a simple but effective initiative which aims to re-recruit those who have got out of the habit of going to church. In 2010, 153 parishes in the diocese of Carlisle took part. 7,000 invitations were given, and 1,000 people took them up, of whom 100 joined the church (one church, St Paul's Grange, doubled its membership from twelve to twenty-four). In the UK as a whole in 2009, members of 6,000 churches gave out 100,000 accepted invitations; a survey six months later showed that 10% of those invited had stayed. See www.backtochurch.co.uk. A survey by Tearfund suggested that 3 million people in the UK would go to church if someone invited them – see Lisa's comment in chapter 1, 'I managed to get an invitation to church.' Christian Schwarz and Robert Warren have developed church audit materials – Christian Schwarz, *Natural Church Development Handbook*, (for use in the UK see www.healthychurch.co.uk); Robert Warren, *The Healthy Churches Handbook*, (Robert's material was developed and published by Springboard, and is still carried by ReSource).

16. Many nurture courses are available – google *Alpha*, *The Y Course*, *Emmaus*, *Knowing God Better*, *Christianity Explained*, *Start*, *Essence*, *Christianity Explored*, or *Evangelium*. Or visit www.resource-arm.net publications and look at *Beyond Ourselves*, a unique new course which helps people with no church background to find faith and leads them into the next stage of their journey as disciples of Jesus. For community action see Lynda Barley, *Community Value*; 21% of church members are involved in local social action projects through the local church.

17. See www.tubestation.org: "It's about people coming together, breaking down boundaries and taking risks. It's about the ride, having fun experiencing the fullness of life and being inspired by the ocean and the beauty of creation. It's about music, art, waves, snow and opening compassionate eyes to our world, encouraging people to reach for their full potential." Tubestation is featured on the DVD 'Expressions making a difference', Fresh Expressions, 2011.

18. To find out more about 'Sorted' or to watch the DVD on youtube visit www.churcharmy.org.uk.

19. Sally Gaze tells this story from her own ministry, with many others, in *Mission-Shaped and Rural*; see particularly ch 4, 'Rural fresh expressions' with its tales of alternative worship in barns, croissants, and drama on third Sundays, youth congregations in schools, and prayer groups in farmers' kitchens.

20. Bob Jackson, *Hope for the Church*, and *The Road to Growth*. Bob was appointed to lead the new diocesan strategy 'Going for Growth' in the diocese of Lichfield, and within four years the pattern of gentle decline had been replaced by one of gentle growth. Bob describes the process in his article 'Signs of growth, signs of life,' ReSource magazine issue 15, summer 2009 (online at www.resource-arm.net). The toilet story is told in Bob Jackson and George Fisher's *Everybody Welcome* course, p.43.

21. Ian Bishop wrote about 'Godly dissatisfaction in Middlewich' in ReSource magazine issue 15, summer 2009, 'Signs of life.' The parish renewal weekend was organised through ReSource and led by Mark Tanner.

22. Bob Jackson, *Hope for the Church*, pp.54 and 62–63.

23. Just a few of the stories told in ReSource magazine – by Richard Morgan (issue 11), Robert Ward and Alex Scott (issue 15). See www.resource-arm.net. For other dramatic stories of turnaround see the excellent *Back from the Brink: Stories of Churches Which Refused to Die* by Heather and Pat Wraight. The key factors? The authors list the following: leadership, vision, prayer, children, outward looking, willingness to change, inspiration, involving people, risk taking, dealing with buildings, use of money, and finally God-incidences! See too Paul Bayes and Tim Sledge, *Mission-shaped Parish*.

24. Bob Jackson, *The Road to Growth*, p.40.

25. Neil Cole, *Organic Church*, p.22.

26. Presenting the 2008 statistics for the C of E, Lynda Barley pointed out that committed membership of anything at all is in decline: "It is important to see [attendance] trends in the context of wider changes in a society where fewer people

are willing to join and take part in membership organizations. Political parties have seen their memberships fall by around 40 per cent in recent years."

27. Martin Down, *Speak to these Bones*, pp.172–73.

28. See Acts 2.42; 1 Corinthians 12.12–27; John 15.1–13. It was a hard lesson to learn even for Jesus' first disciples. Judas never did learn it; James and John had to be unpinned from personal ambition, Peter cut down to size – see John 12.4 and 13.2, Matthew 20.20–24, John 13.8–10.

29. Robert Lewis, *The Church of Irresistible Influence*, pp.28–29. The church decided that the purpose of building community within the church was to build bridges to those outside it. They began a comprehensive programme of engagement with their city, each small group choosing its own focus – mentoring fatherless children, painting local schools, providing bereavement counselling, financial advice and so on. Their key verse was Matthew 5.16, "let your light shine before men so that they may see your good deeds and praise your Father in heaven." The result was a vast increase in motivation and renewed church growth.

30. Luke 4.42; Matthew 25.35–36; Matthew 10.8; Matthew 28.18–20.

31. See www.hope08.com. The initiative has continued each year. The report *The Whole Church, for the Whole Nation, for the Whole Year: An Evaluation of HOPE08*, by Stephen Backhouse, was published by Theos in 2009. See also Debra Green, *Redeeming our Communities*, for an account of the way similar projects are helping to transform communities within the city of Manchester. The Anglican Consultative Council has formulated our shared purpose in the Five Marks of Mission; to respond to human need by loving service is the third of these (see note 37).

32. See www.coretlumenchristi.org. To proclaim the good news of the kingdom is the first of the five marks of mission.

33. Michael Frost, *Exiles*, p.122. It's rather like attending a cancer support group when you haven't got cancer, Frost says; it won't do anything for you, because it doesn't offer you a journey to go on. He comments that for many, Christian community has become little more than a quiet and reflective soul-space (this is the danger of the alternative worship movement) or a spiritual buzz (the danger of the charismatic movement) for people trying to deal with a busy consumerist lifestyle. He points out that church is not meant to be a refuge of work addicts and experience junkies, a spiritual hospital or entertainment centre; it is about something rather bigger than that – it's a bunch of people who are going somewhere. It seems particularly key for young people – surveys show that up to 80% of Christian teenagers drop out of church when they leave home, because

what they have been offered in their church youth group is not the challenge of discipleship but the comfort of entertainment. Robert Lewis – *The Church of Irresistible Influence*, p.42.

34. Robert Lewis, *The Church of Irresistible Influence*, p.42.

35. To teach, baptise, and nurture new believers is the second of the AC five marks of mission.

36. This is how Jesus himself summarised his task – see Luke 4.43.

37. The five marks of mission were developed between 1984 and 1990, and reaffirmed in 1999. See www.anglicancommunion.org 'The Five Marks of Mission'. See notes 23, 31, 32, 35, 39 for examples. See also the stories in chapter 6, the example of Keynsham in chapter 7, and the experience of the Tanzanian *Rooted in Jesus* groups in chapter 9.

38. Stephen's obituary can be read on www.thisisannouncements.co.uk/5861923. For the story, see www.bbc.co.uk

39. John – not his real name – told his story to Martin Cavender during a mission in Axbridge. To seek to transform unjust structures of society is the fourth of the AC five marks of mission.

40. This story was told to me by Matt Barnes, rector of St Thomas Chesterfield, where these events took place.

41. See www.holytrinityleicester.org, where each of the new 'mission-shaped communities' has its own blog. Litter-picking is one aspect of the fifth mark of mission – to strive to safeguard the integrity of creation and sustain and renew the life of the earth.

42. Called 'First Tuesday', its website is www.1sttuesday.info. Modelled on our Questions events in Leicester, First Tuesday is similar too to the Café church initiative now taking place throughout the Costa Coffee chain – see www.cafechurch.net

43. Steven Croft, *Transforming Communities: Re-imagining the Church for the 21ˢᵗ Century*, ch 4. The two other dangers he mentions are quality control (the tick box approach) and mirror of society (the blender approach).

44. William Abraham, *The Logic of Renewal*, p.158. See also Gordon Fee, *Paul, the Spirit, and the People of God*, p.179.

45. 1 Corinthians 9.20. In Acts, see Peter's vision of eating unclean animals, Acts 10.9–16, and the debate about whether non-Jewish believers should be circumcised, Acts

15, particularly verse 28 where the decision is attributed to the Holy Spirit. For an inspiring contemporary account of this process of discernment and adaptation see Vincent Donovan, *Christianity Rediscovered: An Epistle from the Masai.*

46. *Courageous Leadership*, p.23.

Bibliography

We are, as the twelfth-century saying went, but dwarves standing on the shoulders of giants; in so far as we see over new horizons it is only because we rely on what others have seen before us. It would be impossible to offer a comprehensive listing of the many writers to whom I am indebted in this way; what follows is therefore a simple list of works which I have specifically cited in the text or in the notes.

Abraham, William J.: *The Logic of Renewal*, Eerdmans 2003

Alexander, Denis: *Creation or Evolution: Do We Have to Choose?*, Monarch 2008

Alexander, Denis: 'God, Darwin and Evolution', ReSource magazine issue 14, *Science & Faith,* Spring 2009

Alexander, Liesl: *Free to Live and God Heals Today*, Liesl Alexander 2006

Anderson, Norman: *The Evidence for the Resurrection*, IVP, 1950

Appleyard, Brian: *Understanding the Present: Science and the Soul of Modern Man*, Picador 1992

Astley, Nick, and Pamela Robertson-Pearce: *Soul Food: Nourishing Poems for Starved Minds*, Bloodaxe 2007

Atkins, Peter: *Creation Revisited: The Origin of Space, Time and the Universe*, Penguin 1994

Augustine, Saint: *On the Literal Meaning of Genesis*, Paulist Press International, 2004

Backhouse, Stephen: *The Whole Church, for the Whole Nation, for the Whole Year: An Evaluation of HOPE08*, Theos 2009

Baggini, Julian: 'The rise, fall and rise again of secularism' in *Public Policy Review*, vol. 12.4, Jan–Mar 2006

Baker, Rolland and Heidi: *Always Enough: Miraculous Ministry in Mozambique*, Sovereign World 2003

Barclay, William: *New Testament Words*, Westminster John Knox Press 1974

Barley, Lynda: *Christian Roots, Contemporary Spirituality*, CHP 2006

Barley, Lynda: *Community Value*, CHP 2007

Bartholomew, Craig, and Thorsten Moritz (ed): *Christ and Consumerism: Critical Reflections on the Spirit of Our Age*, Paternoster Press 2000

Bayes, Paul, and Tim Sledge: *Mission-shaped Parish: Traditional Church in a Changing Context*, CHP 2006

Beauregard, Mario: *The Spiritual Brain: A Neuroscientist's Case for the Existence of the Soul*, HarperOne 2007

Bell, Rob: *Velvet Elvis: Repainting the Christian Faith*, Zondervan 2006

Berry, Lucy: *Trouble with Church? Provocative Poems for Thoughtful Christians*, Kevin Mayhew 2008

Blanchard, Ken, and Terry Waghorn: *Mission Possible: Becoming a World-Class Organization While There's Still Time*, McGraw-Hill 1997

Bookless, Dave: *God Doesn't Do Waste*, IVP 2010

Bonaventure of Bagnoregio: *Ascent of the Mind to God*, internet edition

Brierley, Peter: *Religious Trends* No.5, 2005–06 Christian Research

Browne, Thomas: *Major Works*, Penguin Classics 2006

Bruce, F. F.: *The New Testament Documents: Are They Reliable?*, IVP 1960, reprinted Eerdmans 2003

Bruce, Steve: *God is Dead: Secularization in the West*, Blackwell 2002

Brueggemann, Walter: *Texts that Linger, Words that Explode: Listening to Prophetic Voices*, Fortress Press 2000

Brueggemann, Walter: *Texts Under Negotiation: The Bible and Postmodern Imagination*, Fortress Press 1993

Brueggemann, Walter: *The Word that Redescribes the World: The Bible and Discipleship*, Fortress Press 2006.

Bryson, Bill: *A Short History of Nearly Everything*, BCA 2003

Burgess, Stanley: *International Dictionary of Pentecostal and Charismatic Movements*, Zondervan 2003

Butcher, Tim: *Blood River: A Journey to Africa's Broken Heart*, Vintage Books 2008

Cantalamessa, Raniero: *The Mystery of God's Word*, The Liturgical Press 1994

Carr, Donald E.: *The Forgotten Senses: A Book About the Sensory Puzzles of Life*, Doubleday 1972

Carroll, Lewis: *The Annotated Alice*, edited by Martin Gardner, Penguin 1981

Cartledge, Mark: *Encountering the Spirit*, DLT 2006

Chadwick, Owen: *A History of Christianity*, Phoenix 1995

Chevreau, Guy: *Turnings: The Kingdom of God and the Western World*, New Wine Press 2007

Claiborne, Shane: *The Irresistible Revolution: Living as an Ordinary Radical*, Zondervan 2006

Clouser, Roy: *The Myth of Religious Neutrality: An Essay on the Hidden Role of Religious Belief in Theories*, University of Notre Dame Press 2005

Cole, Neil: *Organic Church: Growing Faith Where Life Happens*, Jossey-Bass 2005

Collins, Francis: *The Language of God: A Scientist Presents Evidence for Belief*, Pocket Books 2007

Colson, Charles, and Nancy Pearcey: *How Now Shall We Live?*, Marshall Pickering 2000

BIBLIOGRAPHY

Comblin, José: *The Holy Spirit and Liberation*, Burns & Oates 1989

Cray, Graham et al.: *Mission-shaped Church: Church Planting and Fresh Expressions of Church in a Changing Context*, CHP 2004

Crick, Francis: *Astonishing Hypothesis: The Scientific Search for the Soul*, Simon & Schuster 1994

Croft, Steven (ed): *Mission-shaped Questions: Defining Issues for Today's Church*, CHP 2008

Croft, Steven: *Transforming Communities: Re-imagining the Church for the 21st century*, DLT 2002

Cummings, E. E.: *Selected Poems* 1923–1958, Faber & Faber 1960

Davies, Paul: *God and the New Physics,* Simon & Schuster 1984

Davies, Paul: *The Goldilocks Enigma: Why is the Universe Just Right for Life?*, Penguin 2007

Dawkins, Richard: *The Blind Watchmaker*, Longmans 1986

Dawkins, Richard: *The God Delusion,* Bantam Press 2006

Dawkins, Richard: *The Selfish Gene*, OUP 1989

De Bono, Edward: *Simplicity*, reprinted Penguin 2009

De Botton, Alain: *The Pleasures and Sorrows of Work*, Hamish Hamilton 2009

De Chardin, Pierre Teilhard: *The Divine Milieu*, Sussex Academic Press 2003

Deere, Jack: *Surprised by the Voice of God*, Kingsway 1996

Dekker, Ted, and Carl Medearis: *Tea with Hezbollah*, Doubleday 2010

Dillard, Annie: *Pilgrim at Tinker Creek,* Picador 1976

Donovan, Vincent: *Christianity Rediscovered: An Epistle from the Masai,* 2nd edition SCM Press 1982

Dowden, Richard: *Africa: Altered States, Ordinary Miracles*, Portobello Books 2008

Down, Martin: *Speak to these Bones*, Monarch 1993

Drane, John: *After McDonaldization: Mission, Ministry and Christian Discipleship in an Age of Uncertainty*, DLT 2008

Drane, John: *Faith in a Changing Culture: Creating Churches for the Next Century*, Marshall Pickering 1994

Drane, John: *The McDonaldization of the Church: Spirituality, Creativity and the Future of the Church*, DLT 2000

Draper, Brian: *Spiritual Intelligence: A New Way of Being*, Lion 2009

Edwards, Jonathan: *Images or Shadows of Divine Things,* Yale University Press, 1948

Etcoff, N. L.: *Liking, Wanting, Having, Being: The Science of Happiness,* Farrar, Straus & Giroux 2008

Fee, Gordon D.: *Paul, the Spirit and the People of God*, Hendrikson Publishers 1996

Finney, John: *Emerging Evangelism,* DLT 2004.

Foster, Richard: *Life with God: A Life-transforming New Approach to Bible Reading*, Hodder & Stoughton 2008

Fox, Matthew: *Original Blessing,* Bear & Co 1983

Frost, Michael: *Exiles: Living Missionally in a Post-Christian Culture*, Hendrikson

Publishers 2006

Frost, Michael, and Alan Hirsch: *The Shaping of Things to Come: Innovation and Mission for the 21st-Century Church,* Hendrikson 2003

Gaze, Sally: *Mission-shaped and Rural: Growing Churches in the Countryside,* CHP 2006

Gempf, Conrad: *Jesus Asked What He Wanted To Know,* Zondervan 2003

Gilbert, Jack: *Refusing Heaven,* Alfred A Knopf 2005

Griffin, Jo: *The Lonely Society?,* Mental Health Foundation 2005

Gingerich, Owen: *God's Universe,* Belknap Press, Harvard University Press 2006

Gould, Stephen Jay: 'Impeaching a self-appointed judge', *Scientific American,* 267, no.1, 1992, pp.118–21

Graves, Robert: *Selected Poems,* Penguin 1986

Green, Debra: *Redeeming our Communities: 21st Century Miracles of Social Transformation,* New Wine Press 2008

Guest, Robert: *The Shackled Continent: Africa's Past, Present and Future,* Pan Books 2005

Hall, D. J.: *The End of Christendom and the Future of Christianity,* Trinity Press International 1995

Haskins, C. H.: *The Renaissance of the Twelfth Century,* new edition Harvard University Press 1990

Hawking, Stephen: *A Brief History of Time,* Bantam Press, 10th edition 1998

Hawking, Stephen, and Leonard Mlodinow: *The Grand Design,* Bantam Press 2010

Hay, David: *Something There: The Biology of the Human Spirit,* DLT 2006

Hay, David: *The Spirituality of the Unchurched,* BIAMS 2000

Hay, David: *Why Spirituality is Difficult for Westerners,* Societas Imprint Academic 2007

Heelas, Paul, and Linda Woodhead: *The Spiritual Revolution,* Blackwell 2005

Hicks, Robert, and Jill Gupta: *A Boy and his Bible,* Creative Publishing 2008

Hirsch, Alan: *The Forgotten Ways,* Brazos Press 2006

Hope, Susan: *Mission-shaped Spirituality,* CHP 2006

Hull, Bill: *The Complete Book of Discipleship: On Being and Making Followers of Christ,* NavPress 2006

Hybels, Bill: *Courageous Leadership,* Zondervan 2008

Ilardi, Steve: *The Depression Cure,* Vermilion 2010

Jackson, Bob: *Hope for the Church,* CHP 2002

Jackson, Bob: *The Road to Growth: Towards a Thriving Church,* CHP 2005

Jackson, Bob, and George Fisher, *Everybody Welcome: The Course Where Everybody Helps Grow their Church,* CHP 2009

Jackson, Deirdre: *Marvellous to Behold: Miracles in Medieval Manuscripts,* British Library 2007

James, Oliver: *Affluenza: How to be Successful and Stay Sane,* Vermilion 2007

Jamieson, Alan: *A Churchless Faith: Faith Journeys Beyond the Churches,* SPCK 2002

Johnson, Bill: *When Heaven Invades Earth: A Practical Guide to a Life of Miracles*, Treasure House 2003

Kelly, Gerard: *Get a Grip on the Future without Losing your Hold on the Past*, Monarch 1999

Kempe, Margery: *The Book of Margery Kempe*, Penguin 2004

Kingsley, Mary: *West African Studies*, Macmillan 1899

Kreider, Alan: *Worship and Evangelism in pre-Christendom*, Grove Books 1995

Kuppers, Bernd-Olaf: *Information and the Origin of Life*, MIT Press 1990

Lagerkvist, Par: *Evening Land*, translated by WH Auden and S Sjoberg, Souvenir Press 1977

Leax, John: *Grace is Where I Live: The Landscape of Faith and Writing*, WordFarm 2004

Leddy, Mary Jo: *Radical Gratitude*, Orbis 2002

Lennox, John: *God's Undertaker: Has Science Buried God?*, Lion 2007

Lewis, Robert: *The Church of Irresistible Influence*, Zondervan 2001

Lovelace, Richard, 'To Althea, from Prison', *Oxford Book of English Verse*, Arthur Quiller Couch (ed.), Clarendon Press 1953

Lovelock, James: *Gaia*, Oxford Paperbacks 2000 (1st edition 1979)

McCloughry, Roy: *Living in the Presence of the Future*, IVP 2001

McGrath, Alister: *The God Delusion*, Transworld Publishers 2006.

McGrath, Alister: *Science and Religion*, Blackwell 1999

McGrath, Alister: *The Twilight of Atheism: The Rise and Fall of Disbelief in the Modern World*, Rider 2004

McKenzie, John: 'The Word of God in the Old Testament', *Theological Studies* 21 (1960)

McLaren, Brian: *A Generous Orthodoxy*, Zondervan 2004

Maddocks, Morris: *The Christian Healing Ministry*, 3rd edition SPCK 1995

Medawar, P. B.: *Advice to a Young Scientist*, Harper and Row 1979

Merton, Thomas: *Comtemplative Prayer*, DLT 1973

Micklethwait, John: *God is Back: How the Global Rise of Faith is Changing the World*, Allen Lane 2009

Middleton, Nick: *Kalashnikovs and Zombie Cucumbers: Travels in Mozambique*, Sinclair-Stevenson 1994

Montefiore, Hugh (ed.): *Man and Nature*, Collins 1975

Montefiore, Hugh: *The Gospel and Contemporary Culture*, Mowbray, London 1992

Montefiore, Hugh: *The Probability of God*, SCM 1985

Morgan, Alison: *Dante and the Medieval Other World*, CUP 1990, reprinted 2007

Morgan, Alison: *Doing what Jesus Did: A Fresh Look at the Gifts of the Spirit*, ReSource 2009

Morgan, Alison: *Praying with Creation*, Resource 2006

Morgan, Alison: *Renewal: What is it and What is it for?*, Grove Books 2006

Morgan, Alison: *The Wild Gospel*, Monarch 2004

Morgan, Alison: *What Happens When We Die?*, Kingsway 1990

Morgan, Alison: *Who do you say that I am? The Unexpected Jesus*, ReSource 2006

Morgan, Alison, and John Woolmer: *In His Name: A Training Course for Healing Prayer Teams*, ReSource 2008

Morison, Frank: *Who Moved the Stone?*: Faber 1930, reprinted Authentic Media 2006

Moynagh, Michael: *Emergingchurch.intro*, Monarch 2004

Murray, Stuart: *Church after Christendom*, Paternoster Press 2004

Neat, Timothy: *When I was Young: Voices from Lost Communities in Scotland – The Islands*, Birlinn Ltd 2005

Newbigin, Lesslie: *Foolishness to the Greeks: The Gospel and Western Culture*, SPCK 1986

Newbigin, Lesslie: *Proper Confidence: Faith, Doubt and Certainty in Christian Discipleship*, SPCK 1995

Newbigin, Lesslie: *The Gospel in a Pluralist Society*, SPCK 1989

Nicholson, Adam: *Power and Glory: Jacobean England and the Making of the King James Bible*, Harper Collins 2003

Nolan, Albert: *Jesus Today: A Spirituality of Radical Freedom*, Orbis 2008

O'Brien, Brian: *She had a Magic: The Story of Mary Slessor*, Jonathan Cape 1958

Olthuis, James H.: 'On Worldviews', *Christian Scholars Review* 14(2), 1985, and online at www.gospel-culture.org.uk.

Ortberg, John: *Everybody's Normal Till You Get To Know Them*, Zondervan 2003

O'Shaughnessy, Arthur: 'Ode', *Music and Moonlight,* reprinted BiblioBazaar 2010

Owen, John: *The Spiritual Gifts (Pneumatologia Book IX)*, Diggory Press 2007

Page, Nick: *The Church Invisible*, Zondervan 2004

Pannenberg, Wolfhart: *Toward a Theology of Nature: Essays on Science and Faith*, Westminster/John Knox Press 1993

Peacocke, Arthur: *Creation and the World of Science*, Clarendon Press 1979

Péguy, Charles: *The Portal of the Mystery of Hope,* new edition Continuum 2005

Peterson, Eugene: *The Jesus Way: A Conversation in Following Jesus*, Hodder 2007

Peterson, Eugene: *Subversive Spirituality*, Eerdmans 1997

Pinker, Steven: *The Stuff of Thought*, Allen Lane 2007

Pinker, Steven: *Words and Rules: The Ingredients of Language*, Weidenfeld & Nicolson 1999

Polanyi, Michael: *Personal Knowledge: Towards a Post-Critical Philosophy*, Chicago University Press 1974

Polkinghorne, John: *One World: The Interaction of Science and Theology*, SPCK 1986

Polkinghorne, John: *Science and Christian Belief: Theological Reflections of a Bottom-up Thinker*, SPCK 1994

Ponsonby, Simon: *More: How you Can Have More of the Spirit when you Already Have Everything in Christ*, Victor 2004

Ponsonby, Simon: *God Inside Out: An In-depth Study of the Holy Spirit,* Kingsway 2007

Pontzen, Andrew, and Hiranya Peiris, 'Cosmology's not broken so why try to fix it?, *New Scientist* August 2010

Pratchett, Terry: *Lords and Ladies*, Collins 1993

Rack, H. D.: *Reasonable Enthusiast: John Wesley and the Rise of Methodism*, 2nd edition Epworth Press 1992

Riddell, Michael: *Threshold of the Future*, SPCK 1998

Ruether, Rosemary: 'The Free Church Movement in Contemporary Catholicism', *Continuum*, 6 (1968)

Salgado, Sebastiao: *Africa*, Taschen 2007

Sampson, P. (ed.): *Faith and Modernity*, Regnum Books, Oxford 1994

Samways, John: *More to Life: A Model for Mission for the Local Church in the 21st Century'*, Grove Books 2010

Schroedinger, Erwin: *Nature and the Greeks*, reprinted CUP 1996

Schwarz, Christian: *Natural Church Development Handbook*, BGCA 1996

Senge, Peter et al.: *The Fifth Discipline Fieldbook*, Nicholas Brealey Publishing 1994

Simpson, Ray: *Church of the Isles: A Prophetic Strategy for Renewal*, Kevin Mayhew 2003

Smail, Tom: *Charismatic Renewal*, SPCK 1995

Smith, David: *Crying in the Wilderness: Evangelism and Mission in Today's Culture*, Paternoster Press 2000

Spencer, Nick: *Beyond Belief?: Barriers and Bridges to Faith Today*, LICC 2003

Spencer, Nick: *Beyond the Fringe: Researching a Spiritual Age*, LICC, Cliff College Publishing 2005

Spencer, Nick: *Darwin and God*, SPCK 2009

Spencer, Nick: *Doing God: A Future for Faith in the Public Square*, Theos 2006

Spencer, Nick: *Neither Private nor Privileged: The Role of Christianity in Britain Today*, Theos 2008

Spencer, Nick, and Denis Alexander: *Rescuing Darwin: God and Evolution in Britain Today*, Theos 2009

Stibbe, Mark: *Know your Spiritual Gift*, Zondervan 1997

Suurmond, Jean-Jacques: *Word and Spirit at Play: Towards a Charismatic Theology*, SCM 1994

Taylor, Richard: *To Catch a Thief*, New Wine Press 2006

Thigpen, Paul: 'Come, Holy Spirit! – 2000 years of miracles', *Charisma Magazine*, September 1992

Thomas, R. S.: *Selected Poems*, Anthony Thwaite (ed.), JM Dent 1996.

Tillich, Paul: *Life and the Spirit*, Chicago University Press 1976

Tillich, Paul: *Theology of Culture*, OUP 1964

Tozer, A. W.: *The Pursuit of God*, Christian Publications 1982

Trigg, Roger: *Free to Believe? Religious Freedom in a Liberal Society*, Theos 2010

Van der Weyer, Robert, and Pat Saunders: *The Creation Spirit: An Anthology*, DLT 1990

Veneziano, Gabriele: 'The Myth of the Beginning of Time', *Scientific American*, May 2004

Viola, Frank: *Finding Organic Church*, David C Cook 2009

Von Senden, Marius: *Space and Sight: The Perception of Space and Shape in the Congenitally Blind Before and After Operation*, Methuen 1960

Walker, Andrew: *Telling the Story: Gospel, Mission and Culture*, SPCK 1996

Wallace, Kathleen: *This is Your Home: A Portrait of Mary Kingsley*, Heinemann 1956

Warren, Robert: *Being Human, Being Church: Spirituality and Mission in the Local Church*, Marshall Pickering 1995

Warren, Robert: *The Healthy Churches Handbook*, CHP 2004

Washington, James M (ed): *A Testament of Hope: The Essential Writings and Speeches of Martin Luther King, Jr,* Harper Collins 1991

Wilkins, Michael: *Following the Master: Discipleship in the Steps of Jesus*, Zondervan 1992

Wilkins, Michael: *The Concept of Disciple in Matthew's Gospel as reflected in the use of the term "Mathetes"*, Novum Testamentum Supplements, vol. 59, EJ Brill 1988

Willard, Dallas: *Renovation of the Heart: Putting on the Character of Christ*, NavPress 2001

Willard, Dallas: 'The Apprentices', *Leadership Journal*, Summer 2005

Willard, Dallas: *The Great Omission: Reclaiming Jesus's Essential Teachings on Discipleship*, Monarch 2006

Williams, Rodman: *Renewal Theology*, Zondervan 1996

Williams, Rowan: 'On Being Disciples', ReSource magazine issue 12, *Being Disciples*, Summer 2008.

Wimber, John, and Kevin Springer: *Power Evangelism*, Hodder 1985

Woolmer, John: *Encounters: Authentic Experiences of God*, Monarch 2007

Woolmer, John: *Healing and Deliverance*, Monarch 1999

Wraight, Heather and Pat: *Back from the Brink: Stories of Churches which Refused to Die*, Christian Research 2006

Wright, Tom: *Simply Christian*, SPCK 2006

Yancey, Philip: *Prayer: Does it Make any Difference?*, Hodder 2006

Young, William P.: *The Shack,* Hodder Windblown 2008

Yu, Carver T.: 'Truth and authentic humanity', a plenary address presented at the Gospel and Our Culture Consultation *The Gospel as Public Truth*, held at Swanwick in July 1992. See www.gospel-culture.org.uk

Zohar, Danah, and Ian Marshall: *SQ: Spiritual Intelligence, the Ultimate Intelligence*, Bloomsbury 2000

Index